W9-BNY-093

THE LAST DAYS OF UNITED PAKISTAN

THE LAST DAYS OF UNITED PAKISTAN

BY

G. W. CHOUDHURY

INDIANA UNIVERSITY PRESS

BLOOMINGTON

Published in the United States in 1974 by Indiana University Press

Published in Canada by Fitzhenry & Whiteside Limited, Don Mills, Ontario

Library of Congress Catalog Card No. 74-8977

ISBN 0-253-33260-5

Printed in Great Britain

To my Mother

The Late Fatema Choudhury

memories of whose affections enabled me to endure these fateful days

CONTENTS

FACSIMILE DOCUMENTS

PREFACE

When I joined the Pakistan Cabinet in October 1969, I made a plan to write a book on Pakistan's transition from the military to the civilian rule. I had already been associated with the President Yahya Khan's plan for the transfer of power to an elected civilian government as a member of his three-man "planning cell". I had also collected much information and data relating to the fall of Ayub Khan, with whom also I had close contacts. My original plan was to write on Pakistan's political dynamics from the fall of Ayub to the establishment of a popularly elected government. I began to keep regular notes and diaries of important events and developments.

Then when the plan for transfer of power with which I was so closely associated failed and the country was plunged into a civil war, I came to London with my family. In London Mr. Christopher Hurst approached me to write a book on the "Crisis in Pakistan"; I readily accepted his offer, but at that time I was engaged in writing another book', so could not turn to Mr. Hurst's proposal. In the meantime, Pakistan was dismembered and a new state of Bangladesh emerged.

I began the present work in October 1972 when I joined Columbia University, my Alma Mater, for research and teaching. I am grateful to Professor Zbigniew Brzezinski for appointing me a Fellow of the Research Institute on Communist Affairs at Columbia University, and for arranging for me to receive a research grant. I also received a similar grant from the Foreign Policy Research Institute, Philadelphia, and the South Asian Regional Studies Centre at the University of Pennsylvania. My sincere thanks are due to Dr. Robert L. Pfaltzraff, Jr., Director, Foreign Policy Research Institute, and Professor Richard D. Lambert, Chairman, South Asian Regional Studies, University of Pennsylvania. My former teacher at Columbia University, Professor J. C. Hurewitz, never tired of extending his helping hand towards me. I am extremely grateful to him for his valuable suggestions and help in my research. I also received valuable help and encouragement for my research from Professors Ralph Braibanti, Norman Palmer, Howard Wriggins and Karl Von Vorys in U.S.A. and from Professors C. H. Philips, P. N. S. Mansergh and W. H. Morris-Jones and Dr. Peter Lyon in England.

Last but not the least, I must thank Mr. Christopher Hurst for his long patience with me to get the manuscript; for his excellent editing of it and for all his efforts to get the book printed so quickly after its submission.

The book deals with a subject to which my cherished homeland, near relations and dear friends were involved. I was personally involved with it. My opinions and interpretations may be affected by my emotional involvement with the tragic events in my country in 1970–1, but the book is based on original and unpublished material and data which I believe are still unknown to the world. I felt it a duty to reveal this story as objectively as I could. Any shortcomings or limitations are, however, my responsibility. It is my hope that this work will stimulate further studies and publications on the important events of 1970–1 in the Indian subcontinent.

London G. W. CHOUDHURY
January 1974

INTRODUCTION

Why did Pakistan fail to achieve a national identity or produce a viable political order in which the people of both East and West Pakistan could live together as equal partners? Was Pakistan really an "unbridgeable division of language, climate and way of life", and is it true that "the division of Pakistan into two nations (in 1971) was no more than a belated recognition of the unreality of the original state divided by a thousand miles into two parts"?[1] The growth of nationalism in Pakistan was, no doubt, complicated by diversity of language, race, culture and above all, by lack of geographical contiguity. But there are many countries in the Third World with acute regional, racial and linguistic differences and tensions. The federal solution has proved successful in many newly independent Afro-Asian countries with diverse ethnic, cultural, religious, linguistic and racial groups. Why did federation in Pakistan fail to achieve a similar success?

Geographical separation between the two halves of the country was a great challenge to its emerging nationalism, but in the modern age with satellite communications, jet aircraft, etc., geographical distance was not an insuperable factor. It was often said that there was nothing in common between an East and West Pakistani except religion; if that was the sole argument for the break-up of Pakistan, one may inquire what common identity makes a Bengali (Indian) and a Madrassi live together in an Indian union.

The disintegration of Pakistan and the emergence of Bangladesh in 1971 is a sad story of the Pakistan Army generals' misconceptions about their roles as the "guardians of national interests" and of the dubious roles of two unscrupulous and inordinately ambitious politicians – Mujibur Rahman of Bangladesh and Z. A. Bhutto of "New" Pakistan. The crisis in Pakistan in 1971 was also a case of "foreign-linked factionalism" where there are "linkages between internal political factors and the international environment".[2]

Pakistan itself was the product of a national movement on the part of an intolerant majority group which failed to appreciate the legitimate hopes and aspirations of other national groups in undivided India. It is tragic that Pakistan did not profit from its own history. The driving force behind the creation of Pakistan was democracy, but soon after the nation had been created, the democratic process was killed. The eclipse of the democratic process – first under an imperfect parliamentary system and then under military régimes – was the basic factor for Pakistan's failure in national integration and for its ultimate disintegration in December 1971. There were, no doubt, other factors such as economic disparity in *per capita* income between East and West Pakistan, cultural conflicts among the peoples of two geographically separated units, and finally the external complicating factors which intensified the internal diversive forces. But all these factors were, in a sense, products of the lack of the democratic political order in the country.

In this book I have tried to describe and analyse internal and external developments from the fall of Ayub Khan in March 1969 to the fall of Dacca in December 1971. After briefly examining the birth of Bengali sub-nationalism as a result of the conflict of "three Rs" – Religion, Region and Realities – the volume gives an assessment of the Ayub era, during which Pakistan was described in many quarters as a model for developing countries. Apparently the country was enjoying "political stability", "economic progress"; an "independent foreign policy", etc., under Ayub Khan, but a critical and inside analysis of the period will reveal that the death of the democratic process and the rise of an authoritarian system under Ayub was the beginning of the end of united Pakistan. Ayub's political system, in which the Bengalis had lost all initiatives in national affairs, was the root cause of the disintegration of the country. Similarly his ruinous policy of having an armed confrontation with India in 1965 had disastrous effects on the viability of Pakistan as a united country.

When Yahya Khan came to power in March 1969, he and his military régime made a final and sincere effort to solve the East–West Pakistan tensions, but subsequent events proved that Yahya had not the abilities necessary to meet the complicated situation already created by the misrule of the country in the preceding twenty-two years. Similarly, the two politicians with whom he had finally to deal to maintain the country's unity had neither political honesty and integrity nor any broad vision and statesmanship. External factors were also complicating an already explosive situation.

The result was the dismal failure of a plan to transfer power to the elected representatives of the people from a military régime, culminating in a civil war which constituted a great tragedy of modern history. Here was a conflict which could not be resolved, due to a combination of limiting internal factors and a hostile international environment. Why did Yahya's plan for the transfer of power to a popularly elected civil government fail? Was it inadequate to meet the Bengalis' demands for regional autonomy, or had the Bengalis under Mujib already decided on an independent state? Were Yahya and the military régime sincere in handing over power to a Bengali-dominated civilian government? What were the implications of Mujib's six-point plan? Was it a veiled scheme for secession or a demand only for regional autonomy? Was Mujib sincere and straightforward in his dealings with his own people and with Yahya and the military régime? Did not his policy precipitate the confrontation? What were the roles and aims of Bhutto? Was it correct to say that he was more interested in getting power than in the unity of Pakistan? Could not the tragic civil war have been avoided by statesmanship and moderation on the part of the three parties involved in the final dialogue in January–March 1971?

What were the international implications of the crisis over Bangladesh? Was it not connected with the Indo-Pakistan conflict and the tensions in the subcontinent? What was India's role in the crisis? Was it solely guided by humanitarian considerations, as India pretended, or was it seeking an opportunity to destroy its "enemy number one"? How far was the Bangladesh crisis affected by the Sino-Soviet conflict in South and South-east Asia and by the global competition between the two super-powers?

These and similar questions are examined and analysed in this volume. The break-up of Pakistan and the emergence of Bangladesh have great significance. It will demonstrate how a depoliticized régime, however well intentioned it may be, is not capable of dealing with the complex socio-economic problems of a new country in the Third World. It will also reveal how a stronger neighbour can take advantage of the internal conflicts of a smaller country, and how the big powers can carry on their global competition in the Third World by proxy.

REFERENCES

1. See *The Times* (London), editorial, June 9, 1966, and December 15, 1973.
2. See Alan Dowty, "Foreign-linked Factionalism as a Historical Pattern", *The Journal of Conflict Resolution*, Vol. XV, No. 4, December 4, 1971.

I

THE RISE OF BENGALI SUB-NATIONALISM: CONFLICT OF THE "THREE RS"

The immediate causes of the disintegration of Pakistan and the emergence of Bangladesh on December 16, 1971, were military atrocities committed by the Pakistan Army against unarmed Bengalis, the influx of refugees from East Pakistan into India and finally the direct Indian military intervention in the Bangladesh crisis from its very beginning, which culminated in an invasion of East Pakistan in November 1971, backed up by Soviet military and diplomatic support. The rise of Bengali sub-nationalism within Pakistan, however, had its origin in a number of factors – political, economic, cultural and social – which had operated since Pakistan was created in 1947.

When the Muslims of the Indian subcontinent were gathered together in a unique way in the 1940s under the leadership of *Quaid-i-Azam* Muhammad Ali Jinnah for a separate state of their own, Pakistan, they put all emphasis on one "R": religion; though the significance of "religion" was much wider than it usually is in a modern Western society. The Indian Muslims forgot the second "R": region – which is an important factor in determining group loyalty in the Afro-Asian countries. With the appearance of the third "R" – realities – after the creation of Pakistan in 1947, the second "R" – region – could not be ignored. The history of united Pakistan from 1947 to 1971 is one of constant conflict between the Pakistani nationalism, which could barely acquire a definite identity, and the emerging Bengali regionalism or sub-nationalism. Like the Muslim nationalism in undivided India, Bengali sub-nationalism within united Pakistan was the product of conflicting national ideas and aspirations. "Nationalism in Asia is based more on racial or religio-cultural peculiarities.[1] While discussing the nature of nationalistic movements Professor C. J. A. Hayes makes a distinction between two types of nationalism. One is "a veritable religion, a belligerent, expansive and intolerant one"; the key-note of this type of nationalism is "intolerance".[2] Any groups which do not conform are regarded as suspect and are treated as inferior and second-class citizens, if not as downright traitors. As compared with this militant and intolerant nationalism we have the examples of what has been termed "human and idealist nationalism", which was given expression by John Locke, Milton, Mazzini, Renan, J. S. Mill, Woodrow Wilson and Thomas Masaryk. This type is based on a free individual choice with a consciousness of the inherited traditions and values of community life. The beliefs in this type of nationalism and democracy are intermixed.

When nationalism assumes intolerant and extreme postures, as did the nationalism of the majority community in undivided India, nationalistic movements take new turns, and what Professor Miller calls "supplementary nationalism" emerges to safeguard the interests of the smaller national groups. Miller suggests that "the most obvious case is that of Pakistan".[3] The creation of Pakistan can be explained in terms of the conflicting and divergent aims and aspirations of two major national groups in undivided India. "Race, language, religion and to a certain extent the territorial situation, all separate the Indian Muslims from the Hindus. Their whole history deepens the gulf between them. Their past is a past of mutual destruction."[4] These were the words of an eminent scheduled caste Hindu leader of undivided India, B. R. Ambedkar. The nearer the prospect of self-government, the more bitter were the feelings between the two national groups. In British India the quarter-century preceding the transfer of power in 1947 was a time of increasing friction between the major religio-national groups. As pointed out by Alfred Cobban, "India was composed of many communities, some of which, always distinct in their culture, were rightly becoming politically conscious of their separate national identities".[5] Similarly, Professor Hayes noted that the "nationalist impulse throughout the huge and heterogeneous British Empire of

India has issued in the emergence of separate nations not only distinctive in languages but rather of distinctive religion: Hindu India, Muslim Pakistan, Buddhist Burma and primarily Buddhist Ceylon".[6]

There are some similarities between the Muslim nationalism of undivided India and the Bengali sub-nationalism within united Pakistan: "The force that underlies the political agitation", *The Times* of London reported, from Dacca in 1966, "is the same that created Pakistan itself – the desire of an under-group to improve its position by somehow stepping out from beneath those whom it believes to be exploiting or suppressing it."[7] An East Pakistani political leader commented in 1963: "What was the original demand of the Muslim League in India before independence? Fair shares – in appointments, in jobs, in political influence. It was only the blindness and selfishness of the Hindus that translated that into the demand for partition and now the West wing [West Pakistan] is taking the same attitude to us."[8]

The analogy is not, however, complete and cannot be carried too far. First, the Hindu–Muslim differences which gave rise to the Muslim nationalism in undivided India had six hundred years of history behind it, and was the product of fundamental factors characteristic of any well-defined national movement and aspiration. Jinnah based his demand for a separate state for the Muslims on the principle of the right of self-determination, and no serious observer of the Indian political scene before independence could challenge the grounds on which he based his two-nation theory: that the Hindus and the Muslims constituted two separate nations by any accepted definition or criterion of nationalism. Ultimately both the British Government and the Indian Congress led by Gandhi and Nehru were forced to accept his pleas, hence the partition of 1947 was the result of an agreement among the British authorities, the Hindus and the Muslims.

Bengali sub-nationalism or regionalism was, on the other hand, the product of a number of unfortunate and, in a sense, accidental factors connected with the internal political developments in Pakistan in the 1950s and 1960s, particularly after the eclipse of the democratic process of the country which denied the Bengalis their due share in the political process. It created an artificial situation in which the majority group felt itself dominated by an élite from West Pakistan composed of top civil and military officials. The Bengalis were naturally resentful of this state of affairs but there was no fundamental cleavage between the Muslims of East and West Pakistan, as between the Hindus and Muslims in undivided India.

Secondly, the East–West Pakistan internal political tensions were fully utilized by the hostile neighbour of Pakistan, which not only divided the two parts of the country geographically but took an active role in aggravating the internal tensions of the country in the twin expectation of weakening its principal enemy and belying Jinnah's two-nation theory – neither of which seemed to have been achieved by the partition of 1971. The rise of Bengali sub-nationalism cannot be adequately explained without a reference to India's involvement in it.

But the most significant difference between the Muslim national movement in undivided India and Bengali sub-nationalism within united Pakistan is the fact that while Jinnah and the Muslim League had spelled out the goal of the Indian Muslims – a sovereign state of their own choice, Pakistan – in unmistakable terms and the Indian Muslims while participating in the plebiscitory elections of 1946 knew fully the national aspirations for which they stood firmly behind Jinnah, the Bengali Muslims were never told by Mujib or his Awami League that their national goal was a separate state of Bangladesh.

Mujib adopted a deceptive strategy to achieve his goal of dismembering Pakistan. He appealed to the Muslim voters in the 1970 elections on the issue of regional autonomy for the Bengalis and made repeated pledges that he would never break up Pakistan or oppose a constitution based on Islamic principles or ideology. It was not until the Pakistan Army began its brutal assault at midnight on March 25–26, 1971, that the Bengali Muslims were ever told by Mujib or any of his colleagues of their ultimate goal. He presented to the Bengali Muslims a subtle and veiled scheme of secession under the garb of regional autonomy. Once the elections were over, Mujib and his party adopted a rigid and uncompromising stand; put forward a constitutional formula which amounted to the break-up of Pakistan; created an explosive situation which amounted to a unilateral declaration of independence and when the federal Army reacted – which it did in a most stupid and cruel manner – the Awami Leaguers proclaimed their ultimate goal: a separate state of Bangladesh. It is a tragic history. Of all the provinces which made up Pakistan, it was Bengal which gave the most solid support to Jinnah in his struggle for the establishment of a separate Muslim state in the subcontinent. Yet, within a very short period, the Bengalis found themselves in an unfortunate situation which made them have second thoughts about the creation of a state in which they had joined with the Muslims of other parts of the subcontinent in the north, separated by a thousand miles of foreign territory.

Although they were the majority group in Pakistan, they suffered from a deep-rooted fear of domination by the minority group of West Pakistan. In a democracy, the majority should not have to ask for safeguards, such as regional autonomy, reservation of places in the civil service and the Army, and guarantees that the economic development of their region would not be neglected nor their culture threatened. But for two decades the majority Bengali group did feel obliged to seek these guarantees; and when they were not granted, Bengali sub-nationalism gathered momentum until ultimately it became a national movement for the creation of a separate state.

What were the factors that gave rise to Bengali sub-nationalism? First was the political factor. Pakistan began its political career under a parliamentary system modelled on Westminster and under a federal constitution. But neither the parliamentary system nor the federation was genuine. The constitutional forms and trappings of democracy only provided a cloak for rule by the few who were able to concentrate power in their own hands. During eleven years (1947–58) of so-called parliamentary democracy, there was not a single general election, and the provincial elections were described as "a farce, a mockery and a fraud upon the electorate".[9] Well-organized political parties did not exist. With the decline of the Muslim League, there was no national party; the remaining parties were more narrowly based than those in the new Asian democracies, not to speak of Western countries. The failure of parliamentary democracy led to the development of an all-powerful and irresponsible executive, aided and supported by a power ful bureaucracy. Pakistan was dominated by bureaucrats and soldiers.[10]

The emergence of this all-powerful ruling élite had a great impact on the separatist movement in East Bengal. The ruling élite was composed of senior bureaucrats, none of whom was an East Bengali. Up to 1958 they were supported indirectly by the Army; after 1958, Army support was direct and open. There was a cabinet and a parliament, but the political order in Pakistan could be called "an oligarchy under a democratic constitution". It was a "modernizing oligarchy"[11] in which Bengalis had no share. Except during the short thirteen-month interval of H. S. Suhrawardy's cabinet in 1956–7, the Bengalis had hardly any role in national affairs. Every vital decision, whether it related to political or defence or economic or diplomatic matters, was in the final analysis made by the ruling élite, composed of West Pakistani civil and military officers.

In provincial matters the situation for the Bengalis was no better. Even in their own province, all the key posts in the administration were held by West Pakistanis who had direct access to the central ruling clique. The country had, in theory, a federal constitution, but in practice the provincial government was entirely subordinate to the centre, particularly in financial and administrative matters. The Bengalis found a new ruling group set over them in place of the former British officials. The civil and military officials from West Pakistan stationed in East Bengal never bothered to develop any real bonds with the local population, who looked upon them as aliens. There were few social contacts; the West Pakistani officials considered themselves socially superior to the Bengali Muslims, who were regarded as converts from lower-caste Hindus. The result was bitterness and a widening gap.

The Bengali intelligentsia, particularly at Dacca University, became increasingly conscious of their unsatisfactory situation. It must be pointed out, however, that at the time of independence the Indian civil service left behind by the British *raj* contained only one Bengali officer. Similarly, the Bengalis were very poorly represented in the Army because the British authorities had considered them a non-martial race. There were therefore some historical reasons for the preponderance of West Pakistani civil and military officers in East Bengal. But after independence nothing was done to rectify the situation and, in the absence of a genuine democracy, with the country run by an oligarchy of civil and military officials, the Bengalis found themselves in the position of a colonial people.

Region rather than Religion

After Ayub Khan came to power in 1958 there was complete authoritarian rule in the country until 1962; then came a period of Controlled or guided democracy, under which the President and the same old ruling élite dominated the political scene. What had been veiled before 1958 now became more obvious. The result was a further widening of the gap between East and West Pakistan. The political order, as set up by Ayub in his 1962 Constitution, gave hardly any scope to the Bengalis for effective and equal participation in national affairs. They had no share in the decision-making process. In any vital national issue they could only react; they could never act.[12]

No self-respecting group could tolerate this state of affairs. Nationalism or patriotism cannot be expected to grow or flourish in a vacuum. It is only through participation and sharing responsibility that people develop national feelings. There was hardly any scope for the Bengalis to develop common national feelings with the West Pakistanis, apart from the religious bond of Islam, But, as in many other parts of Asia and Africa, they became more and more conscious of region rather than religion. The Islamic ideology, on which Jinnah had based Pakistan, began to fade away, and regional feelings grew fast in East Bengal. Regionalism was the *raison d'être* for the emergence of Bangladesh.

Henceforth, East Bengal became a hotbed for political agitation and unrest. Hardly a year passed without Bengalis revolting against alleged maltreatment by the central government; the result was shootings and killings, which gave further impetus to the growth of Bengali nationalism. By the 1960s, most of the urban professional Bengali groups were beginning to consider seriously whether they could or would live together with the western part of the country. People no longer concealed their hatred of West Pakistan. But the greatest blow to Pakistan nationalism came as a result of the Indo-Pakistan war in September 1965. Neither India nor Pakistan could claim victory or be considered defeated in this seventeen-day war. In fact, Pakistan, with a much smaller army, air and naval force, did quite well in 1965 in comparison with December 1971. But the war of 1965 disastrously weakened the national bond between East and West Pakistan. Until then a common fear of external aggression had, like the religious link, been an important factor in helping the two parts of the country to live together. There was a deep-rooted myth that if India attacked East Pakistan, West Pakistani soldiers would move up to Delhi. The 1965 war shattered that myth for good. Mr. Bhutto, Ayub's foreign minister, proudly claimed in the National Assembly that East Pakistan had been protected by China. If that was so, the Bengalis began to argue, why do we not settle our own diplomatic and external relations? Why depend on West Pakistan, which could give no protection to East Pakistan? Within one hour of the war beginning, East Pakistan was cut off, not only from West Pakistan but from the rest of the world. So the old argument that the defence of East Pakistan lay in West Pakistan no longer held water.

It was under these circumstances that Sheikh Mujibur Rahman formulated his famous six-point programme. Let me also examine some economic and cultural factors in the Bengal separatist movement. The Bengalis' most serious complaint was of what they called the "economic exploitation" of East Pakistan by the Pakistan central government. It had been said by many impartial economists, particularly American and British, that the economic development of East Pakistan was sadly neglected and that something ought to be done about it. I myself, who used to believe in one Pakistan, have pointed out in previous writings that the most serious challenge to Pakistani nationalism was the economic disparity between East and West Pakistan. Many moderate East Pakistani leaders, like Nural Amin and others who also wanted to live in a united Pakistan, strongly urged the government to accelerate the economic development of East Pakistan and thereby remove the most serious grievance of the Bengali separatists. But unfortunately no one listened carefully or seriously to this advice.

But since political power was exercised by a narrow oligarchy which looked at the whole situation entirely from the colonial angle of maintaining "law and order", it was futile to expect any imaginative economic programme or plans. At the time of Independence, gigantic efforts were made to speed up economic growth. But, tragically, the rate of economic growth in the the development plans was much slower in East than West Pakistan. Many figures have been published to illustrate this disparity. Some may have been exaggerated for political purposes but even allowing for this, they convincingly demonstrate the extent to which the East's interests were neglected. The bulk of the country's revenue was spent in West Pakistan because the federal capital was there. Moreover, a high percentage of the budget was spent on defence, which was all concentrated in West Pakistan. A much larger share of development expenditure as well as of foreign aid and loans went to the West. East Pakistan earned most of the country's foreign exchange by the export of jute; yet most of the foreign exchange was spent on the industrialization of West Pakistan. Whether it was revenue or development expenditure, foreign assistance and loans or foreign exchange, East Pakistan did not get its fair share, though it contained the majority of the country's population.

A report made by a panel of experts to the Pakistan Government's planning commission in 1970 provides authoritative documentation of the increasing economic disparity between the two regions. The most striking fact in this report was the widening gap between the income of the average West Pakistani and his Eastern counterpart.[13]

No East Pakistani, whether a regionalist or a nationalist, could watch this situation with equanimity. The economic disparity – or economic exploitation, as it was called by the regionalists – provided them with powerful weapons to win popular support. The situation could be compared to that which prevailed in undivided India when Jinnah convinced the Muslim intelligentsia and the masses that their rights and interests were not safe under Congress rule in India. He catalogued the list of Muslim grievances under Congress rule; whether these allegations were all true or not, the important thing was that the Muslims *believed* in Jinnah's version of their plight. Similarly, Sheikh Mujib and his party were highly successful in convincing the emotional Bengalis that their interests and rights were not safe with a government controlled and directed from West Pakistan. This led the younger and more militant sections of the Awami League to start a movement for secession. Sheikh Mujib himself has confessed in a recent interview with a British journalist that he had been working for the establishment of Bangladesh for some time;[14] the flag of the new nation was already there; the slogan "*Jai Bangla*" (victory to Bangladesh) was heard long before the tragic events of March 1971.

Now turning to cultural factors, it should be noted that when Jinnah declared that by every definition and standard the Muslims of India constituted a nation separate from the Hindus,[15] his two-nation theory was probably more applicable to Northern India than to Bengal. The Bengali Muslims and Hindus had many differences; the Muslims of undivided Bengal had many grievances against the upper-class Bengal Hindus, or *Bhadralok* of Bengal, as they were called. The Bengali Muslims' support of Jinnah's demand for the establishment of Pakistan was based on a negative attitude. The Bengalis are noted for a negative and destructive attitude rather than for hard work and constructive programmes; they also have a tremendous tendency to put the blame on others. In pre-Independence days, they blamed the British and then the Hindus, with whom they could not compete in any sphere of life. Jinnah's demand for a separate state appealed to the Bengali Muslims, not so much because of the two-nation theory, but because they looked upon it as a protective wall against the wealthy and privileged Hindus.

Language an Emotive Issue

But when, with the establishment of Pakistan, they found that the privileged position of the British and the upper-class Hindus had gone to the West Pakistanis, they started stressing their cultural and linguistic affinities with the Bengalis of West Bengal. The Pakistan authorities regarded this as a serious menace to the existence of Pakistan and tried to impose a cultural uniformity based on Islam. The Bengalis reacted sharply. They felt (just as the Muslims of undivided India had felt) that their cherished culture and way of life were threatened. The first tussle was over the language question. In 1948 the Bengalis reacted violently to Jinnah's proposal that Urdu should be the only national language. On February 21, 1952, three students of Dacca University were killed in a riot over this issue – since which time February 21 has been observed as a day of mourning for the cherished language of the Bengalis.

The Pakistan Government failed to appreciate the fact that nations are made up of human beings whose deep feelings about such questions as their language cannot safely be ignored. A federal union can be strengthened by giving cultural freedom and autonomy, but Pakistan's attempt to impose uniformity where diversity was desirable had unfortunate consequences. Every attempt made by the Pakistan Government to foster a cultural uniformity based on Islamic culture in East Pakistan produced a sharp reaction; the Bengalis began to look more and more to West Bengal for cultural affinity and bonds. The Indians, who also had not been happy about Jinnah's two-nation theory, gave encouragement and sympathy to the growing separatist movement in East Bengal. The Bengali Muslim intelligentsia were more at home with the Bengali Hindus in West Bengal than with their fellow-countrymen from West Pakistan. Culturally, and perhaps psychologically, the country was divided long before the crisis of 1971.

When the six-point programme was formulated early in 1966, Mujib might have been willing to make some adjustments and amendments, but Ayub preferred to meet the challenge with the "language of weapons" rather than by political negotiations.

After Ayab's fall, General Yahya made a number of gestures to try to win the confidence of the Bengalis. He allowed free and fair elections on the basis of "one man, one vote", and Mujib won an absolute majority. Yahya also acknowledged that the Bengalis had no share in the decision-making processes and that this state of affairs must be ended. But these measures came too late. Another analogy can be made with the period of British rule. In the 1940s, the Congress tried to make a number of concessions to Jinnah and the Muslims. But by that time the Muslims had already decided to have a separate state. Similarly, the scheme for a transfer of power as formulated by Yahya in 1969 was too late; the Bengal intelligentsia and urban élites had already decided to have a state of their own. Just as Jinnah used the election of 1946 to establish his credentials as the sole spokesman and leader of Muslim India, so Mujib used Yahya's election on the basis of "one man, one vote" to establish his credentials as the spokesman of the Bengali nation.

REFERENCES

1. C. J. A. Hayes, *Nationalism: a Religion*, New York, 1960, p. 157.
2. Ibid., p. 93.
3. *The Politics of the Third World*,
4. B. R. Ambedkar, *Thoughts on Pakistan*, London, 1941, p. 30.
5. Alfred Cobban, *National Self-determination*, London, 1945, p. 127.
6. *Nationalism: a Religion*, p. 157.
7. *The Times*, London, July 1, 1966.
8. Ibid., June 24, 1963.
9. Report of the Electoral Reforms Commission, Government of Pakistan, Karachi, 1956.
10. G. A. Almond and J. S. Coleman, *The Politics of the Developing Areas*, Princeton, N.J: Princeton University Press, p. 572.
11. Almond and Coleman, op. cit.
12. See the author's *Constitutional Development in Pakistan*, 2nd edition, Longman, 1970, p. 247.
13. See the Report of the Experts on the Fourth Five-Year Plan, Government of Pakistan, Islamabad, 1970.
14. Sheikh Mujib's television interview with David Frost, London Weekend Television, January 16, 1972.
15. See M. A. Jinnah's foreword in M. R. T., *Pakistan and Muslim India*, Bombay, 1942.

2

THE FALL OF AYUB: A PERSONAL ACCOUNT

No Muslim since the fall of the Moghul Empire ruled over a wider area in the Indian subcontinent for a longer period or more effectively than Field-Marshal Mohammed Ayub Khan did in undivided Pakistan from October 27, 1958, to March 25, 1969. Pakistan under Ayub used to be cited as a "model" for developing countries. His political innovation, Basic Democracy, was acclaimed by many, including the historian Arnold Toynbee, as a plausible alternative between the Western democratic and the communist systems. Toynbee wrote:

> It [Basic Democracy] does suggest a possible way in which politically and economically backward countries can arrive at self-government on our Western lines. So I should say that the Pakistan experiment in so-called basic democracy deserves our sympathy and support and certainly deserves out attention.[1]

The extensive rural development works under Ayub's Basic Democracy, especially in East Pakistan (Bangladesh), was described as "an example of Jeffersonian democracy in action" by the leaders of the Harvard Advisory Group in Dacca (1968).[2] While Ayub's economic development programme for Pakistan was appreciated like this – "There is hardly a developing country which would not profit from looking over Pakistan's shoulder today"[3] – his foreign policy and diplomatic moves earned him the title of "Asian [or Muslim] de Gaulle". Ayub was credited with putting an end to Pakistan's subservient foreign policy towards the United States and enunciating an independent policy which extracted such comments as the following: "The spirit of revolution of October 1958 had engendered a new approach to Pakistan problems in both economic and foreign affairs. That Karachi was no longer a helpless and a rather hopeless hostage of the West was shown both by the handling of Peking and by its protests in Washington on the action of the U-2 incident." It went on to note the "original approach on the part of President Ayub which characterized the new Pakistan".[4] Commenting on Pakistan's new trends in foreign policy under President Ayub, a "Muslim de Gaulle", *The Economist* wrote that the President wanted essentially what his brother-soldier sought for France: an opportunity for national self-assertion and independence (meaning independence of the United States). Referring to the creation of a "Regional Co-operation for Development" Plan (R.C.D.), a new scheme for economic co-operation between Pakistan, Iran and Turkey, *The Economist* commented: "C.E.N.T.O., like N.A.T.O., is not dead but President Ayub has served notice, much like President de Gaulle, that from now on the decisions that matter to Pakistan will as far as possible (which is an important proviso) be made in Rawalpindi and not in Washington."[5]

Yet Ayub Khan was removed from the Presidency in March 1969 as a result of agitation which began over a trifling incident in Rawalpindi, a scuffle between the students and the police over some allegedly smuggled goods. In November 1969 it appeared like an anomic movement – a sudden sporadic outburst of political activity engendered by the insecurity and frustrations usually characteristic of societies undergoing rapid change.[6] Political movement against Ayub was not organized by the politicians, who were caught unprepared; they took advantage of it only *after* it had begun.

There have been many interpretations of Ayub's fall. Z. A. Bhutto, now Premier of truncated Pakistan, has been given the credit for having played a "revolutionary role" in it after serving Ayub faithfully for about eight years as one of his "nominated" ministers. There were socio-economic interpretations: Ayub's economic policy had resulted in phenomenal growth, but it sadly neglected the distributive aspect of economic growth; the wealth was concentrated in the "twenty-two families". Mahbub-Ul Haq, the Chief Economist of the Planning Commission headed by Ayub himself, disclosed the fact that the wealth of the country was dominated by industries and directors belonging to the 'twenty-two families".[7] Ayub's own family was, significantly, one of the lucky twenty-two. Industrial production had increased by 160 per cent during the Ayub régime, particularly between 1960 and 1968; all inducements by way of tax concessions, import facilities and export bonus were granted to the industrialists to achieve the accelerated rate of growth, but Ayub's economic policy failed miserably in ensuring an equitable and effective distribution of the fruits of development.

During the political agitation in the winter of 1968–9, the Planning Commission issued a document in which it acknowledged that the economic policy put too much stress on a high rate of growth and neglected the social and regional distribution of the benefits of economic development. At that stage, the Commission stressed the need to "make a beginning of the evolution of a synthesis" of economic and social objectives, but it was too late.

More important, Ayub's economic policy and development projects had widened the gap between East and West Pakistan. Ayub initiated the debate on economic disparity between East and West Pakistan; his Constitution laid down that economic disparity must be removed, yet after ten years of his rule, the disparity had increased. In 1959–60 the *per capita* income in West Pakistan was 32 per cent higher than in the East. Over the next ten years the annual rate of growth of income in West Pakistan was 6·2 per cent, while it was only 4·2 per cent in East Pakistan. As a result, by 1969–70, the *per capita* income in the West was 61 per cent higher than in the East. Thus in ten years of Ayub's rule, the income gap had doubled in percentage terms; it had widened even more in absolute terms.[8]

It has, however, to be added that the political movement against Ayub began in West Pakistan, in his capital city and not in East Pakistan. The fact that the movement began in West and not in East Pakistan, where Ayub's political order and economic policy were totally unacceptable, had great significance, and provides the clues to the inside story of the movement. The socio-economic factors and, more important, the regional tensions between East and West Pakistan were, no doubt, sapping the Ayub régime and indeed the viability of a united Pakistan.

However, the immediate causes of Ayub's removal ay elsewhere: in intrigues at the army headquarters at Rawalpindi. The process began in 1966, after the Indo-Pakistani war of 1965 and the subsequent Tashkent Agreement, gained momentum during Ayub's serious illness in early 1968 and finally culminated in the political agitation which began in Rawalpindi in the winter of 1968–9. Bhutto's so-called "revolutionary role" had its roots in his links with the GHQ at Rawalpindi.[8] Political changes in Pakistan were always the product of internal intrigues and power struggles among the factions of the ruling élite composed of the top civil and military officers, sometimes aided and abetted by some political leaders who had the fortune of enjoying good relations with the ruling élite. The dismissal of Khawaja Nazimuddin's cabinet in 1953; of the Mohammed Ali (Bogra) cabinet and the dissolution of the Constituent Assembly in 1954; and of Suhrawardy's cabinet in 1957 as well as the Ayub-Mirza coup in 1958, were all products of "palace intrigues".

Political changes in Pakistan could not take place through the process of ballot because there was no general election in the country except the 1970 election held on the eve of the Civil War over Bangladesh. Ayub's exit, like his coming to power, was basically the product of secret plans and intrigues. It had the appearance of a mass upheaval, and no doubt the mass movement had facilitated the plans and schemes at GHQ, and similarly the "mass movement", particularly that organized by Z. A. Bhutto in West Pakistan, had the secret blessing of GHQ. While there have been many accounts of the fall of Ayub dealing with political socio-economic factors,[8] the "inside story" has not yet been revealed fully.

I had ample opportunity to watch the drama and to inform myself regarding the plot against Ayub by some of his military colleagues. I had been seconded from the University of Dacca to the Ministry of Foreign Affairs in early 1967 to take up a special assignment in the research division of the Ministry. This was done on Ayub's own initiative and directive. From the time of my arrival in Islamabad I had regular and frequent contacts with the President. He was agreeable to me personally and extremely helpful over my work at the Ministry of Foreign Affairs. I had direct access to him and he was never tired of seeing me. As the "Supreme boss" treated me kindly, I had no difficulty in attracting attention among the members of the ruling élite, including some members of Ayub's inner or real cabinet. After Ayub's fall I was, to my utter surprise, summoned by the new military régime to become a member of a three-man planning cell, which was the first civilian body to be associated with the new military régime. Finally, I joined the Pakistan cabinet in October 1969 as Communications Minister – my real role being political communication and to assist President Yahya in formulating his scheme for transferring power to the elected representatives of the people. These contacts with Ayub Khan and his inner cabinet as well as with some generals, and subsequent contacts as a member of the Yahya cabinet enabled me to gather information relating to the fall of Ayub. I also maintained my old contacts with Ayub even after his retirement – a gesture greatly appreciated by Ayub and approved by Yahya.

Ayub came to power in 1958 as the chief of the armed forces; he had no difficulty in dislodging President Iskander Mirza within three weeks because he and not Mirza had the backing of the armed forces. Then from October 27, 1958, to June 8, 1962, he ruled the country under a military system, though with the full co-operation of the bureaucracy. In 1962 Ayub introduced a quasi-constitutional and civil régime. A Constitution was "granted"; it was not made by the people's representatives. There were institutions like "National Assembly", "Cabinet", "Governor's Conference", "National Economic Council", etc. Political parties were also revived, though with restrictions. The press could criticize the Government; even Ayub and his family were not immune from press criticism. Yet Ayub's political order was no more than a depoliticized quasi-constitutional system in which the real decision-making body was composed of the top bureaucrats and army generals. Some members of the cabinet (such as Manzoor Quader in the early years and Bhutto in 1962–5) or some other individual members might have some share, but usually the cabinet would discuss such peripheral issues as a civil aviation pact between one country and another, the prospects of jute or cotton, or the food situation. But the vital decisions – whether related to defence, foreign affairs or economic policy – were decided in the Presidential House with the help of an inner cabinet. A most significant feature of the system was the total exclusion of Bengalis from the decision-making process.

The main objective of Ayub's political order was to create a rural élite – "the Basic Democrats" – and by-pass the urban élite composed of lawyers, journalists, doctors, teachers and other professional groups. Ayub tried to build up his base of support in the rural areas by his scheme of Basic Democracy and the rural development works done through the Basic Democrats. But he was not successful in acquiring a solid base in rural areas; as a substitute for the urban élite, it was not strong or effective. Thus like any other military leader, Ayub rested in the final analysis on the support and loyalty of the armed forces. He enjoyed their confidence and loyalty for a long time. He was the first Pakistani commander-in-chief of the armed forces – a position which came to him in 1950 on the retirement of the British commander-in-chief. From that time Ayub was the real and unchallenged boss of the Pakistani army. He had organizational skill and ability on the one hand and charming personal qualities on the other which enabled him to retain the confidence of his senior colleagues and the loyalty of the rank and file of the armed forces. This happy state of affairs for Ayub continued even after he became an "elected" or "civilian" President and "leader of a political party", the Muslim League (the Convention group). Ayub, however, began to rely more and more on his top civil servants like Qudrutulla Shahab, N. A. Faruque, Fida Hasan and, in the later part of his era, on Altaf Gauhar more than anybody else. This reliance on top civil officials was resented by the army generals but yet Ayub kept the generals in good humour by patronage, such as promotion to ambassadorships, allotment of large landed properties, increased salaries and chairmanships of many autonomous bodies with wide powers and resources. Ayub also took an active part in the selection and promotion of the army officers and he tried to attend regularly the ceremonial functions of the various units of the armed forces. These good relations between the Presidency and GHQ existed up to 1966, particularly with his closest confident General Musa, commander-in-chief till that year.

Ayub at the Zenith

Ayub seemed to reach the zenith of his power and glory after his electoral victory over Miss Fatema Jinnah in the presidential election of 1965. Miss Jinnah, the sister of Quaid-i-Azam Mohammed Ali Jinnah, the Founder of Pakistan, was supported by the combined opposition parties (COP). Though Ayub's victory was mainly due to the indirect method of election, his success in a lively and much-publicized election campaign over a candidate who was a "popular heroine" and supported by all the opposition parties gave a great boost to his prestige, particularly abroad.

Inside the country, the opposition felt more frustrated and seemed inclined to resort to violence after seeing the futility of ballots under Basic Democracy. Ayub seemed to have developed over-confidence and begun to neglect domestic affairs, while he applied himself vigorously to foreign affairs – to play his role as the Asian de Gaulle. He planned a grand triangular visit to Peking, Moscow and Washington soon after the election in the spring of 1965. He visited Peking and Moscow with good results and wide publicity at home. His trip to Washington was cancelled rather discourteously by President Johnson at the eleventh hour. But it only increased Ayub's prestige as he was regarded as following an "independent foreign policy", which incurred the wrath of Washington. So Ayub's adventures in external relations so soon after his electoral victory had enhanced his prestige and image.

Ayub's dialogue with Chairman Mao, Premier Chou-En Lai and other top leaders in Peking and his similar dialogue with the Kremlin leaders in Moscow[9] satisfied the Pakistanis' sense of national pride, as the country was considered to have achieved at last the goal of diplomatic parity with India – a cherished desire of the Pakistanis. Then Pakistan under Ayub took a leading part in organizing the Second Afro-Asian Conference; although it proved abortive, Ayub's role was appreciated. It must be made clear, however, that the majority of the Bengalis had no such thrill over Ayub's successes in external relations. As already pointed out, the Bengalis had begun to think seriously in terms of emerging Bengali nationalism rather than of sharing the "incoherent" Pakistani nationalism (so described by the Bengali intelligentsia). But for Ayub the diplomatic successes were significant for his image in West Pakistan, the base of his military strength.

But adventures in international politics can sometimes cost a dictator dear when he lacks popular support and a firm base. Ayub's over-confidence in his success in foreign affairs entangled him into the biggest mistake of his career – the war between India and Pakistan in 1965.

The Indo-Pakistan War of 1965 and its Effect on Ayub's Fall

Calculations and temptations for intervening in the widespread political unrest and agitation in the Indian part of Kashmir, which began over the theft of the holy relic in 1964*, were great for Ayub and his advisers. India under "Little Shastri" was considered to be weak following the death of Nehru. The mini Indo-Pakistani battle over the marshy lands in the Rann of Kutch in the spring of 1965 gave the Pakistani armed forces a false sense of superiority, and memories of India's military defeats by the Chinese in 1962 were still fresh. Under these "favourable circumstances", a group of the ruling élite – Bhutto being the most enthusiastic among them – felt that a policy of confrontation with India over Kashmir might be fruitful.

The usual procedure for such a crucial decision was as follows. The Pakistani army chiefs used to make a careful analysis of the pros and cons of the proposed course of action, one group presenting the case, while another group acted as opponents of the proposed action. The opposing group might not actually disagree, but for the purposes of clarification and examination, this type of debate used to be arranged.

In 1965, when the Pakistani ruling élite decided the course of action on Kashmir, this well-established practice was not allowed.[10] When I questioned him on his crucial decision, Ayub on more than one occasion during 1967–9 answered me: 'Please do not rub in my weakest and fatal point." He admitted that he was greatly misled by his Foreign Minister Bhutto and Foreign Secretary Aziz Ahmed. The Foreign

* For details see G. W. Choudhury, *Pakistan's Relations with India,* London, 1968, pp. 283–7.

Ministry was severely criticized for its grand miscalculations, and both Bhutto and Aziz Ahmed were removed soon after the war.

India reacted violently by attacking Pakistan on the international frontier on the morning of September 6, 1965. Thus began the full-scale war between India and Pakistan. The war ended in a draw: neither side could claim victory, nor could it be considered defeated. Pakistan, with a much smaller army, put up a brave show particularly when compared with the military débacles of 1971. Yet the Indo-Pakistani War of 1965 had a disastrous effect both on Ayub's authority and image with the armed forces and on relations between East and West Pakistan, as I have already discussed in analysing the growth of Bengali nationalism (see Chapter 1, above). As to its impact on Ayub's authority, many army officers, including some generals, felt that Ayub should have continued the war with Chinese help; Indonesia under Sukarno was also willing to help Pakistan. The younger groups of army officers felt that Ayub accepted the cease-fire and the subsequent Tashkent agreement under external pressures and to the detriment of his internal political order. It was argued that he could not afford a people's war with Chinese help with his narrow political base and the vested interests of his ruling élite, including his own interests. I have described elsewhere Ayub's secret trip to Peking during the 1965 war and the Chinese offer of help.[11] Suffice it to say here that the Chinese offers were not "empty" nor were they "paper tigers". But Ayub had also genuine and serious limitations in prolonging the war. So the cease-fire and the Tashkent Agreement ended the war after seventeen days. Ayub's image was tarnished by his alleged surrender of the "national interests" at the Tashkent Conference – a theme on which Bhutto based his major attack against Ayub during the political upheaval of 1969.

Ayub lost the confidence of his real constituency of power (the armed forces) and with General Musa's retirement in 1966 as the Commander-in-chief of the armed forces, his position was further weakened. After careful thought and considering many factors other than military efficiency or qualities, Ayub selected General Yahya Khan as commander-in-chief, and in so doing by-passed a few generals senior to

Yahya. Yahya was loyal to Ayub, whose calculations seemed to be that Yahya was a non-political and non-serious type who would be content with relaxed social evenings. But Ayub's cardinal mistake was to ignore Yahya's long-standing friendship and close association with Major-General Peerzada, who had been Ayub's military secretary until 1964, when he was removed after a heart attack. Peerzada, who was inordinately ambitious, could never forget his removal from the President's House, and when Bhutto was also sacked by Ayub in 1966, these two developed a close friendship based on their common animosity towards Ayub. The Bhutto-Peerzada axis had great significance both in the fall of Ayub in 1969 and in the dismemberment of Pakistan in 1971.

Ayub might have recovered his position in the army, but a number of factors were working against him. Soon after the Indo-Pakistani war of 1965, Mujibur Rahman put forward his six-point programme for regional autonomy in East Pakistan. Mujib's scheme will be analysed later in discussing political dialogues during Yayha's régime. Here it may simply be said that in the same city of Lahore where Jinnah presented his scheme for a separate homeland for Indian Muslims in 1940, Mujib, twenty-six years later in 1966, presented a veiled scheme of secession under the garb of demands for regional autonomy. Those who cherished the ideals of a united Pakistan were appalled by threats to Pakistan's viability; Mujib's scheme also demonstrated Ayub's failure, in spite of a much-publicized campaign, to achieve national integration.

Then there was an attempt to kidnap and assassinate Ayub in December 1967 while he was on tour in East Pakistan. The plot was unsuccessful and unpublicized – only the foreign press published the news, and All-India Radio also broadcast it with the usual exaggeration. It affected Ayub's image with his armed forces: he was no longer regarded as "supreme boss", and became vulnerable.

The Agartala Conspiracy Case

Soon after the attempt on Ayub's life, the Pakistan political scene was rocked by the startling news of a case of conspiracy with alleged Indian help to bring about secession of East

Pakistan through armed uprisings.* Even before the Government's announcement of the conspiracy on January 7, 1968, the market place was full of reports relating to plots, arrests, coups, and so on. In fact, some arrests took place while Ayub was still in Dacca in late December 1967. A meeting of the professors of political science of various universities in both East and West Pakistan was arranged at the President's House during Ayub's stay at Dacca. The theme of discussion at the meeting was how to project the content and spirit of the Muslim nationalist movement for Pakistan. Ayub's two top civil advisers, Altaf Gauhar and Q. Shahab, were present.

I was also asked to participate and as soon as I entered the President's House, I could sense an "atmosphere of emergency", The meeting was abruptly cut short. Ayub could hardly talk, though he was usually fond of taking his part in such discussions. After the abrupt ending of the meeting, I had a few minutes with him and when I expressed my reaction to the abrupt cancellation of the meeting, his reply was incoherent and inconclusive. I could realize that something grave had happned. The same evening, the usual banquet by the Governor of East Pakistan in honour of the visiting President began late; Ayub appeared after about two hours – an unusual phenomenon on his part. At the provincial Government House, I had a discussion with the Chief of Civil Intelligence (Central), a senior and capable Bengali officer. He gave me the first inkling of the impending crisis or plot although on that occasion I could get little information or data.

The most serious development of the Agartala conspiracy case was Mujib's implication in it – a few days later, the Government announced that Mujib, who had been in jail since the movement for six points in 1966, was also involved in the Agartala case. The reaction to Mujib's arrest in the case was most unfavourable in East Pakistan. I was in Dacca when the government announcements of the conspiracy case and of

* On January 2, 1968, the Government of Pakistan announced the discovery of a plot to bring about the secession of East Pakistan, with Indian help. It was disclosed that twenty-eight persons had been arrested: in collaboration with the First Secretary of the Indian mission in Dacca, Mr P. N. Ojha, they were alleged to have been engaged in anti-state activities and were reported to have contacted the Indian officials to get arms and other material aid across the border at Agartala (India).

the subsequent arrest of Mujib were made. The reaction among the Bengali intelligentsia, particularly those at Dacca University, was one of utter disbelief – and to the masses in East Pakistan Mujib became a martyr overnight. Ayub could do then no greater disservice or harm than to make Mujib a hero.

What were the factors which led the Government to arrest Mujib and to give undue prominence and publicity to the Agartala case? Subversive activities of this kind had not been uncommon in the subcontinent since 1947; both India and Pakistan accused each other of internal subversion and with some justification. Pakistan's hands were not clean in Kashmir nor in the Mizo unrest in Assam; similarly Indian involvement in the agitation and upheaval in East Pakistan was nothing new or unusual.

Some explanations can be given relating to Mujib's arrest. Ayub's Provincial Governor in East Pakistan, Monem Khan, and one of Ayub's Bengali cabinet ministers thought that the best and most effective way to meet Mujib's challenges was to implicate him in an Indian-inspired conspiracy which, it was expected, would ruin his political career. Such calculations may have been made and Ayub may have received such advice, but I cannot vouch for such an interpretation of Mujib's arrest. After joining the Pakistan cabinet in 1969, when the Argartala case had already been withdrawn, I read the intelligence reports, both civil and military, relating to it carefully. According to these reports, which were also vouched for by a senior Bengali intelligence officer whose intgrity I did not doubt and who now holds a top position in Mujib's government in Bangladesh, Mujib's indictment was based on the following data:

Ojha of the Indian Mission at Dacca used to have regular rendezvous with one of Mujib's closest followers, who is now in a key position in the ruling Awami League party in Bangladesh; in fact, he was like a member of his family and was often in his residence at Dacca. Ojha's meetings with Mujib's man were carefully observed by the intelligence service, and there were photographs of his movements. Mujib's man, after lengthy discussions with Ojha, would go to Mujib's residence at Dhanmondhi, Dacca, following a roundabout way from the place of

his meeting with Ojha at an obscure spot in the old quarter of Dacca city. Mujib's wife, though an uneducated woman, began to take an active part in politics after her husband's arrest in 1966; both his wife and Mujib's follower had regular meetings with him at the Dacca Central Jail where Mujib was detained and, thanks to the sympathetic attitude of the Bengali officers and staff of the jail, Mujib had no difficulty in discussing any political plan or plot, even from his confinement. This, according to the intelligence people, was the basis of Mujib's involvement in the case. But the public, who were never told the inside story, were naturally furious over Mujib's arrest. They asked, quite legitimately, how he could be a party to the conspiracy since he was already in prison.[12]

After the creation of Bangladesh, Mujib himself confessed that he had been working for the secession of East Bengal for some time.[13] But the reaction to Mujib's arrest over the Agartala case in East Pakistan could not have been worse. Not only Mujib's arrest but the stupid way the case, which was otherwise based on facts, was handled by the Ayub régime portended ill for Pakistan's viability as a united country; it had an effect in bringing nearer the final dismemberment of Pakistan in the same way as the much-publicized and frequent observance of "Anti-Pakistan Days" by the Indian parties, like Hindu Mahasabha, had made "Pakistan" known and popular among the masses of Indian Muslims in the 1940s.

A special tribunal was set up headed by a former Chief Justice of Pakistan, S. A. Rahman. The trial was public, in contrast to the Rawalpindi conspiracy case of 1951.* There was long debate among the ruling élite about whether the trial should be held *in camera* or be open. Ayub's publicity chief, Altaf Gauhar, was in favour of an open trial not because

* The first Prime Minister of Pakistan, Liaqat Ali Khan, announced in March 1951 that the chief of staff of the Pakistan Army, General Akbar Khan, and other senior officers, had plotted to overthrow the government, who were alleged to have planned "to resort to force with the support of Communist and revolutionary elements" to establish a military dictatorship. The Pakistan Constituent Assembly passed the Rawalpindi Conspiracy (Special Tribunal) Act, 1951, which established a special court to try the case *in camera*.

it would be fair but with the object of exposing the "conspirators". But this was a grand miscalculation: the publicity had just the opposite effect. Mujib and others involved in the case became Bengali national heroes. The reaction to the Agartala case among the Bengalis demonstrated clearly that Bengali sub-nationalism was now a fully-fledged national movement for a separate state of the Bengalis. During the course of the proceedings of the case, all details of the future state of Bangladesh were fully described, such as the colours and design of the national flag, the national anthem, etc. A British lawyer, T. Williams, Q.C., was allowed to come to defend Mujib; he was assisted by the former Chief Justice of East Pakistan, S. M. Murshed, who had been arbitrarily removed by the Government. Justice Murshed is a man of calibre and integrity, and his indirect support in extending co-operation to Mujib's British lawyer had a further impact on the Bengali public, particularly the intelligentsia and journalists over whom Murshed had tremendous influence. His removal as the Chief Justice of East Pakistan had already antagonized public opinion in East Pakistan. The Government's side was taken up by Ayub's former Foreign Minister, Manzoor Quader. At one stage, another former Foreign Minister of Ayub, Z. A. Bhutto, appeared in the court in Mujib's defence, and Mujib was reported to have joked: "The Government has engaged a former Foreign Minister, so I also have one former Foreign Minister."

The drama unfolded in the fullest glare of publicity, and the Dacca newspapers were giving banner headlines to the proceedings of the case. Talk of secession was no longer covert or underground; it was now freely discussed and debated, thanks to the wonderful publicity given by the Ayub régime itself. To draw another comparison with pre-independence days in undivided India, the Agartala case had given the same impetus to the cause of Bengali nationalism as Jinnah's vigorous publicity campaign against Congress rule in the Muslim minority provinces in 1937–9 gave to the creation of Pakistan. Jinnah was successful in making the Indian Muslims realize that there was a conspiracy by the majority Hindu community to destroy the Muslim culture, ways of life, economic and political interests; he observed a "Day of Deliverance" when

Congress rule came to an end in 1939. The publicity in the Agartala case did not expose Mujib or even the Indian involvement; Mujib's chief defence lawyer, Abdus Salam, an Awami Leaguer, himself told me that he had no doubt about India's involvement in the case. It only exposed the Ayub Government's apathy and neglect of the Bengalis' legitimate rights and interests and thereby added arguments in favour of a separate state for the Bengalis.

Ayub's Serious Illness

Soon after the announcement of the Agartala conspiracy case, Ayub was caught with a near-fatal illness – he suffered from a pulmonary embolism. News of the illness was first published on January 29, 1968, saying that he had "an attack of influenza". Subsequently, it was announced on February 6 that he had developed viral pneumonia in the right lung. It was further stated that his physician had advised him to rest "for a few weeks". This piece of advice soon gave rise to all sorts of speculation and rumours. I tried to ascertain the real situation myself by inquiring from the Foreign Secretary, S. M. Yousuf, who till recently had been Ayub's principal secretary. To my utter surprise, Yousef confessed his ignorance of the true condition of Ayub's health; he added that nobody was allowed to see the sick President. Subsequently, I talked to Fida Hasan, Ayub's principal secretary and then promoted to his "Adviser", but again I could not get the full news though Fida Hasan gave me sufficient indication of the seriousness of the illness. Ayub's personal physician, Colonel Mohiuddin, was a friend of mine. It was almost impossible to contact Mohiuddin during those days, but in due course I got the full story from Mohiuddin. In the meantime, my best source of information was my next-door neighbour in Islamabad, Group-Captain T. S. Jan, who was second in command of the highest military intelligence service, the Inter-Services Intelligence Division(I.S.I.D.). The chief of the I.S.I.D., General Akbar, was closely known to me. According to their version, Ayub was a "lost person"; Jan described him as "an umbrella without the cloth-cover – just the steel framework". Ayub was completely debilitated for more than six weeks. Nobody except his family, Altaf

Gauhar, General Yahya and very few others such as Fida Hasan or General Musa was allowed to see him.

According to Ayub's Constitution (Article 16), when the President was incapacitated due to illness or for any other reason, the Speaker would assume the presidential functions. But that was the constitutional provision only; when Ayub used to go abroad, the "Bengali" Speaker of the National Assembly would become the Acting President. But the situation in February 1968 was quite different. As I learned subsequently from Mohiuddin, for about forty-eight hours there seemed scarcely any hope of Ayub's survival. So there the question was not that of an acting arrangement but of succession.

The battle for succession within the military junta began: the generals, air-marshals and admirals were "jockeying and jostling" with each other to take the President's place; the constitutional arrangement was put aside. The three main contenders, according to to my sources of information from I.S.I.D., were General Yahya Khan, the Commander-in-Chief; Air-Marshal Nur Khan, the ambitious chief of the Air Force, and Ayub's Defence Minister, Admiral A. R. Khan. Soon it became evident that Yahya was the strongest contender because in the Pakistan armed forces, the Air Force and Navy were not equal in prestige to the land forces, and as Yahya was the Commander-in-Chief and was living next door to the President, he had a better chance than any of the other contenders. Rumours that some younger officers were trying to capture power against the generals also circulated, but there was no such real threat.

Yahya was reported to have said to a lady sitting next to him at a dinner in February: "Do you know by whose side are you sitting?" Then he gave the answer himself: "The next President of Pakistan." Yahya's long-standing colleague and friend, Major-General Peerzada, was the happiest person; he could never forget his removal from the Presidential House. He now saw the prospect of re-entering the Palace with much greater power and position than before, and was gleefully awaiting the day.

Ayub, however, survived the pulmonary embolism. His publicity chief began to display Ayub's recovery on television.

Ayub used to give "First-of-the-Month" radio-television speeches to the country. On March 1, 1968, Ayub followed this practice, though on television he appeared a sick man. Altaf Gauhar also announced that Ayub would take thc salute at the military parade on Pakistan's National Day, March 23, but that had to be cancelled. Defence Minister A. R. Khan appeared to do the job on March 23, while Yahya, in a self-confident mood, was the real man of the show. The foreign diplomats who were present on the occasion could feel the changed mood in the army hierarchy.

Ayub gradually began to resume his work at the President's House, though on a restricted basis. The number of visitors allowed to see the President was reduced. There was an inner group of three in the ruling élite: Altaf; Ayub's military secretary, Major-General Rafi Khan; and his physician, Colonel Mohiuddin. This trio more or less controlled Ayub's activities and he was gradually cut off from the other powerful members of the ruling élite; this had a prejudical effect on Ayub's continuation in power. Finally, Ayub went to London for a medical check-up in the summer of 1968. He was given, according to Government publicity, "a clean bill of good health".

I met Ayub in London and found him in much better shape than when I had last seen him in later April on the eve of Kosygin's first visit to Pakistan. In spite of his poor health, Ayub made two important decisions almost from his sick-bed. First, he give notice to the U.S. Government to close its military communications centre at Badaber, near Peshawar. Then he had a serious conversation with Kosygin over the provision of Russian arms to Pakistan; thus a move which he had been frantically planning since 1965 had at last been successful, though the Russian arms consisted of nothing more than "nuts and bolts".

After Ayub's return from London with the news of his "full recovery", the celebration of "The Great Decade" was revived with full vigour and enthusiasm. These year-long celebrations, like the publicity of the Agartala conspiracy case, constituted another great miscalculation by the régime and had a most unfavourable effect on Ayub's image in the country.

The programme for a full one-year celebration of the "Decade of Reforms" was mainly the brain-child of Altaf, and it was surprising that a man of Altaf's calibre and intelligence should make such a stupid programme. In a country with so many unsolved socio-economic problems, the Government began to publicize its achievements – phenomenal economic growth; a large number of new universities, colleges and other educational institutions; "grand achievements" in foreign policy, etc. It is true that Pakistan under Ayub achieved remarkable economic growth, but as pointed out earlier, the fruits of this development were not equitably distributed. The economic conditions of the poor and the urban lower middle classes were rather getting worse, particularly after 1965, when development projects had to be cut off as a result of the Indo-Pakistani war and the consequent rise in defence expenditure. At the same time the main source of economic aid, i.e. Washington, was becoming chary of giving aid to Pakistan. In 1967–8, the country's economic situation was not ripe for the Government's to harp in its publicity on "the miracle" of economic growth and prosperity. Instead of enhancing the image of Ayub, it only reminded the people of their unsatisfactory conditions. In East Pakistan, where there was great resentment over Ayub's economic policy, the publicity over the "Decade of Reforms" was a great source of annoyance and provocation. As a counter-move, the Bengalis displayed the skeleton of a starved villager in front of *Shahid-Minar* (memorial to those killed over the language issue) to tell the people that notwithstanding the so-called "miracle" of progress and prosperity, their conditions had not improved. Even in West Pakistan, in cities like Karachi and Lahore, the publicity did harm rather than good to the Ayub régime. It was another ill-planned scheme.

Political Unrest in West Pakistan

Ayub, after his medical check-up in London, began to make preparations for the coming Presidential election in 1969–70. The "Great Decade" performance culminated on October 27, 1968 – the tenth anniversary of Ayub's accession to power. The majority of opposition parties had decided to boycott the election as they were convinced that unless the indirect method of election through the Basic Democrats were not changed, it was no use their contesting the election. The results of the 1964–5 election had demonstrated that the wishes of the electorate were not truly reflected in the results of the election because of the indirect election. Only Mr. Bhutto, whose links with some generals, particularly his old friend Peerzada, were growing, was hoping to enter the Presidential Palace at any cost. So he refused to join in the opposition parties' boycott.

The real and most crucial developments were taking place at GHQ at Rawalpindi. Ayub's recovery, though never full, and his plan to contest the presidential election had upset the plans and calculations of those generals who had been getting ready to enter the Presidential House during his illness in February 1968. It was at this stage that a deal was struck between Bhutto and Peerzada to initiate a movement against Ayub. Peerzada himself told me the story gleefully after his dream of re-entering the Presidential House had been fulfilled in March 1969.

The climate for anti-Ayub agitation was ripe. As described in the preceding pages, Ayub's image and popularity had been declining both among the people and, more important, among his true constituency – the armed forces – since the war of 1965. The dissatisfaction over the Tashkent agreement, the growing East–West Pakistan tensions threatening the viability of a united Pakistan, and economic discontent after the 1965 war were all working against Ayub. Furthermore, in a system of one-man rule like Ayub's political order, constant and vigorous leadership and guidance from the chief boss is vitally important. Ayub was no longer able, after his illness in early 1968, to exercise an active role; he could no longer, for example, attend and preside over the annual ceremonial functions of the various units of the armed forces. He lost the vital contact with his real constituency. This gave his arch-enemies like Bhutto and Peerzada their grand opportunity to topple the régime. Peerzada assured "Zulfi" (as he used to call Zulfiqar Ali Bhutto) that army support for Ayub would be lacking in a mass confrontation, and Bhutto was ready to start the movement on the popular theme of Ayub's alleged sacrifice of "national honour", preserved at the cost of the blood of the brave *Jawans* (soliders) in the battlefield, at the conference table at Tashkent. Bhutto began to make repeated promises to disclose the so-called "secrets" of the Tashkent agreement. Nothing was more popular in the Punjab, "the bastion of power" in West Pakistan, than to whip up anti-Indian feelings. Bhutto became ever bolder in his wild accusations against Ayub in collusion with some generals at GHQ.

This was the background of the sudden outburst of violence in Rawalpindi, the garrison capital of Pakistan, and the role of Z. A. Bhutto, the so-called "revolutionary leader". General Musa, Ayub's trusted Governor, and Khawaja Shahabuddin, the Information Minister, tried to meet Bhutto's allegations against Ayub on the Tashkent agreement. Musa pointed out that although Bhutto might now be criticizing the Tashkent agreement, he had earlier taken the credit for its drafting and had defended it both inside and outside the National Assembly until he was sacked by Ayub. I had the opportunity of reading the entire proceedings of the Tashkent Conference, but could not trace any sign of dissent by Bhutto. At the height of the movement, the Soviet Union made an unusual gesture to Ayub: the Soviet news agency *Tass* came out with a denial of any secret "clauses" in the Tashkent Agreement. But who cared for the truth? Ayub had lost his initial popularity by a number of factors as described earlier, and Bhutto had no difficulty in rousing public passion against his régime. In an underdeveloped country where there are colossal socio-economic problems, it is not difficult to discredit a régime when it has been in power for ten years. Moreover, the Ayub régime had given enough provocation for political agitation; and its record was worsening.

As soon as the student–police clashes took place in Rawalpindi in early November resulting in the death of a student from police firing on November 7, 1968, the undercurrent of popular resentment became articulate and was given vigorous expression. As pointed out earlier, the agitation began as unexpectedly to the opposition leaders, excluding Bhutto, as to the ruling authorities. But the political leaders were quick to react to the situation to bring about the downfall of Ayub. Students, journalists, lawyers, doctors, engineers and labour all joined in the movement for an end to Ayub's political system.[14]

However, once it had spread to East Pakistan, the movement

took a different shape. There it was not merely an agitation against Ayub or his régime, but a revolt against what the Bengalis began to regard as their "domination" by West Pakistan or, more accurately, by the Punjabis. It was the most articulate expression of the emerging Bengali nationalism. While the leaders in West Pakistan demanded the restoration of parliamentary democracy and a direct method of election, the Bengalis raised their voice for *extreme* regional autonomy, namely Mujib's six-point programme. The Bengalis seemed to have adopted the old technique of kicking the enemy when he was already down.

It is true that as the movement progressed, in West Pakistan too, it was not merely a movement for constitutional reforms; it turned into a struggle between the "haves" and the "have nots". The unprivileged group seemed to have got their opportunity to voice their resentment against a privileged élite, who in the name of "Pakistan", "Islamic ideology" and other high-sounding slogans, had grown fat since the creation of the state in 1947. In East Pakistan the grand old Maulana Bhashani was agitating not only for regional autonomy but also as the spokesman of the "have nots". Mujib was still in military custody for his part in the Agartala conspiracy case; his party had been ruthlessly suppressed by the provincial Governor Abdul Monem Khan since the movement for six points in 1966, and as such was not well organized although Mujib had acquired tremendous popularity. The opposition parties, including Mujib's Awami League but excluding Bhutto's People's Party and Bhashani's National Awami Party, formed an alliance known as the Democratic Action Committee (DAC).

Initially, Ayub and his advisers tried to minimize the impact of the movement, and Ayub refused to talk to the opposition leaders. Bhutto was arrested on November 13, two days after an unsuccessful attempt on Ayub's life while he was addressing a public meeting at Peshawar. The reaction among the students to Bhutto's arrest was great, as Bhutto had by this time become a hero of the students for condemning the police excesses against them. The more significant development was that after Bhutto's arrest two new figures, both noted for clean records, joined the movement: Air-Marshal Ashgar Khan in West Pakistan and Justice S. M. Murshed in East

Pakistan. They were newcomers to the political scene and as such Ayub's oft-repeated adverse comments against "old politicians" of the parliamentary era (1947–58) were not applicable to them. They gave fresh momentum to the movement.

Ayub and the Generals

After ten years of unchallenged rule, it was a big shock for Ayub to face the realities of his situation. The army intelligence chief, Major-General Akbar of I.S.I.D., had no hesitation in sending the most candid reports to Ayub; even his top civil service advisers could no longer conceal the unpleasant truth. There was a scene of confusion and panic at the Presidential House. There were regular meetings of a small group consisting of Altaf, Fida Hasan and one or two others to review the situation and plan the strategy for meeting the most serious challenges to the régime.

At first, Ayub's expectations were that the normal machinery of law and order, consisting of the police and paramilitary forces, would be adequate to meet the situation. Ayub was still thinking in terms of law and order, but he soon realized that the situation had gone far beyond the capacity of the normal machinery of law and order. There were two alternatives before Ayub: a political settlement with the opposition – a very complicated task, apart from Ayub's reluctance to "talk to the politicians", because of the lack of a national party or a national leader. The country seemed to have been already politically split: Mujib was a popular hero in East Pakistan but anathema to West Pakistan; Bhutto was popular in West Pakistan but in East Pakistan he was not only uninfluential but thoroughly disliked for his long eight-year association with the Ayub régime. Ashgar Khan and Murshed were newcomers and were listened to respectfully by the urban élites but had no hold over the masses who were getting beyond the control of the centre politicians. Bhasani was never interested in any political or constitutional settlement; along with other leftist forces, he was working for a real revolutionary movement, not one which had the secret blessing of GHQ.

The second option before Ayub was to regain the Army's

confidence. He therefore turned to his real constituency for help. As I gathered from Yahya himself after I joined his cabinet in 1969, a series of meetings between Ayub and the top armed forces leaders look place in February 1969. This account was also substantiated by General Akbar and by some members of the Presidential House staff, who can sometimes provide a better account of the "inside story". The chiefs of the Army, Air Force and Navy and their aides had joint and separate meetings with Ayub. The most crucial meeting took place in mid-February when the three chiefs (General Yahya, Air-Marshal Nur Khan and Vice-Admiral Ahsan) were to tell Ayub to work for "a political settlement" and not to rely on the military forces to suppress the revolutionary movement. The most interesting part of this crucial conference was: who was to break the unpleasant truth to the boss? – there was pause, hesitancy and silence. Ahsan of the Navy would not take the initiative as he wanted to maintain his posture of neutrality; for Yahya it was a delicate time – Ayub had made him Commander-in-Chief, by-passing a few senior generals. Ultimately the task fell to the outspoken chief of the Air Force, Nur Khan. The army chiefs agreed to use the armed forces only to the minimum extent needed to keep the administration functioning and prevent the situation from being exploited by any foreign country, presumably India.

For Ayub the advice to seek a political solution as a remedy for the basic causes of the upheaval was perhaps the biggest shock. He had been the unchallenged chief of the armed forces for the last eighteen years (1950–68). As he told a visiting foreign dignitary, "perhaps they are now tired of seeing my face". There were, however, genuine reasons for the army's "getting tired" of Ayub.

Ayub Turns to Political Leaders

Ayub invited the chairman of the DAC, Nasrullah Khan, to meet him. Nasrullah was also authorized to invite any of his other colleagues. The DAC responded by saying that Ayub must withdraw the state of emergency and Defence of Pakistan rules which had been imposed since the 1965 war with India. Further demands included the release of all imprisoned students;

the lifting of the ban on public meetings, processions, etc., and an end to the suppression of students by the police. Ayub, after some tactical delays, agreed to the four demands of the DAC. Three important leaders with popular support, Mujib, Bhashani and Bhutto, were away from the scene: Mujib was still in military custody, Bhutto was still in prison, and Bhashani declared in unqualified terms his opposition to any negotiations with the Government. Bhutto was released with the withdrawal of the Defence of Pakistan rules under which he had been arrested, but after coming out of prison, he declared his opposition to any negotiations with Ayub. The reasoning of Bhashani and Bhutto differed totally. Bhashani favoured a prolonged confrontation and mass upheaval, which was good strategy for his long-term political objectives, while Bhutto knew that Ayub's days were numbered as the generals refused to back him, so why make a compromise with a sinking man? He rather pleased the rising military group with his negative attitude.

Mujib's case was most complicated. While Ayub could accede to the four demands of DAC, it was difficult for him to withdraw the Agartala case and release Mujib unconditionally. A powerful group of the military junta was still opposed to the withdrawal of the Agartala case. But events overtook all calculations. The agitation against the Agartala case was so great in East Pakistan that the provincial Government virtually collapsed and student leaders were running the administration of the province. Mujib, however, did not get the true picture of the situation while he was living in military custody. So the general officer commanding in East Pakistan, Major-General Muzaffruddin, managed to make a deal with Mujib: Mujib pledged not to work against the viability of United Pakistan, and was thus assured of Ayub's clemency. But strangely enough Mujib, without realizing the depth of public feeling, agreed to go to Rawalpindi on parole. So Ayub did not have to withdraw the Agartala case and yet was able to bring about Mujib's participation in the Round Table Conference (RTC). Ayub's Defence Minister, Admiral A. R. Khan, also had meetings and talks with Mujib in his military custody.

It was at this crucial moment that the same Bengali officer who gave me the full account of Ohja's meetings with Mujib's follower during the Agartala conspiracy, which was referred to earlier, made a shrewd move which saved Mujib's prestige and honour. He arranged a meeting for Mrs. Mujib with her husband at the place where he was held in custody by pleading with General Muzaffruddin that this request should be granted on humanitarian grounds and the General agreed. Mujib's wife thus had the opportunity to brief her husband on the prevailing mood of the people and to tell him that it would be a terrible blow to his prestige if his followers were to see him going to attend the RTC under parole and military custody. She also explained that Ayub was bound to release him if he were to stick to his demand for unconditional release. So a dramatic turn occurred: while the plane was ready to take Mujib to Rawalpindi and the leaders were already at Karachi, Lahore and Rawalpindi airports waiting to meet Mujib, he turned his face and demanded his release before he would participate in the RTC. Ayub had no choice. The final step was also taken: the Agartala case was withdrawn and Mujib went to participate in the RTC as a free man who was also a victor.[15] In the meantime, Ayub announced his irrevocable intention not to contest the presidential election.

Had Ayub lost all his hopes? Not yet. I had two meetings with him in February. It was difficult to assess anything accurately but I had no doubt that the initiative had gone from the Presidential House to GHQ. Ayub began the RTC with all seriousness; but it soon became evident that this much-publicized event would achieve nothing. Events were moving fast.

Ayub's Final Bids

Many of the "leaders" participating in the RTC were self-styled ones without any popular base. Any settlement with these leaders, except for Mujib and Wali Khan of the North-West Frontier Province, would be meaningless. In fact, in the absence of Bhashani and Bhutto, Mujib was the key figure. So serious attempts were made for an Ayub–Mujib understanding. Ayub's closest adviser, Altaf, began the initiative. He had the support of the Haroon brothers, Yousuf and Mahmood. The Haroon family had a feudal type of rivalry with the

Bhutto family. While Bhutto was serving Ayub as his Foreign Minister, the Haroon brothers had a difficult time. Yousuf Haroon was not allowed to enter Pakistan because of his alleged links with a foreign agency. But when Bhutto began his campaign against Ayub in 1968, Ayub made a deal with the Haroon brothers: Mahmood was made Ayub's High Commissioner in London while Yousuf was made Governor of West Pakistan.

Though belonging to one of "the twenty-two families", the Haroon brothers had a long-standing friendship with Mujib, to whom they gave a salary of 3,000 rupees and many other facilities during his long period of political persecution. Now, with the help of Altaf, Ayub utilized the services of the Haroon brothers in reaching a deal with Mujib, which was Ayub's last hope. Secret meetings took place at the Presidential House between Ayub, Mujib and the Haroon brothers in a "cordial atmosphere". The proposed deal was that Mujib would be made Prime Minister of Pakistan under a parliamentary system and with regional autonomy for East Pakistan; Yousuf Haroon was already sworn in as the Governor of West Pakistan and a nominee of Mujib, Dr. M. N. Huda, was appointed as Governor of East Pakistan; and Ayub would continue as President under a system of parliamentary democracy. Again events overtook the working-out of this deal. The generals at GHQ were not happy with any such secret deal between Ayub and Mujib. Bhutto got the news of the secret talks as he had no difficulty in knowing what was happening either at the GHQ or the Presidential House, thanks to his friend Peerzada. Bhutto at once issued press statements denouncing the secret parleys, and this embarrassed Mujib. Bhashani was also terribly upset over Mujib and the Haroon brothers getting power. The latter were regarded as having strong links with the Americans. Ayub's shifts in favour of the Haroon brothers had cost him Bhasani's covert support, which he had enjoyed since the Presidential election of 1965. This was mainly due to his moving away from Washington and closer to Peking. Bhashani and his followers were happy with Ayub's foreign policy, but Ayub's courting the Russians since 1966 and his latest deal with the Haroon brothers annoyed Bhashani and the pro-Peking group of National Awami party. At this stage, Bhashani openly preached violence, destruction, and armed uprisings: *hartal* (strike), *gherao* (encirclement).

Mujib became shaky; in fact, the whole situation was so confusing that hardly any political settlement or serious political negotiations could take place. The small advisory group at Fida Hasan's office in the Presidential House met regularly. I was summoned twice to attend those meetings but nobody could understand what was happening and how the crisis could be resolved. The RTC came to a deadlock when Mujib presented his extreme demands for autonomy bordering on break-up of the country. All the West Pakistani leaders were opposed to Mujib's scheme, and so the RTC met its natural death. When the RTC failed to reach any agreement, Ayub announced his own formula on March 13 – restoration of the parliamentary and federal system and a direct method of election. Ayub wanted to restore the *status quo* as it had existed before his capture of power through the coup of 1958. But the Bengalis were not satisfied with the *status quo* of 1958; much water had flowed under the bridge since they accepted "parity of representation" in 1955 and the federal structure of the 1956 constitution.

The RTC failed; so too did the Ayub–Mujib secret parleys. Mujib was nervous that it might jeopardize his image with the Bengalis. But the final blow to the Ayub–Mujib deal came from GHQ: when Ayub really had good prospects with Mujib, the group opposed to him in the military junta tantalized Mujib with the prospect of getting power through the front door (i.e. through elections) rather than the "back door", which was what Ayub offered him,

After the failure of the talks on political settlement, either through the RTC or by bilateral negotiations with Mujib, the country's situation deteriorated quickly. There was almost a complete breakdown of governmental machinery, and the condition of the country was semi-anarchic. It was obvious that this state of affairs could not be allowed to continue. Ayub summoned a special cabinet meeting in mid-March, which also turned out to be his last. Yahya was specially invited to attend the meeting. The description he gave me of it was as follows.

Ayub summed up the situation after the failure of the RTC

and Mujib's demand for total acceptance of his six points. He told the cabinet, and Yahya in particular, that the only remedy for saving the country lay in the imposition of martial law. The cabinet, as usual, listened to the supreme boss but all eyes were fixed on Yahya who, as he narrated to me, listened to the debate quietly but without much comment; he indicated to Ayub that he would talk to him alone. So the Ayub cabinet was adjourned for good. The two old colleagues and friends, Ayub and Yahya, moved from the cabinet room of the President's House to Ayub's office in the adjoining room. Ayub put the final question to Yahya: would he come to the government's rescue by imposing martial law, which was now the only remedy? Yahya agreed that martial law was now the only solution. But he stipulated certain conditions before he would impose martial law in support of the government: First, Ayub must sack his provincial governors and his Cabinet – to this he agreed at once. Secondly, Ayub must dissolve the National Assembly and the two provincial Assemblies; again came Ayub's prompt affirmative response. Then Yahya, after a pause, proposed: "You must also abrogate your constitution as it has proved totally unacceptable to the people, both in East and West Pakistan. I cannot allow my troops to make an unacceptable constitution operate against the wishes of the people."

At this stage Ayub exclaimed: "Abrogate the Constitution! No, that is impossible; the Constitution is bound in the book of Pakistan and in the soil of Pakistan!"

But soon Ayub realized what Yahya was demanding: in the absence of the Constitution, martial law would be the supreme law of the land and the chief martial law administrator would be the final authority. Ayub's position would be the same as that of President Iskander Mirza from October 7 to October 27, 1958, when Ayub threw him out of the Presidency and sent him abroad into exile for life.

So the drama ended with a significant smile and remark from Ayub: "I know what you want; all right, let us mutually work out the final arrangement." So Ayub decided to hand over power to Yahya and the final preparations for the imposition of martial law began immediately.

It must be added that even if Yahya had been willing to back the Ayub régime with the 1962 Constitution, it would have been a hopeless task. The public mood, the popular uprisings, the new socio-economic forces, the growing regional tensions were all against the continuation of the Ayub régime in any shape or form. It was not merely a question of Yahya's loyalty to Ayub; the movement might have been originated by some green signals from GHQ as a result of Ayub's loss of confidence among the armed forces, but once it started it became a genuine mass upheaval and no secret deal or "palace plan" could save the situation.

On the contrary, it was also not wholly true that the new military régime was a "reluctant" one, as it was interpreted to be in some quarters. The military junta was as "reluctant" as Ayub pretended to be in 1958 when he said: "We solemnly decided to build up a true national army free from politics."[16] It was as untrue as the new military régime's "reluctance" to take over power in 1969.

In his "farewell broadcast" Ayub presented the same dismal picture of the country as he had done when the army coup took place on October 7, 1958. On that occasion Ayub had justified the army's take-over on the grounds of what he termed "total administrative, economic, political and moral chaos in the country".[17] After about eleven years of almost absolute rule, he confessed that the country was on the verge of total collapse and declared with great pathos: "I cannot preside over the destruction of my country."[18] What a sad ending!

An Assessment

Was the Ayub era so unsuccessful and blank as Ayub himself seemed to admit in his last broadcast? Why did he make such a pathetic statement? Some interpreted Ayub's final speech as having been made under duress, but this is not correct. Both Ayub and Yahya told me that the farewell speech was made freely without any pressure or even hint from Yahya. Ayub's sense of frustration, humiliation and failure was the explanation. I began the discussion of the fall of Ayub by referring to some of the most flattering remarks on Ayub, his political order, his economic policy and successes in external affairs, made mostly by foreigners. Inside the country too, Ayub began his political career with wide support even in East Pakistan. People were so frustrated with the unsatisfactory working of the country's parliamentary democracy and the performance of the politicians that they welcomed Ayub in the expectation that their basic problems and interests would be better served by an honest, efficient and stable régime. Ayub was, in a sense, the last hope for a united Pakistan.

But in giving Pakistan its much needed national identity Ayub was a total failure. The crucial question is why he failed so miserably in the task of national integration. In an underdeveloped country, an effective political leader might be successful in developing a broader sense of cohesion in a society characterized by ethnic, linguistic and cultural pluralism. As Howard Wriggins puts it: "In a society made of diverse primordial groupings with parochial loyalties, a personality can be the main focus of common loyalty."[19] First, let it be stressed that Ayub was not a leader with the mass support or calibre of Nehru, Gandhi or Jinnah. To achieve political integration in a Pakistan with two wings geographically separated by a thousand miles was too big a task for Ayub. He could, at best, have contributed to the achievement of that goal; but his political order and his economic policy, instead of contributing to the goal of integration of the country, greatly widened the gap, both political and economic, between the peoples of the two wings.

There was no lack of sincerity. Ayub was a great patriot, and loved Pakistan passionately; he did not even hesitate to risk his own personal security in defending what he genuinely believed to be the "national interest" of Pakistan. When he wrote in his autobiography *Friends not Masters* that "Pakistan is my passion", he meant it.

As for the East–West Pakistan relationship on which the viability of a united Pakistan depended, Ayub's understanding was extremely limited. I had the opportunity to read the reports which Iskander Mirza as the Governor of East Bengal in 1954 used to send to the Governor-General, Ghulam Mohammed, in which Mirza used to offer his solutions to problems facing the "troublesome province of East Bengal". The approach was that of a district officer under a colonial régime.

Mirza suggested, for instance, shifting the campus of Dacca University to a remote place and setting up a few cadet colleges as the panacea for East Bengal! Ayub's approach was different in degree but not in kind. He allocated more money for development work in East Pakistan; his rural works programme no doubt benefited the poorest landless labourers in East Pakistan; agricultural employment facilities were increased in rural areas (facilities the lack of which is now lamented in Bangladesh); a vast extension of roads in villages was made, hospitals were opened, educational facilities were increased. Some of Ayub's social reforms, such as family planning and a family law ordinance prohibiting polygamy were commendable. Ayub's record for modernizing the country was better than that of his predecessors. His economic policy resulted in an increase of the gross national product (GNP) from 2 per cent to about 6 per cent in the 1960s. But, as pointed out earlier, the growth was not being equitably passed on to the poor. This created frustration and bitterness among the lower income groups both in urban and rural areas, notwithstanding Ayub's rural works programme, because they were not adequate to meet the growing demands and expectations.

Turning to his political order, its greatest shortcoming was the lack of effective opportunities for the Bengalis to have their share in the decision-making process. By curbing the power of parliament, by making the cabinet ineffective, Ayub's political order robbed the Bengalis of their share of participation in national affairs. Nationalism or patriotism cannot develop or flourish in a vacuum. The Bengalis could not be expected to be conscious of "Pakistani nationalism" when they "could only react but not act on major national issues".[20] The Army's atrocities during the civil war in 1971 and the Indian military intervention backed by Soviet help were the immediate cause of the disintegration of Pakistan. It was Ayub's political order and his inability to appreciate the political dynamics in East Pakistan in the late 1960s which were the real factors, among others, for the rise of Bengali nationalism and the birth of Bangladesh.

His lack of understanding of the basic problems of the Bengalis was revealed to me when I had my last meeting with him in New York in the summer of 1971. Ayub had gone to the

United States for a heart operation and stopped in New York overnight on his way back to Pakistan. I, with two other friends, went to see him mainly as a courtesy; we had no intention of discussing politics with him in his poor physical condition after a major operation. But the country was in the midst of a civil war and political issues could not be avoided, particularly when he insisted that we join him for dinner at the luxurious apartment of a friend of his (a non-Bengali industrialist from East Pakistan) in Manhattan. So we discussed political issues facing the country. In the course of discussion, Ayub narrated how moderate Bengali leaders like Nural Amin and others who opposed Mujib's six points urged him to grant real autonomy to East Pakistan. Turning to me, he asked: "Tell me, what were they asking for? Did not my provincial Governor Momen enjoy all the powers needed for running the provincial government in East Pakistan? What more could I grant?" After so many years of experience, Ayub equated the delegated powers of his nominated and highly unpopular Governor with the legitimate demands of the seventy-five million people of his country! It was a great shock for me; I wish I had not met Ayub on that occasion as it destroyed my good opinion of his political acumen, although I still have a high regard for his personal qualities and graciousness.

REFERENCES

1. Arnold J. Toynbee, "Communism and the West in Asian Countries", *The Annals of the American Academy of Political and Social Sciences*, July 1961.
2. Quoted in an unpublished paper by Joseph Lelyveld for the Ford Foundation, New York, September 1969.
3. Ibid.
4. *Survey of International Affairs*, London, 1960; *The Economist*, August 15, 1969.
5. G. A. Almond and T. S. Coleman, *The Politics of the Developing Areas*, Princeton: Princeton University Press, 1960, pp. 53–5.
7. See Mahbul-Ul Huq's speech at the 1968 meetings of the Pakistan Management Association in *The Pakistan Observer*, Dacca, May 3, 1968.
7. Edwards S. Manson, Robert Dorfman and Stephen A. Manglin, *Conflict in East Pakistan: Background and Prospects, London:* Bangladesh Action Committee, 1971, Part III, p. 4.
8. See Shahid Javed Bunki, "Ayub's Fall: A Socio-economic Explanation", *Asian Survey*, March 1972; W. M. Dobell, "Ayub Khan as President

of Pakistan", *Pacific Affairs*, Fall 1969; Wayne Wilcox, "Pakistan in 1969: Once Again at the Starting Point", *Asian Survey*, February 1970; Joseph Lelyveld, "Ayub's Hopes Dissolve into Martial Law", *New York Times*, March 30, 1969.

9. G. W. Choudhury, *The Major Powers and the Subcontinent* (forthcoming).
10. I owe this account to a senior civil official of Ayub who held a key position at that time and who was opposed to the proposed course of action.
11. *The Major Powers and the Subcontinent*, op. cit.
12. G. W. Choudhury, "Bangladesh: Why it Happened", *International Affairs*, London, April 1972.
13. See Mujib's television interview with David Frost (London Weekend Television), January 16, 1972; his press interview with Musa Ahmad of the *Bangladesh Observer*, Dacca, on March 23, 1972, and *Bangabandhu Speaks*, published by the Ministry of Foreign Affairs, Government of Bangladesh, Dacca, n.d.
14. See G. W. Choudhury, *Constitutional Development in Pakistan* (second edition), London: Longman, 1970, pp. 250–5; The movement has also been described in Herbert Feldman, *From Crisis to Crisis: Pakistan 1962–1969*, London: Oxford University Press, 1972, pp. 226–76; in Richard S. Wheeler, *The Politics of Pakistan: A Constitutional Quest*, Ithaca: Cornell University Press, 1970, pp. 264–74; and in Lawrence Ziring, *The Ayub Khan Era: Politics in Pakistan 1958–69*, pp. 172–91.
15. I owe this story to the Bengali officers whom I wish to leave unidentified on account of his present position in Bangladesh. Major-General Muzaffruddin also told me the same story; subsequently a student leader belonging to the inner core of the Awami League and a former student of mine gave me the same version of the episode. In fact, I asked Mujib himself about it and though he tried to interpret it in such a way as to prove his strength and political strategy, he had to confess the substance of the episode.
16. See the text of Ayub's broadcast on October 8, 1959, in *Dawn*, Karachi, October 9, 1958.
17. Ibid.
18. See Ayub's last broadcast on March 25, 1969, in *Dawn*, March 26, 1969.
19. W. Howard Wriggins, *The Ruler's Imperative*, New York, Columbia University Press, 1969, p. 8.
20. G. W. Choudhury, *Constitutional Development in Pakistan*, p. 247.

3

YAHYA BEGINS ANEW

Pakistan had been accustomed to kaleidoscopic political changes: the dismissal in 1953 and in 1957 of two Prime Ministers who had the confidence of the legislature; the constitutional coup against the Governor-General, and within a few weeks the dissolution of the legislature by the same Governor-General in 1954; the Ayub–Mirza coup in 1958 and Mirza's exile within three weeks – these are some of the glaring instances at the centre. At the provincial level, a police chief was nominated as chief minister of the North-West Frontier Province in 1953, and when in 1955 the four provinces of West Pakistan were amalgamated into "one unit", the provincial chief ministers, who opposed the seemingly undemocratic process through which the scheme was rushed, were so suddenly and arbitrarily sacked that Pakistan's political order could hardly be described as parliamentary democracy. It was described satirically, though not without justification, as "suddenocracy".

The fact that the great political upheaval in the winter of 1968–9 resulted not in the restoration of democracy but in the imposition of a new military régime was a big shock, but not an unusual phenomenon on the Pakistan political scene. The political leaders were unable or unwilling to take the responsibility of forming a government. They were only demanding the immediate resignation of Ayub. Asghar Khan asked for a "caretaker government", but no political leader with adequate popular support was willing to accept a constitutional arrangement under which such a government and the subsequent elections could be arranged. While the people had revolted against an authoritarian régime and wanted a democratic government, the leaders failed miserably to reflect the popular will.

The result was the imposition of martial law for the second time in a decade. It dismayed the friends of democracy both at home and abroad including the Western press. *The Economist* described the situation with the headline "Tweedle Khan takes over". It also alleged that Ayub seemed to have resorted to martial law "to frustrate" the demands of the regionalists in East Pakistan and those of the leftist parties for distributive justice.[1]

For Ayub it was a great failure to have to ask the Pakistani Commander-in-chief, General Yahya Khan, to "save the country from utter chaos and total destruction". In fact, the political leaders were relieved not to be facing the near-anarchic situation in the country. They seemed to be pleased that the army was called in to tackle a situation which was beyond their calculation. The centre leaders of the DAC were alarmed by the rise of extremist forces and by the militant and highly articulate expression of Bengali sub-nationalism. Bhashani and his leftist forces preferred a military régime with no political base to a bourgeois one with popular backing. For their long-range objectives, leftist forces preferred the military régime to Mujib's coming to power through a secret deal. Mujib was also unwilling to make any compromise; he was afraid of the growing influence of Bhashani. His strategy in 1969 seemed to be to face elections rather than to become Prime Minister under any acceptable political arrangement for the country as a whole, which would mean some sacrifice of his extreme demands for regional autonomy. So, although there was apparent "dismay", the political leaders were neither surprised nor unhappy by the emergence of the military régime. This explained how, although it was not welcomed, it was still accepted quietly. Processions and strikes in various parts of the country vanished in a moment. The behaviour of the faculty members of Dacca University was amusing: they were the loudest in making protests but were also the first to return quietly to their duties. To borrow a Marxist phrase, the 1969 military régime in Pakistan could perhaps be described as "a parasite on society". Marx in his *Eighteenth Brumaire of Louis Bonaparte* describes how struggle among various sections in France created circumstances which made it "possible for a grotesque mediocrity to play a hero's part".[2]

The circumstances in which Ayub and Yahya imposed martial law were, however, entirely different. When Ayub came to power, Pakistan's democratic institutions had been perverted and its politicians discredited. On the other hand, when Yahya became a "military" president, there was great resentment against authoritarian rule and lively agitation in favour of democracy. More important, the Bengalis were no longer prepared to acquiesce in an "ordering framework" in which their demands could be ignored. Bengali sub-nationalism was no longer covert or inarticulate. The four-month-long political agitation against Ayub provided the Bengalis with free opportunities for proclaiming their political goals in clear terms which could be ignored only at Pakistan's peril. Simultaneously the "have nots" revolted against a privileged élite and demanded social justice. The Government's economic policy must aim not only at a high growth rate but also at distributive justice. The problems and challenges facing Yahya Khan and his régime were formidable and complicated. The movement – or more accurately counter-coup against Ayub – was originally hatched by some ambitious generals at GHQ in collaboration with frustrated leaders like Bhutto, but it resulted in the "floodtide of Bengali nationalism" and in the formidable and unprecedented challenges to the privileged élite in Pakistan who monopolized both political and economic power.

Yahya had neither the vision nor the capacity to tackle the gigantic problems facing Pakistan in 1969. His immediate task was "to put the administration back on the rails"; he added "we have had enough administrative laxity and chaos".[3] At the same time, he could not ignore the upsurge of popular demand for democratic government and social justice. So Yahya declared within twenty-four hours of coming into power:

> I wish to make it absolutely clear to you that I have no ambition other than the creation of conditions conducive to the establishment of a constitutional government. It is my firm belief that a sound, clean and honest administration is a prerequisite for sane and constructive political life and for the smooth transfer of power to the representatives of the people *elected freely and impartially on the basis of adult franchise.*

It will be the task of these elected representatives to give the country a workable constitution and final solution to all other political, economic and social problems that have been agitating the minds of the people.[4]

Thus began a new chapter – as it turned out, the last – in the political drama of united Pakistan. Yahya's pledge to restore democracy was at first greeted with considerable scepticism; it was the sort of declaration that had accompanied the emergence of military régimes in the Third World all too often. Yahya's régime was described in certain quarters as Ayub's political order without Ayub. That might have been the original hope of those at the GHQ who were planning a counter-coup in the summer of 1968 when Ayub returned with a "clean certificate of good health" from London. But the four-month political movement had roused too many expectations and encouraged too much political activity not permitted during the Ayub era, and thus a reversion to Ayub's system was simply not possible.

Before discussing Yahya's efforts to convince the political leaders that his pledge was not an empty one but that he meant business, let me describe the new military régime in Pakistan and its *modus operandi*. The Ayub régime had been a civil-military partnership. Some of the top civil officials were as much part of his ruling élite as were some of the generals, A new régime tries to benefit from the mistakes and shortcomings of its immediate precedessor. One of the causes of Ayub's downfall was believed to have been his overdependence on senior civil servants. The new régime, particularly Major-General (soon promoted to Lieutenant-General) S. G. M. Peerzada, who was described by the *Sunday Times* as *de facto* Prime Minister, and in fact the Rasputin under Yahya, was determined to avoid a similar "mistake" and therefore made sure that no senior bureaucrats were able to get near Yahya.

The administrative set-up at the President's House was changed. At the top, Yahya became the chief martial law administrator (CMLA); for a few days he did not assume the title of President. Then, due to diplomatic compulsions, he became the "reluctant" and "shy" President. Foreign diplomats told the Ministry of Foreign Affairs that it would be a complicated affair to present credentials to a martial law administrator. The U.S. Government also raised, not publicly but through diplomatic channels, the question of "recognition" of the new régime. However, once Yahya became President, diplomatic niceties were solved. Yahya, however, continued to be the Commander-in-chief of the army. According to his own order of precedence, he often used to describe himself first as Commander-in-chief, then Chief Martial Law Administrator and lastly President. As Ayub had lost the confidence of GHQ by becoming an "elective" president and ceasing to be Commander-in-chief, Yahya always retained his basic post of Commander-in-chief in the expectation that it would enable him to have direct access to and links with the GHQ.

Next to Yahya at the President's House was Peerzada; his official title was Principal Staff Officer (PSO) to the CMLA and the President. Under the PSO were two brigadiers: Rahim, a Punjabi who was given charge of martial law affairs, and Karim, a Bengali, who was put in charge of civil affairs. These two brigadiers (subsequently promoted to major-generals) were the "super secretaries"; no secretary of any ministry could send a file to the President without going through these two, who were under the direct control and supervision of the PSO. It was an amusing phenomenon to see the top bureaucrats waiting in the corridors of the brigadiers and then at the office of the all-powerful PSO; very rarely did they have occasion to see the President himself. The Ayub–Mirza régime in 1958 had been very prompt in having a civilian cabinet, but the new régime decided to have no such partnership.

The various ministries were divided like this: Yahya was in charge of Defence and Foreign Affairs. General Hamid, the Chief of Staff and number two in the armed forces, took the Home Ministry. The rest was divided between the two chiefs of the Air Force and the Navy: Nur Khan, the Air Commander-in-chief, became the overlord of the Ministries of Education, Labour, Health, Social Welfare, while the Navy chief, Ahsan, was given Finance, Planning, Industry and Commerce. Yahya, Hamid, Peerzada, Nur Khan and Ahsan constituted a small cabinet known as the Council of "Administration".

The secretary of a ministry was summoned before the Council whenever any matter relating to that particular ministry was to be discussed.

Nur Khun, however, recruited a number of talented younger men from outside the civil service, popularly known as "whizz-kids". He began to introduce reforms with far-reaching implications such as the right to strike and other important concessions which had been denied to the workers under the Ayub régime and then proceeded to introduce a new educational policy which, although it had some commendable features, included also such fantastic proposals as giving students the right to participate in the selection and promotion of teachers including university professors. Nur Khan's labour policy had already created panic. Yahya was not prepared to go in the same direction to placate the students to such an absurd extent; he was willing to replace the "black" university ordinances of Ayub and to give the students their legitimate rights, but Nur Khan was too ambitious – he wanted to create an image for himself, as against Yahya, by introducing "radical" reforms. So the first tussle began in the ruling junta between Yahya and Nur Khan. By this time Yahya also set up a three-man "planning cell" following the model of Nur Khan's "whizz kids". As already mentioned, I became a member of the planning cell. My first contact with Peerzada was both surprising and amusing.

Peerzada was unceremoniously removing all the so-called "Ayub men" – the top civil officers who had been close to Ayub, such as Altaf Gauhar, N. A. Faruque and Fida Hasan. Although I had no such important links with Ayub as these officers, I had, as mentioned in the preceding chapter, a close and friendly relationship with him. Peerzada's summons to me therefore came as a surprise. He recognized me at once since I had met him on many occasions while he was Ayub's military secretary. There were a few moments of initial surprise and hesitancy. Then, like a big boss, he communicated to me the order of the CMLA's office "transferring" my services from the Ministry of Foreign Affairs to the CMLA's office. When I explained to him that I was not a regular government official and that my services were lent to the Ministry of Foreign Affairs for a specific assignment on a contract, he first hinted at a threat that defiance of an order from the CMLA's office might lead to termination of my job at Dacca University, but he soon changed the technique and pleaded with me to work as a team member for "important affairs". Finally, I was successful in making a compromise – I continued to be Director-General (Research) in the Foreign Ministry but would also work as a part-time member of the planning cell. I soon found myself a full-time member of the planning cell and only part-time in the Foreign Ministry. I must confess that the work at the planning cell was both interesting and challenging. I was given the task of helping the President on political and constitutional matters. However, it was Nur Khan's educational reforms which gave me the first contacts with President Yahya Khan. I began to attend the meetings of the Council of Administration and witnessed the interesting sight of top bureaucrats being heckled by Nur Khan's "whizz kids". The bureaucrats, however, knew well how to bide their time and adjust to the new situation. Nur Khan soon became the target of "palace intrigues"; Yahya wanted to "kick him upstairs".

By June 1970 Yahya had begun to think in terms of a civilian cabinet and had already started his political dialogue with the leaders of the various political parties, which I shall describe in the next chapter. In order to get rid of Nur Khan and some of his ill-planned reforms, which alarmed the powerful pressure groups (big business, the bureaucracy and most important, some of the generals including Hamid and Peerzada) Yahya made new moves. Unlike Ayub's system, Yahya operated under a "collective leadership", where army generals constituted an "inner cabinet". Nur Khan antagonized many of the inner cabinet.

When martial law was introduced on March 25, 1969, the legislatures, both central and provincial, the cabinet and the provincial governors were all gone as the Constitution itself was abrogated. In the two provinces, the zonal Martial Law Administration (MLA) assumed the role of provincial governors. At the provincial level, the zonal MLAs had to rely exclusively on the top civil officers – "the CSP". So the order of "Junior or concealed partnership", as J. C. Hurewitz described the Ayub régime,[5] continued in the provincial administration; there were no "whizz kids" attached to zonal MLAs.

Ayub's Basic Democracy was one of the main targets of attack. The new régime abolished the electoral role of the Basic Democrats but their functions as local councils for rural development could not be abruptly ended. So after careful analysis and thought, Basic Democracy continued to play its role in local affairs.

In the meantime, the working of the Council of Administration became more and more complicated as a result of the Yahya-Nur Khan differences. Yahya, Hamid, Peerzada and the majority of the generals, as well as Ahsan, were rather conservative and were not prepared to move fast, while Nur Khan and a few others were eager to play an important modernizing role as "harbingers of progress"; they seemed to share Ayub s view that in the new states "the military organization represents the most effective public institution available for leading the modernizing effort".[6] But the Yahya régime had neither the abilities nor the opportunities to play such a role in modernization or progress. The result was a withering away of the Council of Administration.

Nur Khan and Ahsan ceased to be Chiefs of the Air Force and the Navy and became respectively provincial governors of West and East Pakistan. At the centre, Yahya announced his decision to form a civilian cabinet – with five nominated members each from East and West Pakistan – to replace the Council of Administration. In the provinces, a dyarchic pattern of administration developed. The zonal MLAs were supreme in martial law affairs and were directly in contact with the CMLA and President Yahya; while the newly appointed governors were given the same functions and role as under Ayub's Constitution of 1962, which was revived under an "ordinance of continuance". Parallels were being drawn with similar actions of the previous military régime. There was speculation and rumour about the meaning of these new moves. Was the new régime trying to prolong its stay and move backwards from the pledge of an early transfer of power? There were, however, no signs of this. Yahya continued to emphasize, rather too often, the "temporary" character of his régime. However, I gathered from my talks with some generals, that the word "temporary" was not liked. Their arguments, however, were not against the transfer of power itself, because even the hawkish elements in the junta realized that some big moves had to be made. Their objection was that too much emphasis on the "temporary" aspect of the régime was detrimental to its effective functioning.

The role of the bureaucrats, which reached its zenith during the Ayub era, suffered a temporary eclipse. Peerzada was reported to have said: "We took the blame last time when everything was done by the civilians. This time we will do everything and take the credit too."[7] In my talks with Peerzada, I could discern bitter feelings and prejudice against the senior civil servants. He could never forget his removal from the President's House as Ayub's military secretary which, according to him, was not due to his heart ailment but to a "plot" by the civil servants against an army officer who was trying to minimize their influence with Ayub. The new régime terminated the services of 303 civil servants, including some top CSP officers. Most of Ayub's close associates were removed unceremoniously. Although there were charges of "corruption", no proper judicial process was allowed and in many cases decisions were made arbitrarily at the CMLA's office by Peerzada and his two "super secretaries", Brigadiers Karim and Rahim. Some of these unlucky 303 are now restored in the service under Mujib's government in Bangladesh and under Bhutto in "New" Pakistan.

Yahya, in order to give the Bengalis some share in the top positions of the administration, made six Bengali CSP officers "central secretaries", the highest civil service rank in Pakistan. This accelerated promotion of the Bengalis was a step in the right direction but it came too late; it should have been taken in the early 1960s when Bengali nationalism was still inarticulate and undefined. By 1970 measures like this, though commendable, were not adequate to meet challenges to Pakistan's viability as a united country. Yahya also gave directions to all the ministries that whenever a senior post became vacant, Bengali candidates for it should be accorded priority, even if this meant disregarding the principle of seniority. The quotas for Bengali recruitment in the Pakistani armed forces were doubled – again a pious but ineffective move, given the prevailing mood of the Bengalis, who demanded to be masters in their own house and were not satisfied with some "special favours" or "grants", as these moves were interpreted among the Bengali intelligentsia. The Bengali civil servants were the most vocal group in expressing "Bengali nationalism", just as the Muslim officials in undivided India had been great champions of a separate Pakistani state. The Bengali officials' expectations were centred on rapid promotion; they were guided by their own interests and had no broad vision or perspective. Some of these officials were supporters of Mujib's scheme of secession. The Pakistani intelligence service was full of reports on their alleged political activities, but the Government could do hardly anything unless it was prepared to sack the entire group of top Bengali civil servants.

Turning to the formation of the Yahya cabinet, I had my first opportunity to observe at close quarters the process of "selecting" a minister in a military régime. Yahya went to Dacca in July 1969 to select his cabinet members from East Pakistan. As I was the member of his "planning cell" dealing with political matters, I was asked to accompany him. The President used to "grant interviews" to the prospective candidates, talk to them informally and then make inquiries concerning them from various sources including the intelligence services. Ayub used to follow the same procedure. By August, nine of the ten cabinet members were "nominated". Peerzada, Hamid and other top generals were consulted while Ahsan had the role of selecting from East Pakistan. Most of the ministers were older, the average age being sixty. The selection and formation of the cabinet, like its predecessors in the Ayub era, evoked very little interest or comment. It included one retired major-general; one former Chief Justice; one member of the wealthy "twenty-two families", one belonging to a big landlord and industrial group. The Bengali ministers were two former civil servants, one former politician and one from a private firm, hardly known.

My own inclusion in the cabinet as the latecomer in October was a big surprise for me. The political dialogue with Mujib and other Bengali and West Pakistani leaders had already begun. I was constantly associated with these talks as a member of the "planning cell". When Yahya was in Dacca in July selecting or nominating his ministers, he first hinted that he would like me to join the cabinet. I explained my unwillingness as I was apprehensive of being directly involved in politics, but I soon realized that my role in the planning cell had already involved me. By this time, I was also convinced of Yahya's sincerity about transferring power to the elected representatives of the people. Between July and October, when I finally joined the cabinet, I had more meetings and discussions with him than any of his cabinet ministers.

The Role of a Cabinet in a Military Régime

As a political scientist, I had unique opportunities of watching and participating in the political process of a military régime. I had watched the phenomenon during the Ayub era also: I recollect that in November 1967 Ayub asked me to see him on a date when the "Governors' Conference", which was described recently by a Bengali author as "the highest decision-making body",[8] was due to meet. All the high dignitaries – the Governors, the cabinet ministers, the secretaries – were assembled in the committee room of the President's House. I thought that my interview would either be cancelled or be a very short one. But, to my surprise, Ayub kept the "high dignitaries" waiting while talking to me as if no important meeting or engagement was scheduled for him. Finally I interposed politely: "The Governors' Conference is perhaps due to meet." Ayub, with a smile, asked me to continue my business. This is how he used to treat the cabinet and other high-level bodies.

Now it was my turn to participate in the drama. The cabinet used to discuss, sometimes quite lengthily, such issues as labour or education policy. The chief of the civil intelligence service, Mr. Rezvi, used to present to the cabinet a picture of the "current political situation" in the country, but Rezvi's real report was never before the cabinet; that was meant for Yahya and the inner circle of the junta. I had occasion to see some of these "sensitive reports", not as a cabinet minister but in my role as constitutional adviser to the President. Then the cabinet would discuss the food situation, the jute or cotton prospects and other such peripheral matters. Never in my two years as a member of the cabinet did I find any real and meaningful discussion on vital matters such as defence, foreign affairs, administrative or political policies and programmes. The cabinet was a ceremonial body, its members often touring as VIPs in the four principal cities, Karachi, Lahore, Islamabad and Dacca, inaugurating public functions, presiding over innocuous meetings, sitting at the head table at banquets in the President's House. To an outsider, a cabinet minister would appear to be an extremely busy and important person. But in reality, his role in the military régime depended primarily on his relationship with the President, the President's own assessment of the minister's effectiveness and ability to do a particular assignment or assignments, as well as the minister's links with other influential members of the ruling junta.

Socio-economic Problems and Dilemmas

Bhutto compared Pakistan when Yahya came to power in 1969 to "a patient in the last stages of tuberculosis".[9] Although he made this remark two years after Yahya had come to power and when the country was already heading towards break-up on the issue of Bangladesh, the remark contained truth. Apart from complex political and constitutional issues which will be referred to shortly, the country was beset with gargantuan problems in the socio-economic sphere. Whether the new military régime was capable of providing effective political leadership to meet the formidable challenges was very doubtful. In recent years, the social scientists in their new jargon have discussed extensively the role of the military in political development and modernization in the new countries of the Third World.[10] One conclusion drawn from a study of these recent volumes on military rule in new states was summed up by Robert Price:

> A striking characteristic of the literature on military rule in developing countries is the gap between theoretical expectations and political, social and economic reality. On the one hand, practitioners of comparative social and political theory have tended to view the military, at least in the non-Latin American area, as an organization capable of playing an important modernizing role. On the other hand, empirical researchers, often the very same individuals, who at a

different time wear the hat of theoretical practitioner, have found the performance of the military as political agents of modernization to have been rather dismal.[11]

Political and socio-economic realities in Pakistan in 1969–71 were not conducive to the Yahya régime performing any significant role. Further, the régime had its own weaknesses and deficiencies. One requisite for a military régime to achieve success is either to get broad support from the people as Nasser had done in Egypt and Ayub also in the initial years, or to have the co-operation and assistance of powerful segments of society such as the bureaucrats, the business community and other important groups among the urban élite. The Yahya régime had the full support of the army, though the junta was a divided house from the beginning, with Peerzada at odds with Hamid and Yahya with Nur Khan. Yahya was never the big boss among the armed forces as his predecessor had been.

The great debate on the synthesis of economic growth and social and distributive justice had already begun. The pertinent issue was whether such a synthesis could be achieved without fundamental changes in the political and economic order. Yahya's government, being a "temporary" one, was neither capable nor willing to undertake such revolutionary changes in the economic system. As the former chief economist of the Planning Commission, Dr. Mahbub Ul Haq, rightly pointed out,

> A mere reform of the capitalistic system is no longer a viable solution. The capitalist structure was rejected by the mass upsurge of 1969. The "reformed" system which is being demanded by the public and the politicians – with minimum wages for all workers, participation of the workers in profits, social responsibility of the capitalists, etc. – may be in operation in Sweden or Yugoslavia but cannot be built in Pakistan through an evolutionary process.[13]

Yet Yahya with all the limiting factors, the internal and external determinants of his programme, had to take some steps toward planned economic development. At his first press conference on April 10, 1969, Yahya, after reviewing the demands of the various sections of society (labour, peasants, students) and the general economic conditions prevailing in the country, said:

> In our circumstances, there is no alternative to planned economic development. But planned development cannot be isolated from the demands of social justice. The wide gap which separates the different sections of society must be narrowed, and the imbalance which led to social strife and discontent must be removed. . . . The objective of planned economic development should be the general raising of the standard of living all over the country and not the building up of a privileged class to the detriment and disadvantage of others.[14]

This was an admirable goal but was most difficult to achieve without radical changes in the economic and political spheres. Piecemeal measures, such as increased allocation in public health, education and housing, a limited scheme of minimum wages as reflected in Yahya's two budgets (1969–70 and 1970–1) were not adequate for meeting the new and growing demands for distributive justice. Prospects of foreign aid and assistance were also not bright. When the U.S. Secretary of State, Rogers, came to Pakistan in May 1969, Yahya made strong pleas for increased U.S. economic assistance, but without much success. The climate for foreign aid in Washington was unfavourable; the bargaining strength of the countries of the Third World was on the decline. With little scope for raising internal resources and poor prospects for external aid, Yahya's hands were tied in any comprehensive scheme of distributive justice. There could be some "distribution of poverty" but not much scope for raising the living standards of the people, which was the objective as spelled out by Yahya. When the budget for 1969–70, which was already being made up at the time when Yahya came to power in March 1969, was rejected by the new régime on the grounds that it must make more allocation for social justice, the planners' reply was: "No money for increased allocation." The planning commission finally made some adjustments.

But the explosive and vital problem on the economic front was that of regional distribution rather than social distribution. The economic disparity between East and West Pakistan had been given free and articulate expression during the political upheaval against Ayub. The new régime did not make any attempt to censor or restrict the great debate on the economic disparity between East and West Pakistan. A reading of the East Pakistani press, both English and vernacular, in 1969–70, would reveal that "economic disparity" was its dominant theme, regardless of whether a paper's political affiliation was rightist, leftist, moderate or extremist. Even those who disagreed with Mujib's six-point programme were no less vocal in raising the issue as a *sine qua non* for the survival of a united Pakistan, and rightly so. Political factors had worked to turn this disparity into a deeply resented grievance. The disparity had already gone too far to be removed such a short period as, say, ten or fifteen years. It was recognized by foreign experts; yet, if Pakistan were to remain united, this disparity must be removed, or at least the gap must not be allowed to widen any further. But the crucial questions were: first, would West Pakistan pay the economic and political price needed for the viability of a united Pakistan? The bulk of the rupee capital could come from only one source: West Pakistan. And West Pakistani industrialists were also expected to bear the burden of the new measures to correct social inequities. So the prospects as one foreign expert pointed out, were not hopeful: "At best, East Pakistan development will be painful. At worst, the task may be completely impossible even with a monumental effort."[15]

Secondly, would the Bengalis be prepared to wait for an evolutionary process to remove the economic disparity by "step-by-step concessions"? The political climate in East Pakistan in 1970 was not indicative of any compromise or waiting. Yet there was no "magic lamp" to remove the disparity by one or two five-year plans. The alternative was the division of the country. So the problems and issues connected with economic disparity were very grave.

Pakistan's Fourth Five-Year Plan (1970–5) had to be formulated, although it was objected to in some quarters, particularly by Mujib, on the grounds that the new military régime was "temporary and a caretaker government". But it was soon recognized that the plan must be made if the economic growth of the country was to be maintained. Foreign aid, whoever might be the donor, would not be available if the plan were not finalized. The Annual Development Plan for 1970–1 had to be launched in any case. So the preparation of the Fourth Five-Year Plan began, in the midst of a turbulent political climate, with regional tensions and lack of mutual trust and understanding between East and West Pakistan.

The National Economic Council met under Yahya's chairmanship on February 3, 1970. Even the debate in the "nominated cabinet" reflected the widening gap between the ministers and the economic experts belonging to the two wings of the country. Sometimes the debate was acrimonious; there were few voices that could approach this grave issue with proper appreciation and a broad perspective. While the Bengali ministers, aided and supported by the Bengali bureaucrats, were urging a big push for the development of East Pakistan, the West Pakistani ministers, aided by top officials of the planning commission who were mostly non-Bengalis, presented the same old arguments against a substantial redirection of resources and development expenditure to East Pakistan – such as lack of absorbing capacity, inadequacy of administrative machinery and the difficulty of measuring actual regional disparity, and so forth. It was a pity that, even at this stage, they could not understand properly the depth of the Bengalis' feelings on the question of economic disparity. Finally Yahya gave two commendable directives to the planners. The planning commission should recast and firm up the plan, keeping in mind the following guidelines: first, greater emphasis on social justice and secondly, a substantial reduction in the economic disparity between the various regions of the country.

The plan was also submitted to panels of economists in East and West Pakistan respectively for their comments and recommendations. The economists were divided, and submitted two separate reports – one from the East Pakistani economists and the other from their counterparts in West Pakistan. This was not an unusual or unexpected phenomenon. Politics rather than economic issues dominated the Bengali economists. In fact, they had close links with Mujib and his associates. They used the opportunity to ventilate the grievances of the Bengalis and, of course, their findings and analysis were based on past facts which could not be challenged. The Yahya régime, unlike its predecessor, was not critical of any such appraisal of the earlier economic policy which had created this explositive situation. The Bengali economists stated:

> Our analysis indicates that despite the formal commitment of the Government of Pakistan to reduce disparity, the extent of disparity in *per capita* income between East and West Pakistan has widened at an increasing rate over the past decade and the commitment was only honoured in the breach. Disproportionately higher levels of development and non-development expenditure in West Pakistan, supported by fiscal and commercial policy throughout the past two decades, led to the creation of a thriving private enterprise in West Pakistan while that in the East was deliberately left to lag behind.[16]

The West Pakistani economists in their report stated:

> The phenomenon [regional disparity] was inherited at the time of parition. The disparity has progressively worsened during the last two decades and it is now as high as 38 per cent. The removal of this disparity between East and West Pakistan is an important national objective. . . .
>
> But it is obvious that the disparities cannot be removed overnight. . . . The national objective must be to bring about a reduction in disparity not by lowering the growth rate in West Pakistan but by raising it in East Pakistan. . . . The key elements of our approach towards removal of inter-wing disparity during the Fourth Plan are:
>
> (1) a massive increase in the level of net capital inflow into East Pakistan from Rs. 105 crores in 1969–70 to Rs. 325 crores in 1974–5 involving a dramatic shift in its share in the net capital inflow from 40 per cent in 1969–70 to more than 75 per cent in 1974–5;
> (2) a steep rise in investment levels in East Pakistan from Rs. 405 crores in 1969–70 to 991 crores in 1974–5 and an increase in her share in total investment from 39 per cent in 1969 to 54 per cent by 1974–5; and
> (3) a much closer attention to the possibilities of technological change in agriculture, private investment and growth-oriented policies.[17]

The National Economic Council met on June 2, 1970, to finalize the plan with the two divergent reports from the East and West Pakistan economists. The debate on the plan had added fuel to the political situation in the country, which was already overcharged with emotion, tension, hatred and bitterness. The Vice-Chairman of the Planning Commission, M. M. Ahmad, was a man of high calibre who had been closely associated with Ayub's economic policy, which had widened the gap. He now seemed to have realized the gravity of the issue and, unlike other non-Bengali bureaucrats, had at least the foresight to perceive the risks involved in the disparity issue if Pakistan were to be saved from splitting up. The Planning Commission, in its final assessment on the plan, pointed out to the National Economic Council that to secure the widest possible support in both wings of the country, any pattern of regional allocations must, in its judgement, fulfil at least two important criteria:

(1) The total allocation of development expenditure, taking the public and private sections together, must be larger in East Pakistan than the combined allocations for the four provinces of West Pakistan.

(2) While ensuring maximum feasible acceleration in East Pakistan, the allocation for West Pakistan must nevertheless provide for a minimum necessary acceleration to permit a larger social programme and to meet the needs of the less developed areas of West Pakistan.

The final allocations under the Fourth Five-Year Plan, as approved by the National Economic Council, were as follows (in crores of rupees):

	East Pakistan		*West Pakistan*		*Total*
Public sector	2,940	(60%)	1,960	(40%)	4,900
Private sector	1,000	(39%)	1,600	(61%)	2,600
Totals	3.940	(52·5%)	3,560	(47·5%)	7,500

These allocations were expected to give "a big push to the development of East Pakistan during the Fourth Plan and to make a positive move towards a reduction in the inter-regional disparity in *per capita* income".[55] The Bengali cabinet ministers with the exception of two (Dr. A. Malik and Ahsan-ul Huq) were not happy with the final allocations made by the National Economic Council. Non-Bengali members felt that "a good start had been made" towards the objective of removing economic disparity.

But at the same meeting of the National Economic Council on June 2, 1970, when the Annual Development Plan for 1970–1 came up for discussion, the three Bengali ministers raised their voices against the Annual Plan for 1970–1 because it was considered not to be in accordance with the objectives of the Fourth Plan. The allocations for East Pakistan under the Annual Plan for 1970–1 were neither adequate nor in accordance with the supreme objective of removing the regional disparity. Yet Yahya allowed the Planning Commission to go ahead with its proposals, notwithstanding the strong notes of dissent from the three Bengali ministers. This was a big shock for my two colleagues and myself.

Immediately after the meeting of the National Economic Council on June 2, the three of us (Hafizuddin, Shamsul Huq and myself) met together and wrote a joint letter to Yahya expressing our inability to continue in his cabinet in view of what we considered as "most unfair allocations to East Pakistan". We knew our limitations; we were "nominated ministers" without any political or popular support. But our collective resignation – the other two Bengali ministers were bound to follow our course of action because of the prevailing public opinion in East Pakistan – would have compelled Yahya to dissolve the cabinet, and it would have created a big issue in the country. The press in East Pakistan would certainly have taken up a position against the régime by noting that even Yahya's own nominated ministers could not agree to his economic policy toward East Pakistan. These calculations made our decision of collective resignation effective. Yahya immediately met the three of us and assured us of a special meeting of the National Economic Council where Yahya's opening remarks to the Planning Commission were: "My Bengali colleagues in the cabinet have pointed out to me that the allocations to East Pakistan for 1970–1 would not narrow down the gap in regional disparity. If so, I cannot be a party to it; the gap must be narrowed down." The officials of the Planning Commission were taken by surprise by this sudden changed attitude of the President, and like typical civil servants they yielded to the pressure of the boss without much resistance. So the allocations for the Annual Development Plan for 1970–1 were changed.

There are two interesting episodes about this incident. First, when Mujib learned of our threatened resignation from his closest friend in the cabinet, Mahmood Haroon, a member of one of the wealthy "twenty-two families", who opposed East Pakistan's increased allocations on June 2, he "advised" us through Haroon "not to precipitate a crisis" by a collective resignation from the cabinet. We could not, at that time, appreciate Mujib's uncalled for "advice" to us, but it subsequently became evident that Mujib was mainly interested in the promised "free elections" so that he could establish his credentials as the sole leader of the emerging Bangladesh; he was not at all interested in the "allocations" for East Pakistan in 1970–1.

Secondly, while in public Mujib and his economists denounced the 1970–1 allocation for East Pakistan, they cited it as a model in the crucial tripartite negotiations in March 1971 at Dacca before the civil war began on March 25, 1971.[19]

So the great debate on the Fourth Plan was over by June 1970. The plan was formally launched on July 1, 1970, amid government publicity. The Vice-Chairman of the Planning Commission announced that there would be a transfer of resources worth Rs. 750 to 1,000 crores from West to East Pakistan in order to make a substantial narrowing down of the regional economic disparity between the two wings of the country, and to ensure that East Pakistan's share in developmental expenditure would rise from 37 per cent in the "implemented Third Plan" to 52·5 per cent in the Fourth Plan, implying an edge of Rs. 380 crores.[20] Yahya, in his broadcast on July 28, claimed: "The Fourth Five-Year Plan fulfils my promise to the nation that this government will take positive steps to reduce regional disparities and provide a greater measure of social justice."[21]

The plan allotted about 30 per cent of the investments for 1970–5 to health, education and housing. Yahya further stated: "This year we will also begin a determined attack on the problem of flood control in East Pakistan." In the Annual Development Plan for 1970–1, Rs. 150 crores was allocated for flood control in East Pakistan. Yahya and the Planning Commission were willing to spend more on flood control, but we were dismayed to learn that the provincial government of East Pakistan was unable to receive more money "for lack of our adequate number of projects". This was a poor performance on the part of the provincial administration, particularly its planning and development branch, which by 1969–70 was entirely manned by Bengalis. There were some doubts about the feasibility of the "ambitious plan" as a whole: the total size of Rs. 7,500 crores was considered impractical, though the Planning Commission was quite optimistic. The expected foreign assistance for the plan was Rs. 325 crores. Apart from the "consortium for aid to Pakistan" composed of the Western countries (particularly the U.S.A.), the World Bank and Japan, prospects for assistance from China and the Soviet Union were also good.

But all these gigantic efforts were being made for economic development at a time when the country was heading towards massive political changes or, as it subsequently turned out, towards the great confrontation. A Bengali economist working abroad wrote: "Whether or not one accepts the 'immutable' Marxian law, one feels tempted to extrapolate the past empirical experience of Pakistan into the future we are concerned with." He then said: "Let us hope that reason will triumph and the Pakistani people will be able to work out a reasonably viable SS [structure-superstructure]. For a country having two economies, such a SS will make the people of each region master in their own house free to live in it the way they wish without federal let or hindrance."[23] Why such a "structure-superstructure", when offered by Yahya after the 1970 elections, was not acceptable; why reason did not triumph and why the country had to face one of the tragedies of modern history are questions to which I shall turn in subsequent chapters. In the meantime, let me turn to Pakistan's external environment in 1969–70.

The External Environment

Pakistan under Yahya Khan was described in certain quarters "as a country without any foreign policy". In the mid-1950s Pakistan was elevated to "the most allied ally" of the United

States in Asia and consequently a target of Soviet vilification and wrath, culminating in Khrushchev's threat of rocket annihilation at the time of the U-2 incident in 1960. Then Pakistan under Ayub began a policy, which was termed "Bilateralism", the essence of which was to cultivate the friendship of the People's Republic of China and of the Soviet Union without forfeiting that of the United States, particularly its economic aid and assistance. Ayub's foreign policy, as indicated in the previous chapter, had dramatically redefined Pakistan's role in international affairs and its most spectacular aspect was "Ayub's flirting with Mao".

When Yahya came to power in March 1969, Pakistan's internal political dynamics were so desperate that its foreign policy had lost some of its past glamour. Yahya had no foreign minister, a fact which reflected the decreased importance attached by the new military régime to external affairs. The all-powerful Peerzada became the "expert" in foreign affairs. Subsequently Major-General Omar, who became the Secretary of National Security Council, aspired to be the Henry Kissinger of the régime. Both Peerzada and Omar were totally incompetent in handling external problems, but their self-imposed role could not be challenged either by the civil officials of the Ministry of Foreign Affairs or by the Cabinet which, during its existence from August 1969 to February 1971, had not a single debate on foreign affairs. Yahya, however, soon developed his own style and *modus operandi*. He removed the Foreign Secretary, S. M. Yousuf, a man of high integrity and ability, because Peerzada and Yousuf were almost on non-speaking terms; Yousuf was not prepared to be browbeaten by Peerzada. The new Foreign Secretary, Sultan Khan, was able to develop a working equation with both Peerzada and Omar – the "two great experts" on foreign affairs. Yahya, however, knew the worth of his generals as foreign policy makers. So he used to rely on other sources.

When my own contacts with Yahya became closer, I was often taken into his confidence in external affairs. The first occasion was during Nixon's 22-hour visit to Pakistan in August 1969. I was still working in the research division of the Foreign Affairs Ministry and in Yahya's planning cell. Yahya asked me to prepare notes for his dialogue with Nixon, particularly

Pakistan's pleas for U.S. arms aid. I was able to dig up some of the old papers relating to Nixon's sympathetic views on Pakistan's application for U.S. arms when he had visited Pakistan as the U.S. Vice-President in December 1953. Yahya was pleased to have this material and data, and included me in his team for the U.S.-Pakistan talks during Nixon's visit. However, the dialogue was carried on at two levels, at the summit level it was between the two Presidents: Nixon gave Yahya the special assignment to act as "courier" between Washington and Peking – an assignment which the latter carried out with the utmost secrecy and conscientiousness. The second level of discussion was between the U.S. team headed by Henry Kissinger and the Pakistani team headed by the Foreign Secretary.

Though Yahya was neither willing nor had the time to play a significant role in external affairs because of internal complications, yet Pakistan had a number of highly important and complicated external issues in 1969–70. First was Yahya's grand assignment from Nixon which, as already mentioned, he carried out well, his services being appreciated both in Washington and Peking. Yahya's first tour abroad was to attend the Islamic Summit Conference in Rabat, Morocco. He made a mess of this by at first agreeing to India's participation in the Islamic Conference and then realizing that his "mistake" would give India a big edge in support of her claim as a secular country with sixty million Muslims as a religious minority. Pakistan reacts violently to any Indian penetration into the Muslim world; hence Yahya faced a big dilemma. However, King Hassan of Morocco, the host country, and the Shah of Iran came to his rescue. Finally, the Indian delegation, led by a Muslim cabinet minister who had already arrived at Rabat, was unceremoniously asked not to participate. Yahya's "mistake" turned out to be a great diplomatic success for him as nothing pleased the Pakistanis (though not, of course, the Bengalis) more than a setback for India. Yahya returned from his first tour abroad with flying colours.

Yahya made his major speech on Pakistan's foreign policy in the Iranian *Majlis* on October 30, 1969. I participated fully in the preparation of this speech. Yahya's relations with the Shah of Iran were more cordial than those of Ayub, who had offended the Shah by praising Nasser in his political autobiography, *Friends not Masters*. The Shah was reported to have told Ayub: "In the time of your crisis [i.e. the 1965 Indo-Pakistani crisis], you asked me to help but your praises are reserved for Nasser who is a great friend of your enemy, India."[24] The Shah's comments were not without justification. Yahya and the Shah belonged to the same sect, the Shia community of Islam, and Yahya's family had originally come from Iran. A special personal relationship developed between Iran and Pakistan under Yahya.

Turning to Pakistan's relations with the major powers – the U.S.A., the U.S.S.R. and China – Pakistan found her simultaneous friendship with Washington and Peking, which had been a great source of complications in the early 1960s, now not only feasible but appreciated in both capitals. However, Pakistan began to face crude Russian pressures in 1969–70. The Russians were not happy with the exit of Ayub. *Pravda*, commenting on the change of government in Pakistan, wrote that when Ayub agreed to meet the leaders of the opposition parties, "there was no unity of views among them" and then added: "In the meantime, pro-Peking and pro-American elements had begun to appear." At the same time *Izvestiia* wrote that the "introduction of martial law in Pakistan will not solve all the problems facing the country."[25] When the Soviet Defence Minister, Marshal A. A. Grechko, visited Pakistan in March 1969, just before Ayub's exit, he bluntly told the Pakistani generals that their decision to remove Ayub would be a mistake. The Soviet leaders, Kosygin and Podgorny, however, sent greetings to Yahya on April 11, 1969. Then in May Kosygin made his second and, to date, his last visit to Pakistan to talk to Yahya. It was at this meeting that the Russians made it plain to Pakistan that simultaneous friendship with Moscow and Peking would not be tolerated. Yahya asked Kosygin how the Soviet Union could insist on simultaneous friendship with India and Pakistan. The reply was: "What is possible for a super-power is not possible for a smaller power."[27] Ayub's follies in falling into the Soviet trap in exchange for some Russian arms of the "nuts and bolts" type now became evident, and the Chinese warnings to Pakistanis about the illusory Russian friendship with Pakistan proved correct. Yahya was faced with the crucial choice between Moscow and Peking, and this grave issue in external affairs flared up at a time when his attention was diverted exclusively to internal problems. From the time of my entry into the Ministry of Foreign Affairs in 1967, I had consistently pointed out, in my various notes to Ayub and then to Yahya, the Soviet designs and threats to Pakistan. Ayub used to take great pride in what he claimed to be the "unfreezing" of Soviet hostility towards Pakistan. But this was not a correct assessment; the Soviet Union never wished Pakistan well. Ayub's flirting with the Russians had, on the contrary, the risk of costing Pakistan the confidence of China.

When Yahya planned his grand visits to Moscow, Washington and Peking in 1970, Pakistan's triangular diplomacy needed serious study and assessment; but thanks to the neglect of foreign affairs and to the personal feud between Peerzada and Omar to gain prominence to foreign affairs, the complicated problems had not been properly dealt with. I had some roles – Yahya asked me to comment on the papers before his state visits to Moscow (June), Washington (October) and Peking (November) in 1970. I did my best to point out the threats from Moscow and urged closer and friendlier relations with both Washington and Peking, for which Yahya's chances were better than Ayub's had been. Yahya also gave me a choice of going with him either to Moscow, Washington or Peking; as he had no foreign minister he used to "pick up" a member of his cabinet to accompany him for his state visits. I opted for Peking because I had already been to Moscow with Ayub in 1965, and the United States is not only my "academic homeland", but I had also been there more than once as a delegate to the United Nations. I had never been to Peking and moreover, as a researcher, I was keenly interested in the emerging Sino-American relations in which Yahya was playing a significant role, and I was one of the very few whom he took into his confidence about his top secret mission.

Indo-Pakistani relations in 1969–70 were bad and as tense as always. Reports from the Pakistani intelligence services, both civil and military, about India's involvement in the highly explosive situation in East Pakistan since the Agartala conspiracy case of 1968 continued to pour into Yahya's office, but were not given the attention they deserved. A friendly country was also giving a similar version of India's involvement. Yahya realized the truth too late. In all my public speeches as a member of the Yahya cabinet, I voiced the country's concern about Indian designs but my voice was a lonely one.

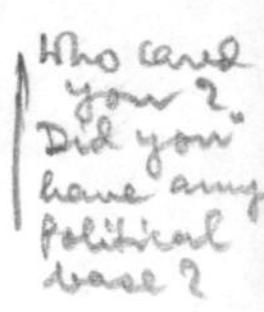

REFERENCES

1. *Economist*, March 29, 1969.
2. Quoted in John Plamenatz, *German Marxism and Russian Communism*, Longmans, London, 1954, p. 144.
3. See the text of Yahya's broadcast on March 26, 1969, in *Dawn*, March 27, 1969.
4. Ibid.
5. J. C. Hurewitz, *Middle East Politics: The Military Dimension*, pp. 179–200.
6. See Lucian Pye, "Armies in the Process of Modernization", in J. J. Johnson (ed.), *The Role of the Military in Underdeveloped Countries*, Princeton: Princeton University Press, 1962, pp. 69–90.
7. Quoted in Fazal Muqeem Khan, *Pakistan's Crisis in Leadership*, National Book Foundation, Karachi, 1973, p. 19.
8. Rounaq Jahan, *Pakistan: Failure in National Integration*, New York, Columbia University Press, 1972, p. 97.
9. Z. A. Bhutto, *The Great Tragedy*, Karachi, a Pakistan Peoples' Party Publication, 1971, p. 9.
10. See M. Janowitz, *The Military in the Political Development of New Nations*, (Chicago, The University of Chicago Press, 1964); J. J. Johnson (ed.), *The Role of the Military in Underdeveloped Countries*, op. cit.; S. E. Finer, *The Man on Horseback*, London and New York, 1962; William F. Gutteridge, *Military Institutions and Power in New States*, London, 1964.
11. Robert M. Price, "A Theoretical Approach to Military Rule in New States," in *World Politics*, April 1972.
12. *Dawn*, April 1969.
13. See Dr. Mahbub Ul Haq, "Pakistan's Choices for the 1970's", a paper at the Conference on Economic Growth and Distributional Justice in Pakistan, the University of Rochester, July 29 to July 31, 1970.
14. *Dawn*, April 11, 1969.
15. From a review paper by Dr. Ralph Smuckler, former representative of the Ford Foundation in Pakistan, dated September 16 and 17, 1969.
16. See the *Report of the Panel of Economists on the Fourth Five-Year Plan (1970–75)*, Planning Commission, Government of Pakistan, May 1970, p. 11.
17. Ibid., pp. 104–6.
18. Based on "Summary for the National Economic Council", June 2, 1970.

19. For details of the Dacca talks see Chapter 7.
20. *Dawn*, July 2, 1970.
21. Ibid., July 29, 1970.
22. Ibid.
23. From Professor Wahidul Haque's paper "Development Policies and Regional Justice in Pakistan" at the University of Rochester conference, op. cit.
24. Based on personal interviews.
25. See *Pravda*, April 10, 1969, and *Izvestiia*, April 11, 1969.
26. Based on personal interviews.
27. For details see my *Major Powers and the Indian Sub-Continent* (forthcoming).

4

THE ABORTIVE SCHEME FOR THE TRANSFER OF POWER

As pointed out earlier, Yahya's pledge, made within twenty-four hours of his accession to power on March 25, 1969, to transfer power to the elected representatives of the people was treated with scepticism. It was recalled that Ayub had made a similar pledge in 1958, but there were some differences. Ayub had qualified his pledge by saying that he would restore democracy of the type which he would consider suitable for Pakistan. Yahya's pledge on March 26, 1969, was unqualified; he elaborated it in his first press conference on April 10, in which he categorically opted for a democratic process: "Our aim must be to establish constructive political life in the country so that power is transferred to the elected representatives of the people." On the subject of elections, he specifically spoke of "election of the representatives of the people on the basis of direct adult franchise" and on the future constitution Yahya's views were that "it will be for the representatives of the people to give the country a workable constitution".[1]

There were three clear and unambiguous promises: first, transfer of power to the elected representatives of the people; secondly, the election would be held on the basis of direct adult franchise – Ayub's system of indirect election through Basic Democrats was rejected; and thirdly, the future constitution of the country would be framed by the elected members. By April 10 the new military régime was in full control of the authority; while Yahya's pledge of March 26 might have been a "panic one" after a four-month-long popular movement for democracy, the unqualified commitments made on April 10, did not arise from a panic decision.

Between April 10 and July 28, 1969, when Yahya again

spoke in detail on his plan for a transfer of power, much discussion and parleying took place between Yahya and the leaders of the various political parties. One significant phenomenon was that though Yahya abrogated the constitution, dissolved legislatures and cabinets, both national and provincial, and imposed martial law throughout the country, political parties were not banned, nor were politicians put into prison as under Ayub in 1958. In fact, the new military junta had made some prior contacts with political leaders like Mujib, Bhashani and Bhutto. Hence the imposition of martial law was no surprise to the political leaders; as for the public, the reaction was one of relief after months of chaos and confusion in the country, although there was no welcome to equal that with which Ayub was greeted in 1958.

Yahya did not summon any conference of political leaders after seeing the fate of the Round Table Conference summoned by Ayub before his departure. Yahya, on the contrary, began quiet and bilateral talks with political leaders; he toured the country from one end to the other and had genuine dialogues with leaders of various parties, and politicians gradually became impressed by his sincereity. He devoted most attention to Mujib – rightly so, since he was the leader of the Bengalis who constituted a majority of the country's population. Mujib, however, was suspicious of the military régime's intentions. He had never forgotten the arbitrary removal in 1957 of the Prime Minister, H. S. Suhrawardy, his political mentor and the founder of the Awami League, by President Iskander Mirza, who a year later presided over the establishment of the first military régime in Pakistan. Mujib showed the greatest anxiety to secure every possible safeguard against similar treatment being meted out to him if – as was bound to happen – he lost some of his popularity after coming to power. Eventually Yahya began to win Mujib's confidence and a good personal relationship gradually developed between them.

As a member of Yahya's planning cell entrusted with constitutional and political affairs, I had opportunities of watching the political dialogues that took place between April and July and again between August and November, when Yahya finally spelled out his scheme for the transfer of power. I used to get full details of Yahya's talks with the politicians and he would then send me to them to find out their reaction as well as to convey their proposals and suggestions back to Yahya regarding a *modus operandi* for the transfer of power. I had lengthy discussions with most of the political leaders including Mujib, Bhutto, Bhashani, Asghar Khan, Justice Murshed, Qayyum Khan, Nurul Amin, Ghulam Azam (Jamaat-i-Islami), Muzaffar Ahmad (pro-Moscow Group) and others. It was a most interesting experience for me; I had similar experiences in 1960–1 while acting as honorary adviser to the Constitution Commission, headed by a former Chief Justice, Shahabuddin, but this time it was a unique opportunity for a political scientist, as well as a rewarding experience. I was impressed by Yahya's straightforwardness in his talks with the politicians.

I shall particularly narrate my own assessment about Yahya's talks with Mujib, Bhutto and Bhashani. Mujib, as already noted, was suspicious of the military régime and its intentions. He had good reasons for it; Yahya was, no doubt, sincere and Mujib gradually became convinced of the sincerity of his pledge, but Yahya was never master in his own house as Ayub had been. He never had more than a limited hold over the army generals, who in fact constituted the ruling junta between March 1969 and December 1971, nor did he seem either anxious or able to acquire a position of complete dominance. Consequently what he did or intended to do was often torpedoed by other members of the junta. Yet between March 1969 and December 1970 Yahya was given a free hand in his constitutional quest; however, he would consult his "inner cabinet" of generals before taking any important move; even his policy statements, made on the 28th day of the month – Yahya had been commissioned in the army on the 28th – at four-monthly intervals which continued till the time of elections in 1970, were discussed paragraph by paragraph by the "inner cabinet", but from my attendance of these meetings I could observe that while some generals had reservations and doubts about the unqualified transfer of power and grave misgivings about Mujib's six-point plan, on the whole Yahya, with the help of his advisers like Peerzada and myself, had a free hand in dealing with the politicians to work out an acceptable formula for the transfer of power on the basis of a united Pakistan.

Any threat to the break-up of the country was to be met effectively; on that there was no difference of opinion. Within the framework of "one Pakistan" Yahya could freely negotiate with political leaders including Mujib, whose alleged involvement in the Agartala conspiracy was never forgotten by the generals. So Mujib's doubts and reservations had some basis. The East Pakistan provincial Governor, Admiral Ahsan, was to some extent successful in removing Mujib's doubts; or, alternatively, Ahsan let himself be fooled by Mujib and his few advisers like Dr. Kamal Hossain, who was Mujib's constitutional adviser (he became Bangladesh's first Law Minister to frame its constitution in 1972), and Rahman Solhan, a pseudo-economist who had failed to obtain a Ph.D. from London University, but he was close to Mujib as his economic adviser. The two met almost daily with Ahsan at the residence of a common friend whose services were recognized when he was given an ambassadorial assignment in 1970. Ahsan was sincere but lacked the capacity to understand the political dynamics of East Pakistan and the external forces at work there. He was all for a deal with Mujib while the zonal MLA, General Yakub, and the intelligence services, both military and civil, were apprehensive of Mujib's ultimate aims – whether these were to become the first Bengali Prime Minister of Pakistan or the creator of a new state, Bangladesh. Yahya was bewildered by the conflicting views of Ahsan, Yakub and his intelligence chiefs. So the Yahya-Mujib dialogue was a most important and complex one. The crucial issues were whether Mujib would modify his six points, and whether the military junta would really hand over power to Mujib.

Dialogues with Bhashani were interesting but not of great significance. The octogenerarian Maulana Bhashani is a legendary figure; he never accepted any office, and is thoroughly dedicated to the causes of the poor and the "have-nots". "Maulana" is sometimes dubbed as "red" or as a pro-Peking communist but he is also a sincere and devoted Muslim; he is a leader of the Gandhian type with a missionary zeal to serve the poorest. At his first meeting with Yahya, Bhashani gave a list of the demands of peasants, workers and students, and told Yahya that the past governments in Pakistan had never cared for the welfare of the "have-nots". Bhashani usually did most of the talking and would allow nobody else to talk; so after hours of one-sided discussion Yahya said to Bhashani "Maulana Sahib, why not join my administration and try to solve the problems as mentioned by you?" Bhashani's reply was: "My job is to find faults with the government and not to join any government." The first meeting ended in cordiality and friendliness, but with no positive suggestion relating to constitutional issues. When I visited the "Red Maulana" I had to listen to his "sermons" for five hours without much opportunity to find out any reaction he might have to any proposal for the constitutional problem; I was, however, thoroughly impressed by his devotion to the cause of the poor and his lack of any personal political ambition. He is indeed a great man.

The non-Awami League Bengali leaders like Nurul Amin, Ghulam Azam and other moderates were most anxious for a genuine political settlement between East and West Pakistan but they had serious apprehensions about Mujib's six points which they considered a scheme for secession.

Bhutto, the dapper and aristocratic leader in West Pakistan, was busy building his political base in West Pakistan as well as cultivating links with various members of the military junta. Like Bhashani, he had hardly any constructive suggestion or plan for solving the constitutional dilemma. Moreover, his task was more complicated than that of Mujib, who had only one theme – "Bengali liberation from domination of West Pakistanis". Bhutto had to speak in one language in Punjab, where he was preaching the gospel of "a thousand years' war with India" and to restore "national honour", which Ayub was alleged to have sacrificed at the Tashkent conference, while in the smaller provinces of West Pakistan like Baluchistan, the North-West Frontier and his own native province of Sind, he had to speak differently on removing poverty and ensuring social justice on the basis of "Islamic Socialism". Bhutto's real and secret dialogues were with Peerzada, while with Yahya he would drink whisky and have general discussions. In my talks with Bhutto, he never spelled out his attitude to Mujib's six points, which was the most involved issue facing the country. He was more fond of talking on international politics, on which he was an impressive talker though very elusive on specific issues. It was a pleasure to talk with him, but not very rewarding while everyone was seriously in search of a formula for a genuine settlement of the country's most complicated political problem.

The rightist groups in West Pakistan, popularly known as "*Islam-pasand*" (Islam-loving) parties, were more interested in ideological issues – the State *versus* Religion in the new constitution – rather than the threatening tensions between East and West Pakistan. They betrayed lack of understanding of real issues but they were patriotic, sincere and honest in their negotiations and talks.

The pro-Moscow group, led by Wali Khan in West Pakistan and by Muzaffar Ahmad in East Pakistan, were extremists, particularly Muzaffar Ahmad. The latter refused to see Yahya during his first visit to Dacca in 1969 but subsequently sought interviews with him, whereupon Yahya in his typical style snubbed him at a dinner in Dacca which was attended by all the political leaders by saying to him publicly: "I am not going to grant you an interview because you refused to see me when I invited you." Muzaffar was very much annoyed and maintained his hostile attitude throughout the period of political negotiations. I had a single meeting with him and was thoroughly disgusted by his big talk.

After four months of discussion, on July 28, 1969, Yahya made a major policy statement. He referred to his talks with political leaders and pointed out acute differences of opinion over such issues as the revival of the 1956 Constitution – Mujib was opposed to its revival while many others felt that the 1956 Constitution should be a legal document under which an early election could be arranged. Then there were disputes over the principle of representation – whether it should be on the basis of "one man, one vote" or on the principle of "parity", as agreed by the leaders of both East and West Pakistan in 1955. But Mujib had made clear his total opposition to any idea of parity, and demanded that the basis of representation should be the democratic principle of "one man, one vote", which would give Bengalis a clear majority in the national assembly. However, West Pakistani leaders were unwilling to accept it unless the federal legislature were composed of two houses – the lower house on the basis of population, or "one man, one vote", and the upper house on some other basis. In West Pakistan, there was controversy over "one unit" – amalgamation of the four provinces of West Pakistan into one province as was done in 1955. The smaller provinces were against "one unit", and Mujib too did not favour it because, although it did not directly affect East Pakistan, its dissolution would – or so it was expected – give Mujib a better bargaining position by coming to a deal with the smaller provinces against "domination of Punjab" – towards which the Bengalis and the people of smaller provinces had a shared antagonism. The most complicated issue, however, was the relationship between the centre and the provinces – whether a viable national government was at all feasible if Mujib's six points were not modified. After reviewing all three controversial issues, Yahya stated:

> So, you see there is quite a variety of opinions and views on these major issues. As for myself, I have already indicated on a number of occasions that my mind is absolutely open on these subjects and that the decision must lie with the people. The only requirement that I would insist upon is that any constitution or any form of government that the people of Pakistan adopt for themselves must cater to the ideology and integrity of Pakistan. . . . We must think, first and foremost, in terms of Pakistan. This is not to say that reasonable and just demands of various regions of Pakistan should be ignored. As long as these demands are in keeping with the integrity of Pakistan, ways and means should be found to accommodate them.[2]

Then, referring to the Bengalis' demands and grievances, Yahya said: "They were not being allowed *to play their full part in the decision-making process at the national level and in certain important spheres of national activity* [my italics]. In my view they were fully justified in being dissatisfied with this state of affairs", and Yahya pledged "to correct this stituation".[3] This was the first occasion when a Pakistani President looked at the problems of East Pakistan in its true perspective and not with the colonial approach of "law and order". The fact that the Bengalis had no effective share in decision-making process was the fundamental challenge to Pakistan's viability as a united nation. The Constitution Commission headed by Justice Shahabuddin referred in its Report to the East Pakistanis' feelings of "being treated like a colony[4]" – it was the first official document of the Government of Pakistan in which the word "colony" was used while analysing the political dynamics of East Pakistan, and Yahya was the first Pakistani President to give correct expression to the Bengalis' sense of frustration over the national issue. I recall with pleasure that with both the Constitution Commission's remarks and Yahya's speech of July 28, 1969, I was closely associated and had a share in their drafting. Anybody who cherished the ideals of a united Pakistan could hardly ignore the true feelings of the East Pakistanis. The vast majority of Bengali Muslims were not asking for secession; but they demanded their legitimate share in national affairs, and it was the failure to tackle this vital problem in time which ultimately led to tragic happenings in 1971.

Yahya expressed the hope that consensus would develop on the vital constitutional issues, but he hinted that if the political leaders failed to agree, he might have to evolve his own scheme for the transfer of power.

The second phase in the preparation of the scheme for transfer of power began in August 1969. By this time, it had become evident that there would be no consensus among the political leaders on the major issues of constitution-making. Mujib now indicated his views on constitutional problems through Governor Ahsan; I too had several meetings with him to find out his reactions to various alternatives relating to the scheme for the transfer of power. Yahya used to ask me to go to Mujib and get his views. As I mentioned earlier, Yahya gave Mujib much attention while preparing his plan.

Yahya Works Out his Plan

Lord Mountbatten, the last Viceroy of the British *raj* in India, claimed to have made his plan for the transfer of power of June 3, 1947, working "hand in glove" with the leaders of Indian national parties, mainly the Congress and the Muslim League. Mountbatten's claim was partly correct; he consulted the Indian leaders in a series of conferences and talks with the Congress, the Muslim League and Sikh leaders, but the final shape and draft of his plan was made by a small group; he relied mainly on his constitutional adviser, V. P. Menon, and the final draft was shown to, and prepared in consultation with, the leader of one party, Congress. Nehru was the only leader who was able to see and comment on the final draft, though the broad features of the plan were known to the other leaders.[5] Similarly, Yahya could claim that he worked out his plan "hand in glove" with the politicians, yet, as with the Mountbatten plan, the final shape was given by a small group. The initial draft was prepared by Peerzada and myself with a very small group of aides and with the utmost secrecy. The politicians' views were constantly assessed and reassessed, and the reports of the intelligence services, both civil and military, were taken fully into account. Finally the "inner cabinet" consisting of Yahya, General Hamid, General Peerzada, two provincial governors and two zonal MLAs, used to have lengthy sessions. The civilian cabinet – including the Law Minister, Justice Cornelius – was completely by-passed. I myself was the only civilian present and I used to attend the "inner cabinet" not as a cabinet minister but as a constitutional expert.

What were the demands from the political leaders? Let me first take the Bengali demands as voiced by Mujib. First, Mujib demanded a definite date for holding the promised "free and fair" elections, and secondly, he was unwilling to accept the 1956 Constitution. His main objections to it were the system of representation, based on the "principle of parity" and not on the basis of population, popularly known as "one man, one vote"; he also strongly objected to the centre–provinces relationship in the 1956 Constitution. Mujib also gave hints that he would favour the break-up of "One Unit" in West Pakistan. He further demanded the restoration of full activities by political parties. The martial law did not ban the parties; it allowed "indoor" political discussions and conferences, and even press statements by the politicians, but not public meetings, processions, mass rallies, etc.

The non-Awami Leaguers in East Pakistan favoured the restoration of the 1956 Constitution, with a flexible amending procedure, for at least one year, so that genuine regional autonomy could be given to East Pakistan; as pointed out earlier, they did not approve of Mujib's six points but were strongly in favour of much larger autonomy than in the 1956 Constitution; they also favoured the representation on the basis of population and not on "parity".

The rightist parties in West Pakistan were in favour of a strong central government and an Islamic constitution; they did not oppose East Pakistan's demand for autonomy, but their concept of "regional autonomy" was out of tune with the prevailing demands in East Pakistan.

Bhutto's was also not happy with the 1956 Constitution, mainly because of its parliamentary form of government. He seemed to agree with Ayub that Pakistan could not afford the Westminster variety of parliamentary democracy which, according to him, would lead again to political instability like that of the pre-1958 period. He kept his options on the centre-provinces relationship, the Islamic character of the constitution and on "one unit" in West Pakistan open for his political strategy; he was in favour of Yahya deciding these issues in the light of his discussions with East and West Pakistani leaders.

The leaders of the smaller provinces in West Pakistan were almost unanimous in demanding the break-up of "one unit" and the restoration of the four old provinces – Punjab, Baluchistan, the North-West Frontier and Sind – while the Punjab leaders were in favour of the retention of "one unit" but did not press it too far; they could realizc the depth of the feelings in the smaller provinces.

Bhashani and both pro-Moscow and pro-Peking groups were stressing the social and economic demands of the people; but Yahya pointed out to them that he was not drafting a constitution; all he was trying to do was evolve a legal procedure whereby elections could be held and a constitution could be framed by the elected assembly. To this Bhashani's reply was that he was not interested in such "secondary issues"; to him the basic problem was the economic uplifting of the "have-nots". The pro-Moscow group had some ideas on constitutional issues but the East and West Pakistani factions within the pro-Moscow elements were divided – there were differences between Wali Khan, the National Awami Party chief in West Pakistan, and Muzaffar Ahmad, his counterpart in East Pakistan. The pro-Peking group and Bhashani were not interested in the immediate constitutional façade; they were busy in the long-term objectives of politicizing the rural masses for real national liberation. There were also divisions and factions within their party.

There were three basic issues which Yahya had to decide. The first was the Bengalis' demand for representation on the basis of "one man, one vote" in an unqualified way and without any reservation such as a second parliamentary chamber or a special voting procedure requiring more than a simple majority in the national assembly. The second and most complicated issue was the relationship between the centre and provinces; this was the crux of the whole constitutional quest for a viable political order in Pakistan.

The third issue related to the break-up of "one unit" and the restoration of the old provinces in West Pakistan.

The Islamic character of the new constitution which dominated constitution-making in its first phase (1947–56) was no longer an important or controversial one. Similarly, as regards the method of election, direct adult franchise, which had been hotly debated in the Ayub era, was already decided by Yahya's unqualified commitment in favour of it.

How did Yahya and his inner group seek to solve these three basic problems?

Yahya and the majority of the junta were willing to concede demands for maximum autonomy for East Pakistan, provided it were within the framework of one Pakistan. It was realized that a stable political settlement with Bengali leaders – or the leader who represented the majority of the population – was essential, and there could be no doubt that Mujib and his party represented the majority view in East Pakistan. Yahya had no plan like his predecessors, who tried to "create" Bengali leaders either by intrigue as during the parliamentary era (1953–8) or by "controlled elections" as under the Ayub era (1958–69). By September–October 1969, when I had developed close contacts with Yahya and used to have lengthy discussions with him on the constitutional problems facing the country, he told me on numerous occasions that East Pakistanis had not had their proper share in any sphere of national life and that this must be rectified. I became convinced that he intended a genuine political settlement between two parts of Pakistan by giving the Bengalis a real share in the decision-making process within a loose federal or even a confederal system. Yahya told me that he was opposed to any idea of a "strong centre", such as Ayub had often stressed. I tried to impress on him and other members of the "inner cabinet" that Pakistan had tried to achieve national integration from above by having a highly centralized government although the nation was legally constituted as a federation – but the experiment had proved to be a total failure. We should try the other way: let the two wings of the country manage their own affairs without any guidance or hindrance from the centre, particularly in the economic sphere. Here the Bengalis could say with ample justification that the all-powerful Planning Commission, which had been entrusted with the task of the country's economic development, had grossly neglected the economic problems and needs of East Pakistan. Pakistan, I continued to argue, should have full decentralization in economic and financial matters. In any political process, the Bengalis could not be made part of a Pakistani nationalism unless they could play their full part in national affairs. They rightly complained: "We hear the big decisions over the radio or television or read them in newspapers; sometimes we hear Pakistan is the 'most allied ally of the United States'; then we hear that the same United States encourages secession in East Pakistan. Even foreigners sometimes know the real situation in Pakistan better than we, the Bengalis." As regards economic and financial matters, even a small project such as a road linking district A to district B had to be finalized by a planning commission sitting a thousand miles away and dominated by the non-Bengali bureaucrats. No important observer of the Pakistan political scene could dismiss the genuine Bengali complaints. There was never a single Bengali finance minister, nor a Bengali chief of the Planning Commission. How could Bengalis consider themselves as part of an elusive Pakistani nationalism solely on the basis of Islamic bonds? If Islam were the only bond, the Bengali intelligentsia might well argue that they could create a larger Islamic state than West Pakistan.

Yahya, unlike Ayub, never pretended to be an expert on

constitutional or political matters, though some members of the junta pretended to be so. So it was easier to argue with him and convince him; he approached the whole problem with an open mind and was amenable to reasoning, although his powers of understanding and of taking imaginative decisions were extremely limited, which had great disadvantages as he could be influenced by others presenting a divergent picture. Yet, when Yahya was engaged in formulating his plan in 1969, he was genuinely interested in a satisfactory solution to the East–West Pakistan tensions and differences.

Both Ahsan and myself pleaded with Mujib that it was the last chance for the Bengalis to be the masters in their own affairs and to capture real power at the centre. Once I reminded him that the Congress leaders in British India were fighting against the British for national liberation, but when they realized in 1946–7 that the British Government was sincere in its intention to transfer power, Nehru developed a unique friendship with Lord Mountbatten which paid India good dividends; I urged Mujib to adopt the same attitude towards Yahya and his policy.

Mujib gave the impression of being satisfied. He told Yahya and Ahsan that his six points were not "the Koran or the Bible" and the plan was negotiable. One morning in the autumn of 1969, he told me, pointing at the photo of Suhrawardy which hung prominently in his room: "How could I think of destroying Pakistan, being a disciple of this great leader?"

So both Yahya and Mujib voiced optimism, and the prospects for a political settlement of the most complicated East–West differences within a viable political order in Pakistan seemed bright. I was greatly encouraged by these trends and began hopefully working out the details of the scheme for transfer of power; there were almost daily meetings and conferences at the President's House in October 1969 after a serious threat of clashes between students and the local martial law authorities at Dacca, which was averted with great skill and patience by both Yahya and Mujib; Ahsan too played a commendable role in averting the crisis. Yahya returned from Dacca on October 5 and I was taken into the cabinet on October 8; Yahya went to Iran for a short visit at the end of October, by which time the broad outlines of the plan were already decided. Peerzada and myself were engaged almost full-time in giving final shape to the plan. Then Peerzada met with a car accident in early November and the main burden fell on me; I drafted the speech of November 28, 1969, in which Yahya announced his proposals for the future of the country.

The Plan

Yahya began his speech by referring to the basic issues relating to the constitution which have already been pointed out. He expressed regret that political leaders could not arrive at a consensus on these three major issues, but he was careful in not blaming them for their failure to do so. He said: "It is regrettable that they have not been able to do so but one can understand and appreciate their difficulties."[6] In not putting all the blame on the politicians he differed from Ayub; this was a wise gesture. He then referred to the four possible alternatives to the holding of elections. These were: (i) "to have an elected constitutional convention whose task would be to produce a new constitution and then dissolve itself"; (ii) "to revive the 1956 Constitution"; (iii) "to frame a constitution and have a referendum on it in the country"; and (iv) "to evolve a Legal Framework for general elections on the basis of consultations with various groups and political leaders, as well as the study of past constitutions of Pakistan and the general consensus of the country. This proposal from me would only be in the nature of a provisional Legal Framework."[7]

After pointing out the merits and demerits of the various alternatives, Yahya opted for the fourth alternative.[8] Turning to the three basic issues: "First, the question of 'one unit'; secondly, the issue of 'one man, one vote' *versus* parity; and thirdly, the relationship between the centre and the federating provinces."[9] Yahya rightly pointed out that the first two issues were connected with the holding of elections and must be solved before the election. So he decided these two issues: elections on the basis of "one man, one vote" for a single-chamber national assembly and the abolition of the amalgamation of West Pakistan into "one unit".

Yahya's plan conceded all the demands put forward by

Mujib: representation on the basis of population and single-chamber legislature at the centre, where all matters would be decided by a simple majority. He merely expressed a pious hope that on constitutional matters there would be a consensus of opinion from various parts of the proposed federation.

There was strong opposition on this particular point from some members of the "inner cabinet" like Nur Khan and Hamid. Their contention was that in a legislature without a second chamber, elected on the basis of population, the Bengalis who constituted the majority of the population would be in a position "to impose" a constitution on other federating units of West Pakistan by what they termed "brute majority". So they insted on a special procedure for constitutional matters requiring a 60 per cent vote from among the total of members of the proposed legislature. The provision for "60 per cent" was in the plan up to the last moment. When it was put before the Cabinet just one day before its announcement, the "60 per cent clause" was still there. At the eleventh hour, by most skilful manoeuvring, Yahya dropped the clause from the plan. It was a real concession to the Bengalis and came as a pleasant surprise to many in East Pakistan. It had required serious effort and persuasion for the "60 per cent clause" to be dropped at the final meeting of the "inner cabinet" on the morning of November 25.

The most important constitutional issue, however, remained the relationship between the centre and the provinces. Mujib did not want this issue decided by Yahya but left to the legislature, in which there would be a clear Bengali majority. On this vital issue too, Yahya complied with Mujib's wishes, and as a result was criticized, by the West Pakistani leaders, for not deciding this issue as he had done in the case of "one unit" and representation on the basis of "one man, one vote". Yahya, on the contrary, had pledged maximum autonomy to the provinces. He stated:

> As regards the relations between the centre and the provinces, you would recall that in my July broadcast I pointed out that the people of East Pakistan did not have their full share in the decision-making process on vital national issues. I also said then that they were fully justified in being dissatisfied with this state of affairs. We shall, therefore,

> have to put an end to this position. The requirements would appear to be maximum autonomy to the two wings of Pakistan as long as this does not impair national integrity and solidarity of the country.
>
> One of the main aspects of the whole relationship between the Centre and the provinces in Pakistan today lies in the financial and economic spheres. Federation implies not only a division of legislative powers but also that of financial powers. This matter will have to be dealt with in such a manner as would satisfy the legitimate requirements and demands of the provinces as well as the vital requirements of the nation as a whole. People of the two regions of Pakistan should have control over their economic resources and development as long as it does not adversely affect the working of a national government at the Centre.[10]

Could there have been better gestures and incentives for a confederal solution of the regional conflicts between East and West Pakistan than that given by Yahya in his speech on November 28, 1969? There was wide appreciation of Yahya's speed, both inside and outside the country. Pakistan seemed about to show that it could carry out a peaceful transfer of power from a military to a democratic régime. The world's press welcomed Yahya's "bold" and sincere proposals for restoring the democratic process in Pakistan and for solving the complicated regional conflicts of the country. *The New York Times* wrote under the headline "Pakistan sets an example": "Pakistan President Agha Mohammed Yahya Khan has set a prudent example for other military rulers with his move to restore democratic civilian rule in his country. . . . The principle of 'one man, one vote' will give the restive Bengalis of East Pakistan majority representation in the Assembly consistent with their numerical strength";[11] while the *Christian Science Monitor* commented: "To his credit General Yahya Khan has now announced a crisp time-table for elections throughout the country on a one man, one vote basis and drafting of a constitution which should give the Bengalis of East Pakistan virtual autonomy and a voice in national affairs, at last commensurate with their numbers."[12] In the U.S. Congress, Mr. Sikes said: "President Agha Mohammed Yahya Khan is providing an encouraging example which other nations should observe and appreciate. His quiet but effective policies are steadily moving democratic process forward in Pakistan."[13] President Nixon was reported to have advised the Greek Ambassador in Washington that the example of Yahya should be followed in Greece.[14] All those, whether inside or outside the country, who wanted to see Pakistan united and stable welcomed Yahya's plan for the transfer of power. It was the first – and the last – attempt to put the complicated relationship between East and West Pakistan on a sound political footing, and it looked as if Pakistan was set on the right road. Pakistan's firm steps towards democracy as outlined in Yahya's speech were expected to contradict the old truth that dictators never give way voluntarily.

Many questions may be asked about a plan which aroused such strong expectations. Did the army – not Yahya alone but the ruling junta – really want to hand over power? Did Mujib want a settlement on the basis of a united Pakistan or did he only intend to use elections to establish his credentials as the sole leader of an emerging Bangladesh? What were the aims of the West Pakistani leaders, particularly Bhutto? Were they prepared to pay the price needed to fulfil the demands of Bengalis as pledged by Yahya? The whole plan was based on three fundamental premises: first, Mujib would modify his six-point plan, and would be satisfied with genuine provincial autonomy and not aim at secession; secondly, the West Pakistani leaders, both the politicians and the big industrialists, would be willing to make the necessary sacrifices and concessions to satisfy the legitimate aspirations, political demands and economic dues of the Bengalis as a condition for keeping Pakistan united; and thirdly, the military junta must give up the power to which it had become accustomed since 1958; it must not think in terms of any "qualified" or "limited" transfer of power of the "Turkish" type – the Turkish model sometimes arose in conversation with the generals. I was often asked by some of the generals if I consulted the Constitution of Turkey while advising Yahya on the constitutional problems of Pakistan.

A single declaration – or a plan, however carefully and sincerely worked out – could not solve the complicated problems of a country like Pakistan. The plan itself was a step in the right direction, but its success depended on many conditions, many of which were lacking. For the twenty-two years since its founding, Pakistan had not had a direct general election for its governing bodies. There had been no democratic process of representation; the majority of the country's population were denied their political rights and economic dues. For much of the time, there had been either a "modernizing oligarchy" or dictatorial rule. There were deep-rooted fears and suspicions between the peoples of the two geographically separated regions. If Yahya's plan were to go through, Pakistan would survive as a united nation but this "if" was a big one.

Yahya between the Generals and Mujib

One thing that was soon apparent was that some of the army generals and the West Pakistani leaders including Bhutto thought that Yahya had gone too far in placating the Bengalis – at the cost of the "national interest", as they interpreted it. However, Governor Ahsan and even General Yakub, the Zonal MLA in East Pakistan, were happy with the wide acceptance of Yahya's plan and it was a pleasant surprise to me that the chief of military intelligence, General Akbar, and Rezvi, the chief of civil intelligence, were giving Yahya favourable reports supporting his plan. Many army officers, unlike senior bureaucrats, the big industrialists and some narrow-minded politicians, were willing to make major sacrifices to maintain the unity of Pakistan. Among the young army officers and enlightened generals, Pakistani nationalism was not a vague and incoherent concept; with them, as with many patriotic elements in both East and West Pakistan, its ideology and its flag were too dear to be preserved at any cost; they were determined to preserve and value the ideals and ideology which were the driving forces behind the creation of Pakistan. I myself shared these views wholeheartedly.

Yet Yahya was subjected to severe pressures from some quarters at GHQ in Rawalpindi and from Bhutto, who was backed by some generals and top bureaucrats, to modify his plan as outlined in his famous speech of November 28, 1969. Between November 28, 1969, and March 30, 1970, Yahya was in real difficulty. In order "to protect the country against a

Bengali-dominated assembly", some members of the "inner cabinet" put forward two particular demands. The first of these was that the Legal Framework Order (popularly known as L.F.O.) which – sincc the country had no constitution – had to be promulgated before elections could legally be held, must contain a definition of the limits of provincial autonomy, and the second was that in the new assembly, constitutional matters must be decided not by a simple majority but by a two-thirds vote or at least 60 per cent of the total membership – the rider clause which was dropped at the eleventh hour from Yahya's plan of November 28. It was argued that there was no reason why Yahya should not take a definite decision on the extent of provincial autonomy, just as he had decided on the basis of representation and on the break up of "one unit". The non-Awami League leaders from East Pakistan also joined with the West Pakistani leaders in making this demand; their fear was that unless provincial autonomy were defined, Mujib would have a strong edge on them by preaching the gospel of Bengali nationalism and his six points which had become popular in East Pakistan. They feared – and subsequent events proved their fears justified – that if the explosive issue of regional autonomy were not defined in the L.F.O., the flood of emerging Bengali nationalism could not be checked. They also argued that Yahya had pledged genuine and maximum autonomy, in economic-financial matters among others; so why did he not put an end to this potentially dangerous issue by giving real autonomy and then firmly declaring "This far and no further"?

There was good reasoning behind these arguments. However, Mujib made it clear through Governor Ahsan that if the extent of provincial autonomy were defined or if the principle of "one man, one vote" were modified by any special procedure of voting on the constitutional issue, it would mean an end to negotiations and the beginning of an armed confrontation. Some of the generals seemed to prefer to have a confrontation before elections, i.e. before Mujib could consolidate in East Pakistan and emerge as the sole leader of the Bengalis. But Governor Ahsan warned Yahya that a united Pakistan would not survive a confrontation with Mujib. Yahya too at that stage seemed convinced of it. Mujib, the subsequent founder of Bangladesh, was paradoxically the last hope for a united Pakistan – provided he could be persuaded to modify his six points. I carefully examined the substance of the Yahya–Mujib and Mujib–Ahsan talks in 1969–70 and can vouch that Mujib repeatedly assured that he would modify his six points once the elections were over.

Another significant and encouraging development took place in February 1970 when Mujib told me that the L.F.O. should provide for elections not only for the national assembly but also for provincial legislatures. I pointed out that the L.F.O. was not supposed to be a constitution but was to be a just *modus operandi* for electing a national assembly – the first task of which would be to frame a constitution; the provincial legislature could come into existence only *after* the constitution was framed. Mujib, with a significant smile, replied: "You are a political scientist; I am a politician; how could Yahya expect me to modify my extreme demands?" I could appreciate his reasoning and believed that Mujib honestly wanted an agreed constitution on the modified version of his six points. I considered it a very encouraging hint. From Dacca I went to Karachi to meet Bhutto and tried to find out his reaction to the simultaneous holding of elections for both the national and provincial legislatures. Bhutto, with his usual style of talking, asked me if it were Mujib's suggestion; I avoided giving an answer by telling him that my assignment was to talk to all political leaders including Mujib and himself. Bhutto agreed to the proposal, though he termed it "putting the cart before the horse", but he added that it would enable the political leaders to adopt a flexible attitude. On my return to Islamabad, I reported this to Yahya, who immediately accepted it and asked me to draft the L.F.O. accordingly. Turning to the two specific proposals relating to the special procedure for voting on constitutional proposals and the definition of provincial autonomy, the matters were thrashed out at a series of meetings of the inner cabinet. Yahya was firm against any special procedure of voting by saying that he could not compromise on the principle of "one man, one vote"; he argued, with the support of Ahsan and myself, it would destroy confidence in the intentions of the military régime among the Bengalis, and once that confidence was lost, Yahya concluded, the whole process might as well be given up. So the inner cabinet had to yield.

The question of limiting the extent of provincial autonomy was much more complicated. I had almost daily sessions with Yahya in January–February as to how this delicate issue could be tackled. Finally, in an attempt to find a way out of the impasse, I proposed at a meeting of the inner cabinet in late January that instead of trying to define the extent of provincial autonomy, the L.F.O. should define the minimum requirements that were essential for the existence of a united Pakistan. I had prior consultation about my plan with Yahya, Ahsan, Yakub and Peerzada; Ahsan was quick to assure me of his full support, and Yakub said he would discuss it with "open mind" – he had faith in my convictions regarding one Pakistan. Yahya, though surprised initially about what I termed "defining one Pakistan", was prepared to give me a chance to elaborate it in the inner cabinet. Only Hamid, Tikka and a few others like Omar were angered by this "soft" policy towards Mujib. Peerzada had consultations with Bhutto and when the latter was reported to have no objection, Peerzada adopted a neutral posture.

It was a big day for me; I began my discussion with an analysis of the political situation in East Pakistan; I conceded that by not defining provincial autonomy Mujib could cause damage if he were planning to do so. But our whole approach, I continued, was based on expectations of a reasonable attitude from Mujib as well as others and therefore no step should be taken to precipitate a crisis – a view strongly supported by Ahsan. When I finally elaborated the "five principles" of *one* Pakistan, to the great relief and surprise of Yahya, Ahsan and myself, it was eventually accepted by the generals. But though the crisis seemed to be over, events after the elections showed that it had only been postponed for a year.

The Legal Framework Order

The L.F.O., which was at last announced on March 31, 1971, contained five points or principles which were regarded as the minimum requirements for a united Pakistan. (1) Pakistan must be based on Islamic ideology – Mujib did not object to this; on the other hand, the Awami League's election manifesto pledged: "The Awami League affirms that a clear guarantee should be embodied in the constitution to the effect that no law repugnant to the injunction of Islam as laid down in the Holy Quran and Sunnah shall be enacted or enforced."[15] It was only after the creation of Bangladesh that Mujib provided in his country's constitution the principle of secularism by the "elimination of granting by the State of political status in favour of any religion and the abuse of religion for political purposes". Mujib won the election of 1970 by pledging a constitution on the Islamic ideology because he knew that Islam and its ideology were as dear to the Muslims of East as of West Pakistan. Here was one glaring instance of the gap between Mujib's professions and his practice.

Turning to other principles of the L.F.O.: (2) the country was to have a democratic constitution providing for free and fair elections – no one could object to that. (3) Pakistan's territorial integrity must be upheld in the constitution – Mujib could not object to this because, whatever his ultimate goal, he could not openly challenge the "oneness" of the country. (4) The disparity between the wings, particularly in economic development, must be eliminated by statutory provisions to be guaranteed in the constitution – again neither Mujib nor any other political leader, either of East or West Pakistan, could have any objection to this. (5) The distribution of power between the centre and the provinces must be made in such a way that the provinces enjoyed the maximum degree of autonomy consistent with giving the central Government adequate power to discharge its federal responsibilities, including the maintenance of the country's territorial integrity. No doubt the intention was to set up a genuine federal system. But since the wording of this stipulation was deliberately vague, it was capable of more than one interpretation; it allowed Mujib to base his election campaign on his six points while those who wanted a united, federal Pakistan could still hope they had got it. This particular point or principle in the L.F.O. was the most complicated one, and it was agreed upon after much discussion and debate in the inner cabinet; the civilian cabinet was presented the final draft for mere formality and there was not much discussion in the cabinet; there were only few questions seeking clarifications and the President's interpretation was final and unchallenged.

The L.F.O. had a preamble, twenty-seven articles and two Schedules; it looked like a provisional constitution. It was Article 20 which laid down the five "Fundamental Principles of the Constitution" and which was thus the vital one.[16] The other articles related mainly to composition of the national assembly and provincial assemblies, provisions relating to the holding of election, qualifications and disqualifications for membership, the election of the Speaker and Deputy Speaker – peripheral matters which were needed for setting up an assembly to frame the country's constitution.

The L.F.O. provided that the national assembly must complete its task of framing the constitution within 120 days. This time-limit was made because of the past experiences of constitution-making in Pakistan: it had taken two constituent assemblies nine years (from 1947 to 1956) to frame a constitution for Pakistan, and everyone wanted to prevent a repetition of this tragic delay. The time-limit also demonstrated Yahya's sincerity regarding the handing over of power to the elected representatives of the people in the shortest possible time. The political leaders agreed to the time-limit, and it was further agreed that the majority group or groups responsible for producing a constitution would show the draft to the President before formally presenting it to the assembly. The President was given power to "authenticate the constitution" (Article 25).

The L.F.O. was criticized, particularly in East Pakistan, as a retreat from the plan put forward by Yahya on November 28, 1969. In a sense, this was true. But those who knew from the inside how the document had been drawn up realized that some compromise had been essential and were not dissatisfied with the outcome. Mujib, who learned what had gone on from Ahsan, accepted the outcome. The five principles, though not palatable to everyone, could not be criticized openly as they did not violate the demands of any group or party. The President's power of authentication of the constitution was criticized as curtailing the sovereignty of the national assembly or the constituent assembly. On April 4, 1970, soon after the promulgation of the L.F.O., Yahya went to Dacca and declared that there was no intention to curb the people's sovereignty. At Dacca airport while talking to newsmen, he stated: "I do not think there is any curb on anybody's sovereignty. My desire is to lead the nation, towards democracy. My action so far does not conflict with what I have been telling the people about sovereignty."[17] He reaffirmed it when he was leaving Dacca on April 10; on this latter occasion, he disclosed to newsmen at Dacca airport that he had explained the authentication clause to the various leaders during his stay in Dacca, and that the L.F.O. had been "accepted and hailed" by the vast majority of the people, and a few other people "who are worried about one or two things here also accepted 99 per cent of it". He said unambiguously that if the constitution were made according to the broad principles laid down in the framework, then there was no reason why he should not authenticate it. It was unthinkable that he would refuse authentication just for the sake of refusing it. After all, during the last year he had taken a number of steps to move the nation towards democracy. Yahya added that if the nation had faith in him, it must realize that "I am not doing all this for fun". He termed authentication "only a procedural formality".[18]

Did Yahya really mean to fulfill his pledge and restore democracy? I asked him these questions many times and reported to him discouraging hints dropped by some of his generals and the doubts that still lingered in the minds of some politicians about his ultimate objective. His answers were: "Am I such a fool as not to be able to see the writing on the wall?" During the four-month-long agitation in 1968–9, the people's revolt against the authoritarian régime of Ayub was unqualified; he assured me that the urge for democracy was too strong for any general to ignore. However, he would stress again and again that as the Head of State and also as Chief of the Armed Forces he would not tolerate any scheme or plan to split the country. Of course, if seventy-five million people in East Pakistan were to ask for separation in clear terms and not in a veiled scheme (referring to Mujib's six points) then it was a different story. Pakistan, he added, was demanded by the people of East Pakistan; they gave Quaid-e-Azam more support than the people of any region of West Pakistan during the national movement for Pakistan (1940–7).

Yahya strongly believed that if the Bengalis were given their share, there was no reason why they should want to see Pakistan dismembered; they, he used to tell me, would not only have maximum autonomy in their own province but, thanks to "one man, one vote", they would also dominate national politics. Then one evening in late February when the L.F.O. was being hotly debated in his inner cabinet and I expressed my dismay at the attitude of some members of the junta, he told me categorically: "Look at the fate of Ayub for whom both you and I myself have regard! What is his condition? He is virtually leading a self-imposed exiled life; do you want me to have the same fate or should we not save the country from the terrible challenge to its very existence as a result of East–West Pakistan tensions?" I confess that I was impressed by his words, and I still believe that he meant business, otherwise he would not have given a free and fair election. Tampering with elections in an underdeveloped country is not a difficult task. Yahya could have got at least fifty seats from East Pakistan by unfair means and could have had a fake "representative" government. I was also present on an occasion when an influential member of the ruling élite hinted at such a course of action with the plea that Mujib might get out of control if, as developments were indicating, he obtained nearly all the seats from East Pakistan. Yahya's reply was: "If seventy-five million people like Mujib's face, who am I to oppose him provided he does not destroy our cherished homeland? My commitments are for transfer of power and certainly not for splitting the country." Then he would always advise patience and faith. "Pakistan can be saved through mutual faith and trust between the people of East and West Pakistan and not through fraud and unfair elections."

In the meantime political activities, which had been partly suspended, were restored from January 1, 1970. The leaders of various parties began a long election campaign. In fact it was overlong: it lasted a whole year. In one of his early public speeches, Mujib declared: "Pakistan has come to stay and there is no focrce that can destroy it."[19]

In the light of all these statements in favour of "one Pakistan", could anybody foresee the tragic happenings which began on the night of March 25, 1971, and ended with the triumphant entry of Indian troops into Dacca on December 16, 1971?

Things, however, were not moving in the way that Mujib was saying in public. When his party was debating Yahya's scheme of power under the Legal Framework Order of 1970, Mujib was reported to have said to his inner cabinet that his sole aim was to establish Bangladesh. Yahya was presented with a tape-recorded account of these talks of Mujib with his close associates. Mujib was clearly heard to say: "My aim is to establish Bangladesh; I will tear the L.F.O. [the Legal Framework Order] into pieces as soon as the elections are over. Who could challenge me once the elections are over?" He also hinted to his colleagues about help from "outside sources",[20] presumably from India. When Yahya listened to this "political music" played by his intelligence services, he was bewildered. He could easily recognize Mujib's voice and the substance of his recorded talk. The next morning when I saw him he was still in a bewildered state; but he was never a serious administrator, so he soon recovered from his shock and told me: "I shall fix Mujib if he betrays me." Yahya also seemed to have more than one contingency plan, just as Mujib seemed to have.

The Confusing Scene

In political talks and election campaigning, Mujib and his followers were freee to preach the idea of Bangladesh to every house in every village without hindrance; cries of *Joy Bangla!* (Victory to Bangladesh) were heard everywhere. Again, making a comparison with the past, Mujib's election campaign was the same as Jinnah's in 1945–6 for the establishment of Pakistan. As the campaign progressed, it was clear that Mujib's Awami League was the only representative party in East Pakistan; the other parties could hardly organize any meetings, and when they did, the militant Awami Leaguers would disrupt them.

There was a martial law regulation that anybody talking against "territorial integrity" would be severely dealt with, yet a campaign for Bangladesh was freely allowed. Yahya would make some speeches now and then reaffirming his determination to "protect" the country against any threat of a break-up; yet the young and student followers of Mujib were freely carrying the gospel of Bangladesh everywhere in East Pakistan. On August 14, 1970 – Pakistan's independence day – the students of Dacca University had displayed a new map showing the creation of Bangladesh, and the flag of the emerging country was prominently displayed at a meeting to celebrate independence day. The meeting was presided over by the Vice-Chancellor of the University, Justice A. S. Choudhury, former President of Bangladesh. He was summoned by the Martial Law Administrator, Lieut.-General Yakub Khan, to "explain" his open challenge to the country's unity and existence. The matter ended over a cup of tea, thanks to Governor Ahsan's intervention.[21]

All-India Radio, from its station in Calcutta, was broadcasting a programme every evening entitled *Apper Bangla, oupper Bangla* (This Side and the Other Side of Bengal), openly supporting the cause of Bangladesh. There were reports – not only from the Pakistan intelligence services but also from others, including some friendly foreign countries – that Indian money and arms were being sent to East Pakistan both for the success of the Awami League in the election and for the eventual confrontation with the Pakistan army. There was evidence of India's involvement in the affairs of East Pakistan. The non-Awami League political leaders of East Pakistan made similar reports to Yahya.

Ahsan was the only optimistic person in East Pakistan, and he used to tell Yahya: "Sheikh Sahib [Mujib] will not break up Pakistan." Yahya would be satisfied; he was regularly paying visits to East Pakistan and always had "lengthy" and "friendly" talks with Mujib; on every occasion after his talks with Mujib he was happy and would say: "Thank God all those reports [i.e. those supplied by his intelligence services and from other sources] are not correct." My interpretation of Yahya's reaction is that he was not capable of understanding the political realities or dynamics of East Pakistan. It was Ahsan who was largely responsible for leading Yahya into a false sense of optimism; but neither Yahya nor Ahsan seemed to have any other option. Mujib was given a long rope, and it was now difficult for him to retreat without a confrontation, which neither Yahya nor anybody who had any hope of preserving a united Pakistan could afford to think of.

Then came the two terrible natural calamities in East Pakistan – floods in August 1970 and a cyclone and tidal bore in November. During the flood in August, Yahya and his government dealt with the situation well – he and his cabinet ministers toured East Pakistan from end to end and met the people. Yahya's image went up; it is not difficult to get applause or censure from the emotional Bengalis. So no special significance could be attached to this. Yahya had to postpone the elections, but nobody could challenge the decision as it was not possible to hold an election when large areas of East Pakistan were under water. Mujib had to accept the decision.

But the situation was different when East Pakistan was ravaged by a cyclone and tidal bore. Yahya was in Peking when the cyclone struck in November 1970. On his return journey to Rawalpindi he stopped at Dacca and stayed for two days. Governor Ahsan and the provincial government told him that his presence in Dacca was not needed and that newspaper accounts of the havoc caused by the cyclone were highly exaggerated. So Yahya left Dacca, but soon there were cries and protests everywhere. Yahya returned to Dacca, but the damage had already been done. There were widespread protests and dissatisfaction over what was termed as "gross" if not "criminal" negligence by the central government in dealing with the victims of the cyclone. There could not have been a more favourable climate for Bengali nationalists and Mujib to preach the idea of a separate state for the Bengalis. The centre's alleged neglect in handling the situation provided the most convincing argument for having a separate state for Bengalis, just as widespread Hindu–Muslim riots from August 16, 1946 (the great Calcutta killings), provided Jinnah and the Muslims of India with powerful evidence that they could no longer live together with the Hindus.

The Secret Talks between Yahya and Mujib

There were demands by all non-Awami League political leaders including Maulana Bhashani that elections should again be postponed. Mujib, however, was not prepared to sacrifice such a golden opportunity to realize his cherished aim of becoming the creator of Bangladesh. All evidence and reports indicate that he had now reached the conclusion that the creation of Bangladesh was the only solution for the Bengalis. If he had had any reservations or doubts earlier, all were swept away by the "unpardonable apathy" of the "West Pakistanis" towards the suffering Bengalis.

Yet Mujib had three secret meetings with Yahya during the latter's stays in Dacca in late November and early December 1970. Yahya had already decided that elections would not be postponed – a decision which was favourable to Mujib. Yahya did not even grant an interview to the "eleven leaders" of East Pakistan, including Nurul Amin, who appealed to him to postpone the election. They were bitter at Yahya's decision just as it made Mujib happy. Bhashani made it clear to Yahya through an emissary that if Yahya would concentrate his relief operations in cyclone-affected areas by devoting his entire administration to relief work rather than preparations for holding the election, and if Mujib should then challenge him for postponing the elections, he and his party would support Yahya and not Mujib; his party's slogan at that time was "food before vote". If Ayub Khan and not Yahya had been in power, Bhashani's offer would most likely have been accepted. Similarly all other parties and groups were prepared to back Yahya if Mujib started an agitation against the postponement of elections – he openly threatened that a million people would be killed in the confrontation if the elections were postponed. The West Pakistani leaders, including Bhutto, were prepared for a postponement of elections.

Yet Yahya decided to go ahead with the "free and fair election" he had promised to the nation. His great expectation was that this would make Mujib happy and that a compromise would be possible. Before Yahya made his decision, there were exchanges of secret messages between him and Mujib which led Yahya to place trust in Mujib's words: "Pakistan shall not be broken."

So the three secret meetings at the President's House in Dacca in later November and early December were held in a most cordial atmosphere – the outside climate at Dacca at the beginning of the mild winter was very pleasant – and no less bright was the picture inside the conference room of the President's House. Mujib made a solemn promise that he would show the draft constitution before presenting it to the assembly. He was reported to have assured Yahya that his six-point programme did not imply a division of the country, and that Yahya's five points, as laid down in the L.F.O., and his own six points would both be incorporated in the future constitution. After three meetings with Mujib, Yahya sent for me on December 3, 1970, and gleefully told me: "Pakistan is saved"; he also boasted that his decision not to postpone the election was "correct and far-sighted". I could not, however, share Yahya's optimism; I only hoped and prayed that he was correct. The whole Yahya–Mujib dialogue during the three secret meetings was, as usual, taped and I heard the tape-recorded version of the talks. Nobody listening to the tape-recorded version could blame Yahya. However, I also obtained a copy of the preliminary draft constitution prepared by experts of the Awami League in which there was no hope for a united Pakistan. The division of the country was not formally proposed but a rigid and comprehensive interpretation of the six-point programme was in the draft. If the six points were incorporated *in toto*, there could hardly be a federal union.

In the following account of the disintegration of Pakistan I shall try to enable the reader to judge who was truly the betrayer – Yahya or Mujib.[22]

The West Pakistan Scene

I have, so far, discussed the Yahya–Mujib talks and political developments in East Pakistan because it was the tensions between East and West Pakistan which were to determine the fate of Pakistan. But that did not imply that the roles of political leaders or the ruling élite in West Pakistan could be ignored or minimized. Yahya, unlike his predecessor Ayub, did not have absolute control over the ruling army junta. There were currents and cross-currents within the junta, but until January 1971 it gave Yahya and his principal military adviser Lieut.-General Peerzada a free hand to negotiate with Mujib in the effort to find a solution, provided the unity of the country was maintained. The junta had neither much ability nor much enthusiasm for studying the various constitutional devices and formulae. They seemed over-confident that if anything went wrong they would step in, whereupon, as in March 1969, another period of rigid martial law would bring "sanity". What could the non-martial Bengalis, who were looked down upon as Muslims converted from the lower caste Hindus, do once the brave *jawans* (soldiers) were on the streets of Dacca? They were living in a world of illusion and had no ability to read the writing on the wall. Of course, there were exceptions. Many enlightened and well-intentioned army officers were watching the situation with dismay and genuine concern. But like so many, they too could only hope and pray for the best and were perhaps getting ready for the worst, although nobody could imagine at that time that events would soon overtake all calculations and turn the whole situation into one of the greatest tragedies of modern history.

Among the West Pakistani leaders there was no single leader like Mujib who had absolute control over the whole of West Pakistan. Bhutto himself told me in June 1970 that he would get "at least" forty seats out of the 132 allotted to West Pakistan; that was his greatest expectation. Then there were orthodox rightist parties like Jamaat-e-Islami, who had enjoyed the blessing of some of the generals. General Sher Ali (a member of Yahya's cabinet) was a great champion of the *Islam Pasand* (Islam-loving) parties, as they were known. Qayyum Khan's Muslim League was also reported to have enjoyed the patronage of members of the ruling élite. Wali Khan and his party, the pro-Moscow faction of the National Awami Party (NAP), was active only in Baluchistan and the North-West Frontier; it was taken for granted that Wali Khan would have some success in these two smaller provinces of West Pakistan. But as the election campaign progressed, Bhutto's chances became ever brighter. His theme of a "thousand years war with India", restoring national honour supposed to have been sacrificed by Ayub at the Tashkent conference, and his promise of "Islamic socialism" attracted the younger elements in the Punjab.

But more significant, if not sinister, was the deal between Bhutto and the "Rasputin" of the Yahya régime, General

Peerzada. The Bhutto–Peerzada alliance had a long history – both were sacked by Ayub, and common hostility towards Ayub had made them good friends since 1966. Bhutto was also coming closer to other members of the military junta such as Lieut.-General Gul Hasan, Major-General Omar who was a close friend and colleague of the chief of the army, General Hamid, who had already started dreaming of becoming the third military President of the country, following Yahya just as Yahya had followed Ayub.

Yahya seemed to be presiding over not only a divided house but also a bewildering situation. However, he continued to relax and have pleasant social evenings. With all his limitations, he was – I still believe – making an honest effort to reach a political settlement between East and West Pakistan. In his L.F.O. he conceded all the legitimate demands of the Bengalis. He sincerely believed that the only way to save Pakistan was to win the confidence of Mujib by granting him all the concessions – minus the disintegration of Pakistan. As pointed out earlier, Yahya was a non-serious type of administrator; he did not like reading official files and letters except for brief summaries. He used to describe himself as a "part-time" president. There were two matters which attracted his full-time attention – the constitutional formula by which the unity of the country could be saved and the assignment given to him by President Nixon to act as courier between Washington and Peking in the light of Nixon's new China policy. Yahya did both these jobs conscientiously.

Incidentally, these two important tasks of Yahya brought me in close contact with him, not as his cabinet minister. I was also a "part-time" Communications Minister: my main job was to assist him in his constitutional and political dialogue with leaders of various parties, and as I worked as Head of the Research Division of the Pakistan Ministry of Foreign Affairs for more than two years immediately before I joined Yahya's cabinet, he took me into full confidence in his foreign policy matters.

REFERENCES

1. See text of Yahya's press conference in *Dawn*, Karachi, April 11, 1973.
2. See the text of Yahya's broadcast in *Dawn*, Karachi, July 29, 1969.
3. Ibid.
4. See *Report of the Constitution Commission*, 1961, Government of Pakistan, pp. 34–7.
5. See V. P. Menon, *The Transfer of Power im India*, Longmans, London, 1957; Lord Ismay, *Memoirs* (Heinemann, London, 1969); Ian Stephens, *Pakistan* (Ernest Benn, London, 1962); Leonard Mosley, *The Last Days of the British Raj* (Weidenfeld and Nicolson, London, 1962).
6. *President's Address to the Nation: General A. M. Yahya Khan, President of Pakistan*, November 28, 1969, published by the Department of Films and Publications, Government of Pakistan, Karachi, p. 5.
7. Ibid., p. 6.
8. Ibid.
9. Ibid.
10. Ibid., pp. 9–10; one may compare my *Democracy in Pakistan* (1963) p. 234 and pp. 243–4, for almost identical words in this part of Yahya's speech.
11. *New York Times*, December 2, 1969.
12. *Christian Science Monitor*, December 13, 1969.
13. The U.S. *Congressional Record – Home*, December 15, 1969.
14. From an unpublished report by the Pakistani Ambassador in Washington, January, 1970.
15. See Awami League Manifesto in *Bangladesh Documents* published by the Ministry of External Affairs, Government of India, n.d. pp. 67–8.
16. See *The Legal Framework Order*, 1970, President's Order No. 2 of 1970, published by the Department of Films and Publications, Government of Pakistan, Karachi, n.d.
17. *Pakistan Observer* (Dacca), April 5, 1970.
18. Ibid., April 12, 1970.
19. *Bangladesh Documents*, op. cit., Col. I, p. 82.
20. This account of Mujib's speech to his inner circle was reported to Yahya by his intelligence service. For some reason, presumably to continue the path of negotiations, he decided to ignore it.
21. I owe the story of this incident to Lt.-Gen. Yakub and to Governor Ahsan.
22. See *Banglabandhu Speaks; a Collection of Speeches and Documents*, Dacca, Ministry of Foreign Affairs, Government of Bangladesh, n.d., pp. 42–3. Mujib now claims that he was struggling for Bangladesh since 1948.

5

THE FIRST AND LAST GENERAL ELECTION

Periodical elections on the basis of direct adult franchise, contested freely and fairly by more than one party, is regarded as a *sine qua non* of any form of representative government. Democracy was the driving force behind the creation of Pakistan, but its eclipse was nowhere more prominent than in the absence of any genuine general elections in Pakistan during its two decades of existence as a united country. Parliamentary democracy, or a parody of it, existed from 1947 to 1958, but the country did not have a single general election during that period. Pakistan provided a unique example of "democracy without any genuine elections". Two federal legislatures during this period were indirectly elected by the provincial legislatures. The first provincial elections had been held under the British *raj* in 1946 on a restricted franchise; then between 1951 and 1954 provincial elections were held on the basis of direct adult franchise. What was the nature of these elections, and to what extent were they fair and free?

The best account of these elections in the provinces of West Pakistan was given by the Electoral Reform Commission which was set up under the chairmanship of a judge of the Superior Court in 1955. The Commission's Report, recalling the pledge given by the founder of Pakistan, Quaid-i-Azam Jinnah, that Pakistan "would be a democratic state", lamented that the people's faith in democracy was tarnished by

> feelings of frustration and despondency chiefly on account of the alleged malpractices perpetuated and underhand tactics used, during the elections held on the basis of adult franchise in 1951 in most of the regions now constituting the province of West Pakistan. . . . These elections were *a farce, a mockery and a fraud upon the electorate* [author's italics]. It

> was alleged that pocket constituencies lacking in geographical compactness or homogeneity in other material particulars were carved out to suit the convenience and fortune of particular politicians. It was maintained that persons on a large scale were purposely registered as bogus voters in the electoral rolls and made to vote under undue influence, coercion and inducements of all sorts. Ballot boxes . . . were surreptiously forced open and clandestinely stuffed. . . . Officials at the bidding of the party in power interfered with the free exercise of ballot and that hosts of tricks were played upon the electorate. . . . Rival candidates were kidnapped; political opponents were . . . harassed and thrown behind bars on the pretext of their being dangerous to the state. . . . Illegal tactics constituted a blot on the fair name of democracy . . . and created serious doubts and fears in the mind of the general public as to the fate of democracy in Pakistan.[1]

The Commission made a comprehensive list of recommendations in order to avoid these malpractices, and concluded: "If we honestly wish to work democracy in this country, we should let the democratic evolution and ideals take their shape."[2] But the country had no free elections. Soon parliamentary democracy was abolished, and the country was governed under martial law from 1958 to 1962. It has to be added, however, that there was one fair provincial election in East Bengal in 1954 when the ruling party, the Muslim League, was completely routed: it was only able to capture nine seats in an assembly of 304 members. There were 1,285 candidates for the 304 seats. The percentage of voters participating in the election, including women voters, was fairly high judged by the criterion of an election in a new Asian democracy.

When Ayub Khan came to power in 1958 he introduced an indirect method of election through the Basic Democrats. The will of the electorate is not properly reflected in an indirect method of election, which is why most of the democratic states have abandoned it in favour of direct elections – except in some cases for electing an upper house. Ayub's system of election demonstrated clearly, in the presidential election of 1965, that there was a big gap between the verdict of the people and the actual results of the election. As I have already pointed out, one of the major complaints against Ayub's political order – if not the major one – was the indirect method of election which failed to reflect the people's wishes in the election results.

So Yahya's pledge of "free and fair" elections on the basis of direct voting and giving the Bengalis, for the first time, their due share of representation on the basis of "one man, one vote" was in a sense a revolutionary development in Pakistan's politics.

The Election Machinery

Yahya in his speech of July 28, 1969, announced the formation of an Election Commission headed by a Bengali judge of the Supreme Court of Pakistan, Justice A. Satter. I had frequent and regular meetings with him and can say that he was absolutely free in his assignment to arrange a fair election; at no stage was the Election Commission subjected to any pressure or even given any hint as to how it should function. Justice Satter, like myself and others who sincerely hoped for a political settlement between East and West Pakistan, was optimistic and seemed to be fully satisfied in the free and independent role he was exercising. Yahya used to show him all courtesy and respect; sometimes Justice Satter was specially invited to attend cabinet meetings when any important decisions relating to elections were to be made; his views and recommendations were always given high priority and attention.

The Election Commission's first task was to decide whether to accept the electoral rolls already prepared under Ayub's system for the 1970 elections. The main objections to accepting the existing rolls were that Ayub's method of election was indirect, and therefore these electoral rolls had been prepared for electing the members of the electoral college, the Basic Democrats, and not the members of the legislatures, central or provincial. Yahya, as already pointed out, had pledged direct elections on adult franchise. Secondly, the Election Commission under Ayub had not been headed by a judge of the Supreme Court but by an executive officer, who was Ayub's principal secretary for a number of years and a member of his inner cabinet. The work of Ayub's Election Commission could not inspire public confidence, which was badly needed to remove doubts as to whether the military régime sincerely intended to transfer power through "free and fair" elections. So after careful consideration, Justice Satter decided to go ahead with the preparation of new electoral rolls. It was not an easy task to prepare electoral rolls for a country with a population of about 115,000,000 (according to the 1961 census), the vast majority of whom were illiterate, living in remote villages where the means of communications were poor.

Yet the Election Commission did the job with commendable speed and with as much care as possible to avoid any possible criticism that "bogus voters" were being registered, as had been the case in Pakistan in the past. All possible precautions were taken and an elaborate machinery consisting of 285 registration officers, 1,404 assistant registration officers, 14,121 supervisors and 45,766 enumerators was set up to carry out the gigantic task of enumerating the 56,421,198 voters throughout the country.[3] The Election Commission completed the task by June 15, 1970 – a remarkable feat; the preparation of new electoral rolls began on August 27, 1969. The electoral rolls were published with a view to inviting any claims and objections, which would then be promptly disposed of by 315 "revising authorities" recruited with the help of the High Courts of East and West Pakistan. The total number of "applications" against the published rolls in East Pakistan was 20,650, of which 15,007 were accepted while 5,643 were rejected. Corresponding figures for West Pakistan were 6,904, of which 5,776 were accepted while 1,128 were rejected.[4] Of the total number of registered voters, 31,214,935 were from East Pakistan and 25,206,263 were from the West. The number of registered voters was about 50 per cent of the country's population, which was regarded as an "ideal" proportion.

Another important aspect of the elections in 1970 was that adult franchise was extended to some of the tribal areas, which had always been excluded in the past. The people of "Azad" Kashmir – the part of the disputed state Jammu and Kashmir under the control of the government of Pakistan since the ceasefire in 1948 – were also included in the voters' list.

The next job for the Election Commission was the delimitation of constituencies, which could begin only after Yahya's

Legal Framework Order of March 1970 had allotted the number of seats to East Pakistan and the four provinces of West Pakistan in the National Assembly, and the number of seats for the provincial assemblies in the four provinces and in East Pakistan. The schedules as given in the L.F.O. were as follows:

THE NATIONAL ASSEMBLY OF PAKISTAN[5]

	General	*Women*
East Pakistan	162	7
The Punjab	82	3
Sind	27	1
Baluchistan	4	1
North-West Frontier Province	18	1
Centrally Administered Tribal Areas	7	
TOTAL	300	13

PROVINCIAL ASSEMBLIES[5]

	General	*Women*
East Pakistan	300	10
The Punjab	180	6
Sind	60	2
Baluchistan	20	1
North-West Frontier Province	40	2

A Delimitation Commission was set up with Justice Satter as chairman and two judges – one each from the High Courts of East and West Pakistan respectively. Objections and suggestions in respect of East Pakistan constituencies were heard by the Commission from May 11 to May 22, 1970. Modifications were made in respect of 58 constituencies for the National Assembly and 96 for the East Pakistan Provincial Assembly. The final list of constituencies both for the National Assembly and for the provincial assembly in East Pakistan was published on June 5, 1970. A similar process was carried out in the four provinces of West Pakistan by the Commission from May 26 to June 20. Modifications were made for 39 constituencies for the National Assembly and for 89 constituencies for the four provincial assemblies in West Pakistan. The final list of constituencies in West Pakistan, both for the national and provincial assemblies, was published on June 25, 1970.

The work of the Election Commission in preparing electoral rolls and of the Delimitation Commission in setting up the constituencies was well received in the country. Neither any major political party nor the press cast any reflection or doubt on the good faith of the two Commissions headed by Justice Satter. Everybody seemed to be happy with the procedural arrangement for holding the country's first general election.

The Longest Election Campaign: January to December, 1970

As pointed out earlier, Yahya did not ban political parties when he imposed martial law on March 25, 1969. As he said in one of his speeches in 1970: "This caused both surprise and relief. . . . The first action of any martial law régime is to ban political parties, for the existence of a martial law régime side by side with political parties is a most unusual phenomenon."[6] After many years of controlled or quasi-controlled democracy, in which political parties had been denied the freedom to propagate their views and explain their policies and programmes freely, full political activity was revived in Pakistan from January 1, 1970. The Martial Law Regulation 60, promulgated on December 21, 1969, allowed unrestricted political activity in the country. It is true that Regulation 60 provided certain "guidelines" for political activity, as they were called, such as that no political party or group nor any individual would be permitted to preach violence or regional hatred, or speak at all against Pakistan's ideology, i.e. the Islamic ideology on which it was claimed that Pakistan had been established.

But the Regulation was only honoured in its breach. There was open and violent preaching of regional hatred, mainly by Mujib's party in East Pakistan. The younger and militant groups, mainly students and industrial workers, adopted seemingly fascist techniques for disrupting the political meetings and processions of other parties. Various parties made charges and countercharges of hooliganism and vandalism. The Government was accused of being too weak, particularly in East Pakistan towards Mujib's party. Yahya pointed out the real dilemmas facing his régime:

> The plan under which the martial law authorities had, on occasions, to ignore breaches of martial law regulations and

> orders has, I know, been misconstrued in certain quarters as weakness. These people did not understand that this attitude was deliberate and was, in fact, inherent in the situation obtaining in the country. The task of my government has been a difficult and delicate one. On the one hand, we had to keep the forces of disorder in check, and on the other we had to ensure that the development of political activity was not discouraged in any way.[7]

Those who cast reflections and doubts on the sincerity of Yahya's desire to have free elections and a smooth transfer of power should read his repeated pleas to political leaders for tolerance. Democracy, he pointed out, presupposes tolerance; "let us show we are fit for democracy". In his private talks with political leaders, particularly those who had broad political support like Mujib and Bhutto, he urged and begged them for mutual tolerance and understanding and to observe the fundamental "rules of the game" in a democratic process. Unfortunately, those counsels of restraint and moderation fell on deaf ears. I have already described the political scene, both in East and West Pakistan, when election campaigning started in 1970.[8] Let me now discuss the political programme, policies and issues as presented to the electorate by the various parties. It was, incidentally, an election in which there was no ruling party contesting the election. True to its nature as a "caretaker government", no member of the Yahya cabinet was permitted to seek election – it was specifically provided in the L.F.O. that "a person shall be disqualified from being elected as, and from being a member if he has been a member of the President's Council of Ministers at any time following 1 August 1969, unless a period of two years or such lesser period as the President may allow in any particular case has elapsed since he ceased to be a minister" (Article 9*d*).[9] This was done to ensure that no misuse of political power could be made by any member of the cabinet and also to demonstrate the impartiality of the Yahya régime towards the election process. Elections in underdeveloped countries can be, and often have been, rigged. Pakistan's past record, as pointed out earlier, was most discouraging. To what extent did political leaders respond to Yahya's elaborate and well-meaning steps towards democracy?

Parties and their Programmes

Twenty-four parties participated in the 1970 elections. The Election Commission gave symbols to each of these parties. Most of the electorate in an Asian country like Pakistan or India cannot even read the name of a political party to which a candidate belongs and for whom he may wish to vote. So symbols such as a boat for candidates belonging to the Awami League or a sword for Bhutto's party, the Pakistan People's Party, were given. Many of these twenty-four parties were of very small significance. A total of 800 candidates, belonging to various parties and including independents, contested 138 seats in the National Assembly from the four provinces in West Pakistan, while 781 candidates contested 162 seats from East Pakistan. The break-down of candidates for the National Assembly from East and West Pakistan according to party affiliation is given in Tables 5.1a and 5.1b.

Table 5.1a

CANDIDATES FOR THE NATIONAL ASSEMBLY ACCORDING TO PARTY AFFILIATION: EAST PAKISTAN

Name of Party	*No. of candidates*
1. All Pakistan Awami League	162
2. All Pakistan Central Jamiat-Ulama-e-Islam and Nizam-e-Islam	49
3. Islami Ganatantri Dal	5
4. Jamaat-e-Islami, Pakistan	70
5. Jamiat-Ulama-e-Islam, West Pakistan	15
6. Jatiya Gana Mukti Dal	5
7. Krishak Sramik Party	4
8. National Awami Party (Bhashani Group)	14
9. Pakistan Daradi Sangha	1
10. Pakistan Democratic Party	79
11. Pakistan Muslim League (Convention)	93
12. Pakistan Muslim League (Council)	50
13. Pakistan Muslim League (Qayyum Group)	65
14. Pakistan National Awami Party (Wali Khan Group)	39
15. Pakistan National Congress	4
16. Pakistan National League	12
17. Independents	114
TOTAL	781

Table 5.1b

CANDIDATES FOR THE NATIONAL ASSEMBLY ACCORDING TO PARTY AFFILIATION: WEST PAKISTAN

	Name of Party	*Punjab*	*Sind*	*N.W.F.P.*	*Baluchistan*
1.	All Pakistan Awami League	3	2	2	1
2.	All Pakistan Central Jamiat-Ulama-e-Islam and Nizam-e-Islam	4	—	2	—
3.	Baluchistan United Front	1	1	—	—
4.	Jamaat-e-Islami, Pakistan	44	19	15	2
5.	Jamiat-Ulama-e-Islam, West Pakistan	47	21	19	4
6.	Jatiya Gana Mukti Dal	—	1	—	—
7.	Khaksar Tehrik	2	—	—	—
8.	Markazi Jamiat-e-Ahle Hadees, Pakistan	2	—	—	—
9.	Markazi Jamiat-e-Ulama, Pakistan	36	8	1	—
10.	National Awami Party (Bhashani Group)	2	2	—	1
11.	Pakistan Democratic Party	21	3	2	1
12.	Pakistan Masihi League	1	1	1	—
13.	Pakistan Muslim League (Convention)	24	6	1	—
14.	Pakistan Muslim League (Council)	50	12	5	2
15.	Pakistan Muslim League (Qayyum Group)	33	12	17	4
16.	Pakistan National Awami Party (Wali Khan Group)	—	6	16	3
17.	Pakistan People's Party	77	25	16	1
18.	Sind-Karachi Muhajir Punjabi Pathan Muttahida Mahaz	1	5	—	—
19.	Sind United Front	—	1	—	—
20.	Independents	115	45	45	6
	TOTAL	463	170	142	25

As already mentioned, some of the parties were of no significance. Some had a long history behind them, such as the Muslim League, which was, however, divided into three factions. The two rightist parties, Jamaat-e-Islami and Jamat Ulama-e-Islam, also dated back to pre-independence days.

Among the parties created after 1947, the Awami League was the oldest and the most powerful political force in East Pakistan. The most recent, but an emerging powerful force, was Bhutto's Pakistan's People's Party (P.P.P.). The Communist Party in Pakistan was banned from the mid-1950s when Pakistan became "the most allied ally" of the U.S.A. But pseudo-leftist parties affiliating with communist ideology were not lacking. The National Awami Party which was formed as a result of a split with its parent body, the Awami League, over differences on foreign policy in 1956–7, was divided into two groups popularly (though not officially) known as "pro-Peking" and "pro-Moscow". The section of the Indian National Congress which was included in Pakistan in 1947 redesignated itself as the Pakistan National Congress; however, it had had very little strength since the beginning of the 1960s.

In Table 5.2, I have attempted to categorize the political forces in Pakistan over a left-right spectrum:

Table 5.2

POLITICAL FORCES IN PAKISTAN

Left	*Centre*	*Right*
(1) National Awami Party (both Bhashani and Wali groups)	(1) Awami League	(1) All Pakistan Central Jamiat-Ulama-e-Islam and Nizam-e-Islam
(2) Jatiya Gana Mukti Dal (National Peoples' Liberation Party)	(2) Pakistan People's Party	(2) Jamiat-e-Islami
(3) Sind United Party (confined to Sind Province only)	(3) Pakistan Democratic Party	(3) Jamiat-Ulama-e-Islam
	(4) Pakistan Muslim League (all three groups)	(4) Markazi Jamiat-e-Ahle
	(5) Krishak Sramik Party (Peasants and Workers)	(5) Markazi-Jamiat-e-Ulama
	(6) Pakistan National League	
	(7) Pakistan National Congress	

The most disquieting feature of the political forces working in Pakistan in 1970 was the lack of any national leader or national party. Some parties, like the Muslim League (three factions), Jamiat-e-Islami and the Pakistan Democratic Party, doubtless had an all-Pakistan organization and set up candidates in both East and West Pakistan. But it soon became evident that none of these parties had any real popular support in East Pakistan, and they were also rapidly losing their hold in West Pakistan to Bhutto's party. The two principal political parties which ultimately emerged as successful in the election were regional and not national. The Awami League had acquired an absolute hold in East Pakistan but had no support in the West, while the emerging West Pakistani leader, Bhutto, did not dare to set up even a single candidate in East Pakistan. Regional polarization became increasingly evident as the election campaign developed. This was most disheartening for those like myself who had been working hard for the unity of Pakistan.

Without going into the details of the programmes of all the parties, most of which were routed, let me examine the political programmes of Mujib and Bhutto, the two principal actors in the final drama of united Pakistan.

Mujib's political manifesto was based on his six-point plan which will be fully analysed in the next chapter. Apart from this, the manifesto of the Awami League included the following:

> Islam is the deeply cherished faith of the overwhelming majority of the people. The Awami League affirms that a clear guarantee shall be embodied in the Constitution to the effect that no law repugnant to the injunctions of Islam as laid down in the Holy Koran and Sunnah shall be enacted or enforced in Pakistan.[12]

Mujib thus appealed to the sentiment of the rural Muslims of East Pakistan by pledging an Islamic Constitution; yet after the break-up of Pakistan, he imposed a "secular" Constitution on the Muslims of Bangladesh!

Similarly, while his six-point plan was nothing but a veiled scheme of secession, Mujib declared in one of his early election speeches: "Pakistan has come to stay and there is no force which can destroy it."[13] In fact, though Mujib claimed on many occasions that the election would be a referendum on his six-point plan, he gave repeated assurances that his policy or programme would protect "the viability of the Federal Government of Pakistan".[14] Again after the creation of Bangladesh Mujib said that he had been working for a separate state for Bangladesh since 1968: "The struggle for independence began in 1948 and through movements in 1952, 1954, 1962, 1969 and 1970."[15] These provide some of the glaring instances of the gap between Mujib's professions and pledges before the election and his real role in the break-up of Pakistan.

Mujib's manifesto had also promised that a "socialist economic order" would also prevent the transfer of resources, or the flight of capital, from East to West Pakistan. It pledged "an independent non-aligned foreign policy".

Mujib's election campaign and strategy were simple: their sole purpose was to carry the gospel of Bengali nationalism and the ideal of Bangladesh everywhere in Pakistan. Thanks to the naïveté and incompetence of Governor Ahsan, Mujib and his followers had a free hand and were able to preach secession without the least hindrance. Bhashani told me that if the Government were leaving Mujib free to preach the idea of Bangladesh, he had no option but to speak in terms of an "independent East Pakistan". However, his speeches in favour of an "independent East Pakistan" were misunderstood by the Government as well as by sections of the public in West Pakistan. He did not favour the break-up of Pakistan, as he could foresee that Bangladesh would be nothing more than a client state of New Delhi, like Bhutan or Sikkim; his call for an "independent East Pakistan" was one of anguish and warning to the Government. But again Ahsan prevented any understanding with Bhashani. He was unhappy over my meetings with the "Red Maulana" and reported them to Yahya as being highly detrimental to the cause of an understanding or deal with Mujib. Ahsan may have been sincere in his conviction that it was necessary to have a deal with Mujib, but he lacked the political acumen needed to understand the political forces inside the Awami League working against a united Pakistan. I repeatedly suggested to Yahya that he should hold a straight dialogue with Mujib and find out if he was prepared to modify the six-point plan. If Mujib refused, I recommended that Yahya should arrange a referendum in East Pakistan to ascertain if the Bengali Muslims wanted to live in a United Pakistan or to separate. I reminded Yahya of de Gaulle's bold steps in the Algerian crisis. But Yahya was not of de Gaulle's calibre. Moreover, he was misled both by Mujib and by his own Governor, Ahsan.

Mujib's task was simple and easy compared with that of other political leaders. His only theme was the exploitation of Bengal by the West Pakistanis; his ideal was that of a "*Sonar* [golden] Bengal". This was a most successful appeal to a poverty stricken people of 75 million. Just as the Muslims of undivided India were convinced that a separate state of their own would give them a land of opportunities, so the Bengalis in rural areas, to whom Mujib had tremendous appeal, listened to his ideal of a golden Bengal. The only requirement was to give him and his party votes in the elections. Jinnah's strategy in the 1946 elections seems to have been the same and he too had no difficulty in getting votes. Similarly Mujib had no threat either from rightist or leftist elements.

Bhashani subsequently decided to withdraw from the election because of Ahsan's policy of persecuting his party and finally as a protest at the elections being held after the cyclone in November 1970. The pro-Moscow faction of N.A.P. had no popular leader; its leader in East Pakistan, a self-styled "professor" Muzaffar Ahmad, had no real hold on the people. The leftist forces in East Pakistan were also divided and had no well-organized or reliable power base. They were weakened by the manoeuvring of various factions. Bhashani's group was weakened by the defection of a splinter party led by Mohamed Toaha, who was opposed to parliamentary tactics; he believed in a long-term politicizing process among the masses in rural areas. The other pro-Peking factions remained with Bhasani, who had a strong peasant following; but after the resignation of Toha, the N.A.P. (Bhashani group) was increasingly divided; the faction led by Abdul Matin advocated the same revolutionary tactics as those used by India's Naxalite groups, particularly in West Bengal.

Apart from their internal divisions, the provincial Government headed by Governor Ahsan did everything possible to crush the leftist forces in East Pakistan. Why Ahsan adopted this policy is difficult to ascertain, but it might be due to his former long association with SEATO. One big problem with the members of the military junta was their lack of understanding of international issues. In the heyday of SEATO it might have been the policy of the Pakistani Government to be vigilant with pro-Chinese elements, but when China became Pakistan's real and most valuable friend, Ahsan's policy was either simply naïve or inspired by some foreign influence. Whatever the true interpretation of Ahsan's intentions, his policy toward the "Red Maulana" seemed suicidal for Pakistan's national interest, and it gave Mujib a wonderful opportunity to preach his gospel of secession. The rightist or moderate groups were no threat to Mujib; the only person who could expose his scheme of veiled secession was Bhashani, and Ahsan torpedoed all chances of an understanding with him. That the Pakistan Army was ruthless against a friendly force was demonstrated by their killing of so many pro-Peking party leaders during the civil war. When Bhutto went to Peking in November 1971 to enlist China's support against the imminent military intervention by India in East Pakistan, the Peking authorities presented Bhutto with a list of sixty pro-Peking leaders who had been killed by the Pakistan Army. This action by the Army was a legacy of the policy of Ahsan who is his reports characterized the pro-Chinese leaders as "anti-state elements" while ignoring the real anti-state groups. Bhutto was right when he complained:

> The provincial administration [in East Pakistan] gave complete support to the Awami League, and during the elections the Awami League workers were allowed a free hand and took full advantage of it. . . . There are many reasons but the main reason was to be found in the prejudice against the left. . . . Mujibur Rahman boasted that he would liquidate the leftists in East Pakistan. . . . Throughout this period the military governor of East Pakistan [Ahsan] sympathized with the aspirations of Mujibur Rahman.[17]

The pro-Moscow group faced a dilemma as to where to place their allegiance and which party offered them the greatest hope of increasing their influence. The Soviet propaganda media supported Wali Khan's N.A.P., ignoring the existence of Bhashani's N.A.P. A Moscow "Radio Peace and Progress" broadcast on August 16, 1970, gave almost equal praise to Mujib's Awami League and Wali's N.A.P. It should be added that as late as 1967 the Soviet attitude toward the Awami League was not at all favourable. Thus on March 16, 1967, the same "Radio Peace and Progress" voiced the opinion that "reactionaries from the Awami League have exposed themselves for the whole country to see as American hirelings and traitors to the nation's unity." By August 14, 1970, the Awami League was elevated to the rank of "standing in the vanguard of the left-wing forces". The Soviet attitude seemed to have been influenced by Indian support for Mujib, which became palpable in 1970, and also by Mujib's constant antipathy toward China. Mujib used to describe Pakistan's friendship with China as "provocative". When one day I told Mujib that as future Prime Minister he might find China's friendship "valuable", his reply was "friendship of China against whom? I have no dispute with India, why should I need China's help and assistance?"

The Western press had correctly predicted Mujib's success in the election, on which there was no doubt. U.S. policy towards Pakistan, which had been bogged down with mutual suspicion and prejudices during the presidency of Johnson – who was annoyed at Pakistan's links with China – began to grow friendly with the entry of President Nixon into the White House in 1969. But the role of the U.S. Consul General in Dacca, Mr. A. Blood, was dubious and seemed to be detrimental to Pakistan's vital national interests. Blood's secret meetings with Mujib were known to the authorities; his sympathy for Mujib and his aspirations, as well as that of a group of American economists in Dacca who were financed by the Ford Foundation, was too obvious. These people were not aware of Nixon's sympathetic attitude towards Pakistan or Yahya's role on behalf of Nixon in his new China policy. Blood had to be recalled from his ultra-Mujib sympathy. We met several times and he left me in no doubt as to where his sympathy lay. The U.S. policy was made clear to Mujib by Ambassador Farland, who advised him not to look towards Washington for any help for his secessionist game in early 1971; but it was too late. Mujib, who had no experience or depth of understanding of foreign affairs, accepted Blood's personal views as the US governmental policy. This emboldened him in his intransigence in any compromise on the issue of one Pakistan.

Though foreign policy was not a very hot debating issue in the 1970 election campaign, foreign influences were very active in East Pakistan, the most serious one being from New Delhi and subsequently from Moscow.

The rightist parties, as well as moderate or centre groups like the Pakistan Democratic Front and the Council Muslim League, were no less enthusiastic to protect the legitimate hopes, aspirations and rights of the people of East Pakistan. An analysis of their manifestoes and of the speeches made by the leaders of these groups would leave no impartial observer in any doubt that they also wanted genuine regional autonomy for East Pakistan, so that the people of the two regions of Pakistan could live together as equal partners. But with them the unity of Pakistan was a cherished ideal, as it was to many other Bengali Muslims, particularly in rural areas. So they could not, or did not wish to go to the extreme position adopted by Mujib and his younger and more militant groups, for whom the unity of Pakistan or Pakistani nationalism meant nothing.

These supporters of Mujib were going about with the cry of "*Joy Bangla*" (Victory to Bangladesh). The rightist and moderate groups had financial difficulties and, with few exceptions, had no support from the Bengali press. The Bengali urban élite, composed of the intelligentsia, journalists, writers, government officials and businessmen, was behind the demand for a separate state of Bangladesh. Although my birthplace is in East Bengal, I had never toured the rural areas of East Bengal as extensively as I did in 1970. As Communications Minister this was part of my duties, but I was interested as a political scientist in studying the political dynamics prevailing in East Pakistan when the unity of the country was in serious doubt. Many of the district and subdivisional officers, who used to run the administration in the rural areas, were my direct or indirect students – directly those who had studied political science, indirectly those who were students in other fields – at the University of Dacca since 1950. During my tours I talked to them freely and frankly, and they in turn used to treat me more as a former teacher than as a minister. From my talks with these young officials and with local political leaders, I had serious doubts about the viability of Pakistan as a united country. Trends in West Pakistan, to which I shall turn later, were no less discouraging. It was a frustrating experience for persons like myself who cherished and valued the driving forces which led the Indian Muslims to establish Pakistan.

Bhutto and his Programme

Bhutto told me once: "Mujib has only one slogan: 'prevent exploitation of Bengalis by giving votes to my party'." Bengali nationalism, as pointed out earlier, had already acquired sufficient momentum from various factors as analysed in earlier chapters. But Bhutto had no such simple path. The Bengalis of East Pakistan constituted a homogeneous group, but in West Pakistan there were sub-regionalisms in Sind, Baluchistan and the North-West Frontier province. Then in West Pakistan, the rightist elements were not altogether discredited as they were in East Pakistan. Being a non-Punjabi, Bhutto also had to capture the imagination of Punjabis, who, to quote his own words, were the "bastion of power" in West Pakistan, if not in all Pakistan.

To give one example of the complicated issues facing Bhutto, "one unit" was still popular with the Punjabis but was anathema in the smaller provinces of West Pakistan. Then in the Punjab, Bhutto could give hours-long speeches on "confrontation with India" and "a thousand years war with India", and on Ayub's alleged sacrifices of the national interest at the Tashkent Conference of 1966, but such emotional issues did not have much appeal in Baluchistan or the North-West Province or even in Bhutto's home province, Sind. Finally, in West Pakistan the big landlords still constitute a pressure group while in East Pakistan, where they were mostly non-Muslims, their influence was a thing of the past. Bhutto had to speak of "land reforms" and "Islamic socialism" with the object of gaining the support of newly awakened have-not groups, particularly in industrial cities, while he had to be careful not to push the big landlords or businessmen too far. His task was formidable. Finally, as pointed out in the preceding chapter, he was carefully cultivating his links with some members of the ruling junta.

Bhutto's chief slogans were: "Islam is our faith; democracy is our policy; socialism is our economy." His party's manifesto pledged radical changes in the economic system, the overthrow of capitalism and the ushering in of Islamic socialism.[16] Bhutto significantly did not oppose or try to expose Mujib's six-point plan. It was only *after* the outbreak of the civil war that he described Mujib's plan with the significant words: "In essence, the six-point formula was meant to strike at the roots of our nationhood." He also disclosed that, several months before the elections, he had told General Peerzada, one of his best friends in the junta and Yahya's *de facto* Prime Minister, that Mujib's aim was nothing less than "separation". He accused Yahya and his Government of tolerating Mujib's preaching of his six-point plan. In a sense, Bhutto's charge against the Yahya Government was correct, but Yahya relied on Mujib's repeated and firm pledges that he would modify his six-point plan as soon as the elections were over. But was it not a duty on the part of Bhutto as the leader of an important party to warn the nation of the serious threats to its territorial integrity, which he claimed to have discovered before the elections? In one of my lengthy talks with him at his luxurious home in Karachi, I urged him to go to East Pakistan and address the people there, and warn them of the dangers of separation and of the "foreign influences" working in East Pakistan. Both Bhutto and I agreed on the impending crisis, but he ignored my sincere appeals to take up the issue. He preferred to devote all his efforts and energies to capturing as many seats as possible in West Pakistan. He even castigated the rightist parties, such as the Muslim League, who spoke of the dangers facing the country. What did Bhutto's election strategy prove? Was he not more interested in power politics than in the unity of Pakistan?

The rightist parties' position seemed better initially in West Pakistan than in East Pakistan. The same was the case with the centre parties like the Council Muslim League and the P.D.P. But the "old guard" of these parties belonged to the past rather than to the Pakistan of today; half the country's population was born after its creation in 1947. The old guard's appeals to "Islamic ideology" and "strong central government" were of little interest to the newly awakened masses in West Pakistan. The political awakening based on socio-economic factors was hastened during the four-month agitation against the Ayub régime in 1969 and during the year-long election campaign in 1970. During both these periods Bhutto's performance was more successful than that of the old guard's out-dated programmes and policies. Though Bhutto's electoral success in West Pakistan was less than Mujib's in East Pakistan, his achievements – in view of the more formidable forces, more complicated issues, and sub-regional and linguistic tensions which he had to tackle – were no less remarkable.

The Government decided to give facilities to the leaders of various parties to project their political manifestoes and policies through television and radio. This was the first time that politicians were freely and impartially given the chance to use the government-owned radio and television for their political activities. During the presidential election of 1965, the candidate of the combined opposition parties (C.O.P.) was denied the use of this facility by Ayub, while he himself utilized radio and television in his own election campaign. Similarly, during the parliamentary era (1947–58), when provincial elections were held in the 1950s, the politicians were never given the use of such facilities – television was not yet there in the 1950s but radio did exist and could have been made available to the opposition parties, as is the well-established practice in Western democracies.

In their television and radio speeches, the various leaders did not add much to what they hae been saying in their public meetings and rallies. Political broadcasts began on October 28 and continued until November 19, 1970, during which time the leaders of fourteen parties made speeches. The series began with Mujib, who was given the chance to speak first, and ended with the leader of the Sind United Front, G. M. Syud. By this time there was no doubt as to who among the leaders had real political support: Mujib, Bhutto and a few others in West Pakistan such as Wali Khan and Qayyum Khan, leader of one of three factions of the Muslim League; both of the latter two leaders had chances of success in the North-West Frontier province.

That the rightist groups like Jamiat-e-Islam and other orthodox groups would be almost totally routed was not yet certain. Two of the rightist groups, All-Pakistan Jamiat-e-Ulema-e-Islam and Markazi Jamiat-e-Ulema, did better than the older and better organized Jamiat-e-Islam. Among the three factions of the Muslim League, the Qayyum group did better in the North-West Province while the Council Muslim League's performance was better in the Punjab.

Though Bhashani had by this time almost given up the idea of participating in the elections, yet his speech was listened to with great interest. He alone spoke in two national languages: in Bengali from the Dacca radio station and in Urdu from West Pakistan. His speech was a masterpiece and it met with a good reception in both wings. Mujib is not good in television and radio broadcasts; he excels as a demagogue in a mass rally. Yet his speech was listened to with great attention in both regions, as he had already emerged as *the* Bengali leader who spoke for the majority of the country's population. Bhutto had appeared on television previously, both at home and abroad, so his performance was better than that of Mujib. His voice was also listened to with interest as he was seen as the emerging leader of West Pakistan, though even at that time, i.e. six weeks before the elections, nobody could expect that he would gain such a big success.

The leaders in their speeches dealt with almost all the issues facing the electorate: democracy; basic civil rights; socialist or any other state-controlled economic order ensuring a just distribution of the fruits of economic growth; educational reforms; agricultural improvement and land reforms; the role of Islam in the new Constitution; the nationalization of banks and insurance companies; foreign policy, and so on. Mujib's main theme was regionalism or emerging Bengali nationalism, though he also talked about socio-economic reforms. Bhutto's main emphasis was on his concept of "Islamic socialism" and on foreign affairs, including Indo-Pakistani disputes such as the Kashmir problem. The rightist groups emphasized Islamic ideology and threats to it from foreign "isms" like socialism. Wali Khan's basic approach was secular politics and the regional problems of his home province. Bhashani's speech spoke for the "have-nots"; he talked little of constitutional or political issues, his main stress being on the improvement of the lot of the poorest section of society.[19]

The television speeches by political leaders on the whole provided an additional impetus to election campaigning, though a number of them were dull and boring. In an atmosphere full of tension and political activity, the speeches provided the Pakistanis, particularly the urban population, with a good picture of the intensifying election campaign which had now been going on in the country for about a year.

Finally, on December 3, only four days before the elections, Yahya made a passionate appeal to the political leaders "for a spirit of give and take and trust in each other . . . at this particular juncture of our history". He recalled that "many doubts are expressed regarding the sincerity and intentions of this régime, but despite this we remain steadfast in our aim of bringing back democracy to our land".[20]

In a press conference at Dacca on November 27, 1970, Yahya reaffirmed his pledge for "maximum autonomy for East Pakistan". He said that he would not stand in the way of maximum autonomy for the people of East Pakistan, but would rather encourage it so that they could have "full charge of their destiny, planning and utilization of its resources *within the concept of Pakistan*". He added that because of its geographical distance, "East Pakistan must have maximum autonomy to run her own affairs within the overall framework of one Pakistan".[21] Could there be a more unqualified pledge for autonomy for East Pakistan? If Mujib had *only* been interested in autonomy, as he told the Bengali Muslims while he was campaigning for their votes, there should have been no conflict; Yahya could not have been more explicit on the granting of autonomy. But the vital question was whether the issue was one of "maximum autonomy" or a conflict over the dismemberment of the country.

Election Results

Elections were held on December 7, 1970, and were by any standard free and fair – ironically the first and last genuine election in united Pakistan. Contrary to views expressed in many places, the results of the elections, in so far as they related to East Pakistan, caused no surprise to the ruling élite or to any serious observer of political developments there. After Yahya's decision to hold the elections following the violent anti-Pakistan feelings which had arisen after the cyclone in East Pakistan, there was not the slightest doubt that Mujib would monopolize all the seats there. Bhashani and many other political leaders had withdrawn from the contest as a protest against Yahya's decision; only Nurul Amin contested and won a solitary seat and another seat was won by a "*raja*" of the Chakma tribe in the Chittagong Hill Tracts.

However, it was the results of the election in West Pakistan which caused surprise, particularly the total defeat of the right-wing and orthodox parties there and the emergence of a non-Punjabi, Bhutto, as the leader of West Pakistan or, more precisely, of the Punjab. The detailed election results for both the national and provincial legislatures and the statistical data showing the number of votes secured by each political party and its percentage of the total votes polled are given in Tables 5.3 and 5.4.

These data and figures reveal that Pakistan emerged after its first free election as politically split. The Awami League won 160 out of the 162 seats allotted for East Pakistan and secured 74·9 per cent of the votes polled in East Pakistan. But in West Pakistan it could not secure a single seat and the percentages of votes secured by the Awami League in the four provinces of West Pakistan were: 0·07 (Punjab), 0·07 (Sind), 0·2 (North-West Frontier Province), and 1·0 (Baluchistan).

Similarly, Bhutto's party, the P.P.P., which won 81 out of the 138 seats for West Pakistan, did not even dare to set up a candidate in East Pakistan. Those West Pakistani parties which won the remaining seats (fifty-seven seats – shared among seven parties and fifteen independent candidates) were likewise unable to get a single seat in East Pakistan. In fact, these seven parties, none of which could even get ten seats in the National Assembly, could not be regarded as representing West Pakistan.

To say that Mujib's success upset Yahya's plans or calculations would not be fair. When he decided to go ahead with holding the elections after the cyclone in November, I said to Yahya: "I hope you fully realize the implications of your decision." His answer, in the usual non-serious way, was: "You mean, it will ensure Mujib's total success? Yes, I am aware of it and have no worries about it. Ahsan and Peerzada had long sessions with Sheikh [i.e. Mujib] and they assured me, as Mujib assured me himself, that he would modify his six-point plan. *Inshallah* [by the grace of God], Pakistan will be saved. Don't worry."

Table 5·3

(*a*) PAKISTAN NATIONAL ASSEMBLY ELECTIONS, 1970–1

Party	*Punjab*	*Sind*	*NWFP*	*Baluch-istan*	*West Pakistan*	*East Pakistan*	*Total*
AL	—	—	—	—	—	160	160
PPP	62	18	1	—	81	—	81
PML(Q)	1	1	7	—	9	—	9
CML	7	—	—	—	7	—	7
JU(H)	—	—	6	1	7	—	7
MJU	4	3	—	—	7	—	7
NAP(W)	—	—	3	3	6	—	6
JI	1	2	1	—	4	—	4
PML(C)	2	—	—	—	2	—	2
PDP	—	—	—	—	—	1	1
Ind.	5	3	7	—	15	1	16
TOTAL	82	27	25	4	138	162	300

(*b*) PAKISTAN PROVINCIAL ASSEMBLY ELECTIONS, 1970–1

Party	*Punjab*	*Sind*	*NWFP*	*Baluch-istan*	*West Pakistan*	*East Pakistan*	*Total*
AL	—	—	—	—	—	288	288
PPP	113	28	3	—	144	—	144
PML(Q)	6	5	10	3	24	—	24
NAP(W)	—	—	13	8	21	1	22
CML	15	4	1	—	20	—	20
MJU	4	7	—	—	11	—	11
JU(H)	2	—	4	2	8	—	8
PML(C)	6	—	2	—	8	—	8
PDP	4	—	—	—	4	2	6
JI	1	1	1	—	3	1	4
Others	1	1	—	2	4	1	5
Ind.	28	14	6	5	53	7	60
TOTAL	180	60	40	20	300	300	600

ELECTIONS TO THE NATIONAL ASSEMBLY 1970

Number of votes secured by each political party and its percentage of total valid votes polled

		PROVINCES				
Totals	*Pakistan*	*East Pakistan*	*The Punjab*	*Sind*	*N.W.F.P.*	*Baluchistan*
Total of Registered voters	55,207,547	29,479,386	16,364,495	5,335,523	3,072,098	956,045
Total of valid votes polled	32,364,280	16,454,278	10,879,056	3,117,988	1,439,718	373,240
Total of invalid votes polled	1,059,152	550,885	367,584	07,460	38,728	14,495
Total votes polled	33,323,432	17,005,163	11,246,640	3,205,448	1,478,446	387,735
Parties						
1. Pakistan People's Party	6,148,623	—	4,532,501	1,401,660	205,593	8,869
	19·5%		41·6%	44·9%	14·2%	2·3%
2. Pakistan Muslim League	1,465,377	175,822	589,150	333,694	325,884	40,827
	4·5	1·0	5.4	10.7	22.6	10.9
3. Pakistan Muslim League (Convention)	1,083,912	464,185	555,712	55,759	8,256	—
	3·3	2·8	5·1	1·7	0·5	
4. Pakistan Muslim League (Council)	1,963,562	274,453	1,377,006	213,383	57,690	41,030
	6·0	1·6	12·6	6·8	4·0	10.9
5. Jamiat-e-Ulama Islam (West Pakistan)	1,306,038	158,058	571,351	135,507	366,471	74,651
	4·0	0·9	5·2	4·3	25·4	20·0
6. MJUP	1,308,878	—	1,076,439	232,195	244	—
	4·0		9·8	7·4	0·0	
7. National Awami Party (Wali Group)	757,499	310,986	—	11,427	266,282	168,804
	2·3	1·8		0·3	18·4	45·1
8. Jamaat-e-Islami Pakistan	1,937,183	991,908	515,538	321,471	103,935	4,331
	6·0	6·0	4·7	10·3	7·2	1·1
9. Pakistan Democratic Party	737,960	483,571	265,955	2,398	4,642	1,394
	2·2	2·9	2·2	0·04	0·3	0·3
10. All Pakistan Awami League	12,361,868	12,338,929	8,089	7,713	3,170	3,965
	38·3	74·9	0·07	0·07	0·2	1·0
11. Independents	2,300,627	561,083	1,292,285	335,366	86,488	28,405
	7·1	3·4	11·8	10·7	6·0	6·8

Note: The above figures do not include the number of contesting candidates in constituencies where proceedings were terminated due to the cyclones and the death of three of the contesting candidates in East Pakistan.

The intelligence reports, particularly the military one by General Akbar, had clearly indicated Mujib's total victory in East Pakistan. One of my speeches, made in London on September 10, 1970, taken out of its total context, was quoted in two books after the creation of Bangladesh to give the impression that I, as Yahya's constitutional adviser, had miscalculated the election results. The speech was given at the Pakistan Society in London, and a student from West Pakistan asked me whether by advising Yahya to grant "one man, one vote" I had not arranged a "perpetual domination" of East Pakistanis over West Pakistanis. My answer was that if a "confrontation" took place between East Pakistanis as a single group against all the West Pakistanis, it would "mean the end of the state". This particular remark of mine expressing my concern over the unity of Pakistan led the writers of the two books to state that Yahya and his advisers did not understand the people and their prevailing mood.[22] This was unjust. After my extensive tours in East Pakistan during the serious floods in August 1970, I had no difficulty in understanding political realities in East Pakistan, and I was always candid and frank in my talks with, as well as in my written notes to, Yahya. Yahya's whole plan was based on his faith in Mujib's repeated and unqualified assurances that he would modify his six points after the elections. It will be recalled that it was on this expectation that provincial elections were also held, so that Mujib might take a flexible attitude.

REFERENCES

1. From the unpublished Report of the Electoral Reform Commission, 1955, Government of Pakistan.
2. Ibid.
3. These figures are from the papers of the Election Commission, received through the courtesy of Justice Satter.
4. Ibid.
5. The Legal Framework Order 1970, Presidential Order No. 2 of 1970, Government of Pakistan, Karachi, pp. 15–16.
6. See Yahya's Broadcast on July 28, 1970.
7. Ibid.
8. See Chapter 4.
9. See Legal Framework Order, op. cit., p. 5.

10. Figures from papers of the Election Commission.
11. For a concise but useful account of various parties and their programmes, see G. G. M. Budruddin, *Election Handbook 1970*, Karachi, 1970.
12. See the full text of the Awami League Manifesto in *Bangladesh Documents*, published by the Ministry of External Affairs, Government of Pakistan, n.d., Vol. I, pp. 66–82.
13. Ibid., p. 82.
14. For Mujib's various speeches during the Election campaign in 1970, see *Bangladesh Documents*, op. cit., and also *Bangladesh, My Bangladesh: Selected Speeches and Statements by Sheikh Muijbur Rahman*, New York, Fernhill House, 1972.
15. *Bangabandhu Speaks: A Collection of Speeches and Statements*, Dacca, Ministry of Foreign Affairs, Government of Bangladesh, n.d., p. 42.
16. See *Election Handbook 1970*, op. cit., p. 31.
17. Z. A. Bhutto, *The Great Tragedy*, Karachi, 1971, p. 14 and pp. 60–1.
18. Ibid., p. 13 and 75.
19. For text of the television-radio broadcasts of the political leaders, see *Information Handbook*, Part I, Vol. 11, ed. by M. Naeem Tahir, Pakistan Television Corporation, Rawalpindi, 1970.
20. See the text of Yahya's broadcast in *Dawn*, December 4, 1970.
21. See *Morning News*, Dacca, November 28, 1970.
22. See Fazal, Muqueem Khan, *Pakistan's Crisis in Leadership*, Karachi, 1973, p. 41; and see also Anthony Mascarenhas, *The Rape of Bangladesh*, Delhi, 1970, pp. 58–8.

6

TRIPARTITE POLITICAL NEGOTIATIONS BEFORE CONFRONTATION

The arrangement left by the British authorities when they voluntarily liquidated the *raj* in the subcontinent in 1947 has been destroyed by the tragic events which began on the night of March 25, 1971, in East Bengal culminating in the dismemberment of Pakistan and the emergence of a new – and problematical – state of Bangladesh in South Asia on December 16, 1971. Before the division of India in 1947, a series of political negotiations took place between the British Government, the Congress and the Muslim League in search of various formulae – one such being the Cabinet Mission Plan of 1946 to maintain the unity of India; sincere and honest efforts were made to resolve the conflict between the divergent aspirations of the Indian National Congress and the Muslim League, so that the division of India could be avoided.[1] Contrary to widespread popular belief, Pakistan was not the product of the "wicked British policy of divide and rule".[2] The British authorities made sincere efforts to maintain the unity of India, which they considered the greatest achievement of their *raj*.[3]

Similarly, before the disintegration of Pakistan, a series of political talks was held to find some workable means of maintaining the unity of Pakistan – at least to keep the green and white crescent flag flying in both East and West Pakistan. There were serious and sincere efforts to resolve the conflicting aims and aspirations of the emerging Bengali nationalism (or regionalism as it used to be termed at that stage) and those of Pakistan nationalism, which had begun to face various challenges in the previous decade. Again, making an analogy with the events of 1946–7, the biggest hurdle in the way of the transfer of power from the military régime headed by Yahya Khan to the elected representatives of the people was the Bengali and West Pakistani controversy, like the Hindu-Muslim controversy in undivided India – whether Pakistan should remain united or the Awami League's demand for a separate Bengali state be conceded.

Of course, unlike the Muslim League and Jinnah, the Awami League or Mujib could not openly ask for secession or the creation of Bangladesh. Jinnah was free to demand a separate state for the Muslims from a foreign ruling authority which had declared its policy of winding up the empire. Mujib and his party were living in an established state – constitutionally a federal union which was regarded as indivisible – and the Pakistan central Government was legally and morally committed to uphold the territorial integrity of the country. Any federal authority would feel such a commitment as of paramount importance and value. Mujib's *modus operandi* was, therefore, entirely different from Jinnah's and sometimes appeared as ambivalent, if not sometimes vague and contradictory. But the fact remained that the Bengali intelligentsia, like the Muslim intelligentsia in undivided India, seemed to have come to the conclusion in the 1960s that it could no longer live with the West Pakistanis and that a separate state was not only possible and desirable, but inevitable because of the growing tension between the unresponsive ruling élite in Islamabad and the militant Bengali nationalists in Dacca.[4]

The final blow to the concept of a united Pakistan came as a result of the Indo-Pakistan war of 1965 when the last argument in favour of living together – that federal union, however unsatisfactory it might otherwise be, at least provided a guarantee against external aggression – was also destroyed.[5] The war of 1965 had a disastrous impact on the viability of Pakistan as a united country. It was immediately after that war that Mujib put forward his famous six-point programme which, on close scrutiny, proves to be nothing but a veiled scheme of secession. Mujib could not produce another "Lahore Resolution" of 1940 but ironically it was in the same city of Lahore that, twenty-six years later in 1966, he produced his subtle scheme of another separate state. As the political negotiations between the ruling authority (i.e. the Army), the Bengalis and West Pakistanis centred on how Mujib's six-point programme could be accommodated in some federal or (at the final stages) in any confederal scheme for a United Pakistan, I shall begin my discussion of political talks in 1969–71 with a brief analysis of Mujib's scheme.

The Six-Point Programme

Mujib's programme, on which he based his election campaign and won a landslide victory in East Pakistan, was like many other political programmes – capable of more than one interpretation.[6] The identity of its real authors or draftsmen is still a matter of speculation. Rumour went so far as to make the author Altaf Gauhar, one of the most trusted and close members of the ruling élite during the Ayub era; the hint was made in certain quarters that Ayub himself asked Altaf Gauhar to do this job at a time when there was great unrest in West Pakistan over the Tashkent agreement, and that Ayub wanted to divert the attention of West Pakistan by raising the spectre of the secession of East Pakistan. But during my four years stay in Islamabad, both during and after the fall of Ayub, I could find no basis for such a rumour. Nor can I believe that Ayub with his very real patriotism could resort to such a trick; with all his limitations, Ayub was a great Pakistani leader and a statesman. A shrewd document like this was most likely the joint product of several intellectual advisers and associates of Mujib.

The first point laid down was: "The constitution should provide for a Federation of Pakistan in its true sense" – but it significantly added "on the basis of the Lahore Resolution".[7] Many interpretations of the Lahore Resolution claim that it envisaged "two independent and sovereign states; thanks to its most unsatisfactory wording, the Lahore Resolution was capable of such interpretation. So the commitment in favour of a federal union was not unqualified. There were certain other sub-points such as parliamentary form of government, supremacy of the legislature, election on the basis of direct elections and adult franchise, but all these were made in the context of Ayub's constitution of 1962 which denied them.

When Yahya began his political dialogue with Mujib, these issues were of no significance because Yahya had conceded all these demands; as pointed out already, he in fact, went one step further by providing the representation in the federal legislature on the basis of "one man, one vote" thus ensuring a clear Bengali majority in the National Assembly.[8]

Point 2 laid down that "Federal Government shall deal only with two subjects, defence and foreign affairs, and all other subjects shall vest in the federating states." Point 3 provided for either a common currency with so many limitations as to make it almost unworkable, or "two separate but freely convertible currencies" for East and West Pakistan.[9]

Mujib tried to justify the demand for a central government with two, or if currency was added, three subjects by citing the Cabinet Mission Plan of 1946, in which the British Government proposed a complicated three-tier union with a central government having three subjects.[10] But he did not add that the Congress leaders like Nehru and Patel preferred to accept division of India rather than such an absurd arrangement.[11]

If one examines the existing federal systems of the world, one could hardly find a federation with only two powers. But the significant part of Mujib's scheme of a centre with only two subjects was that while it gave defence and foreign affairs to the centre, it deprived the centre of any financial or administrative means to carry out its obligations even with regard to those who subjects. As the renowned author on federalism, K. C. Wheare, points out, a power without financial resources is meaningless.[12] A federal form of government requires both the national and regional governments of the country to be independent of each other within their own spheres. To give the centre defence responsibilities without any financial resources is something like the elaborate collective security system provided under the United Nations Charter. It might have been anything but a true federal union. So Points 2 and 3 were contradictory to Point 1, which claimed to seek a "Federation of Pakistan".

Then turning to foreign affairs, Mujib's proposal made a subtle distinction between what may be termed political or diplomatic aspects and economic aspects of foreign affairs. His Points 4 and 5 made it clear that the federal government would have nothing to do with the country's external or internal economic policies. There was good and ample justification for Mujib's demand that the Bengalis should be masters of their own economic development and even in external economic relations. He cited unchallengeable data and material proving how the economic plight of the Bengalis was intensified by the policies and actions of the ruling élite in West Pakistan. No impartial observer of the economic growth of Pakistan could challenge these figures.[13] But the point here is how a federal government could carry on its foreign policy without any say in external economic relations. Mujib's scheme gave powers to the federating units "to establish trade and commercial relations; to set up trade missions in and enter into agreements with *foreign countries*"[14] [my italics].

In a developing country like Pakistan, foreign affairs are closely connected with economic issues and problems such as foreign aid, foreign loans and regional economic co-operation. I once asked Mujib whether the purchase of tanks or planes counted as external trade, or did it concern diplomatic and political relationships between the seller country and the purchasing one? His answer was, as usual, blank and vague.

In short, under Mujib's six-point programme the centre was made a paper one; it would have no control over the country's fiscal, monetary and budgetary policies or their execution. In external affairs, it made the work of a foreign ministry meaningless, and the defence obligations of the centre would have worked something like those of the United Nations – dependent on the federating units for financial contributions to enable it to carry out any of its responsibilities in the defence of the country. So my earlier contention that Mujib's six-point plan was nothing but a veiled scheme of secession is borne out by any objective analysis of the proposal.

As pointed out earlier, Mujib could not adopt Jinnah's clear-cut demand for a separate state because he was operating in entirely different circumstances. So his strategy had to be a veiled one. Nor was he sure whether the Muslims of East Bengal would opt for a separate state even in 1970 if a clear-cut proposal were put before the electorate. The vast majority of the Bengali intelligentsia, civil service and business community would most likely back him even if he demanded a mandate for a separate state; but it was doubtful whether the Muslim voters of the rural areas would so easily give up their cherished ideals and ideology which had made them the most enthusiastic supporters of Jinnah in the plebiscitory election of 1946. It was only the Army's ruthless atrocities on the innocent villagers, including their women and children, that turned the whole of East Bengal to secession.

Dilemmas and Problems

The pertinent question is how any meaningful dialogue with Mujib was possible when the six-point plan struck at the very existence of a united Pakistan; how could Yahya reconcile his five points, as laid down in his L.F.O., with Mujib's six-point plan? There was no doubt that the provisions for one Pakistan as laid down in the L.F.O. – or for that matter any concept of a united Pakistan – was irreconcilable with Mujib's six-point plan if the latter were not modified. This particular "if" is of greatest significance in the history of Pakistan's dismemberment. The whole political dialogue between Yahya and Mujib from 1969 up to their crucial meeting in January 1971 *after* the elections were over was based on Mujib's unqualified and repeated pledge *to modify* his six-point plan. There were tape-recorded versions of the Yahya-Mujib talks – I do not know if the Mujib-Ahsan dialogues were also tape-recorded. I was also present during some of the political dialogues, and I used to visit Mujib regularly at the time of finalizing the L.F.O. and had lengthy discussions with him. As pointed out earlier, provincial assembly elections were also held simultaneously with those for the national assembly at Mujib's own suggestion so that he did not need to face the electorate again in six months' time; if so, he argued, how could he modify his six points?

Many people, including Bhutto, now accuse Yahya of simplicity, if not stupidity, in placing reliance on Mujib's words. But was it an unfair game? After all, the public in East Pakistan was behind his demand for regional autonomy, although it must be made clear the Muslim masses in rural Bengal who voted for Mujib did not realize that the six-point plan, if it were not modified, would mean the end of one Pakistan. After all, the illiterate voters in an Asian country can hardly be expected to understand the fine distinction between "maximum autonomy" and a veiled scheme of secession. Furthermore Mujib, as is apparent from an analysis of his election speeches during 1970, never for a moment told the Bengali Muslims that his aim was the creation of a separate state of Bangladesh – as he claimed after its establishment with the triumphant entry of Indian troops into Dacca on December 16, 1971.

It is true that by August 1970 the government had received authentic reports concerning Mujib's real intensions. General Akbar's periodical (fortnightly) reports and the civil intelligence service, of which the regional chief in East Pakistan was a Bengali officer, gave Yahya enough indications that Mujib's strategy seemed to be to use the elections to establish his credentials as the sole leader of the Bengalis, and after it he would "show his teeth". At this stage (August–November) serious discussion took place as to whether Mujib should be allowed to face the electorate without autonomy being defined, or whether Yahya should challenge Mujib on substantive evidence including a press statement which he had given to a foreign journalist, expressing his ultimate goal of establishing a separate state for Bengalis. Mujib asked the foreign journalist not to publish his interview; however the intelligence service in Dacca obtained a copy of it from a local journalist who accompanied the foreign journalist to Mujib's residence. There were also reports that Mujib had begun to have contacts with New Delhi.

While Yahya might have been justified in formulating his plan for transfer of power in November 1969 on the basis of his honest belief in Mujib's words, developments in the latter part of 1970 were too serious to be ignored. I had taken a leading part in finalizing the L.F.O., and it was on my suggestion that provincial autonomy was not defined in the L.F.O. and instead "five principles" relating to the minimum requirements for one Pakistan were spelled out in L.F.O.; however, when I heard Mujib's own voice in a tape-recorded conversation in his inner cabinet giving clear hints of his ultimate aim as referred to earlier (as also when I read the full contents of Mujib's press statement to the foreign correspondent as referred to earlier) my own doubts about the success of the plan for transfer of power as laid down in the L.F.O. began to grow. I also held discussions with Bhashani, Nurul Amin, Ghulam Azam and some of the student leaders inside the Awami League who were my students I carefully read various intelligence reports, particularly those of Akbar for whose integrity and sense of patriotism I have a high regard. It was a terrible dilemma for me: the L.F.O., which I had helped to draft, conceded all legitimate demands and aspirations of East Pakistanis, and I knew that Yahya was thoroughly sincere in implementing these provisions relating to maximum autonomy for East Pakistan. But when it became evident that, instead of appreciating Yahya's gestures, Mujib now seemed to be moving along the path of separation, I could no longer, while remaining true to my deep-rooted convictions in favour of a united Pakistan, remain silent.

When Yahya returned home from his extensive stay in Dacca during the floods in August 1970, I was busy organizing a conference on international affairs which was attended by many foreign scholars. Yahya was to inaugurate the conference and my task was to prepare his speech for the occasion. During this period Yahya with his family including his wife came to my residence at Islamabad for a dinner on August 25. On that evening I requested him to give me a "lengthy session" with him "to discuss some most urgent problems"; he at once agreed and we met two days later at the President's House for a three-hour session. I gave my candid views on the growing threats to Pakistan; I also showed him a copy of the preliminary draft constitution prepared by Mujib's constitutional advisers, which had no trace of any compromise on the six-point plan.[15] Yahya was very grave after my exposition of the situation; he raised the question of how we could now retreat. My answer to this was that there was no question of retreating over the matters of transfer of power or free elections on the basis of "one man, one vote", neither should there be any going back on the pledge to give East Pakistan "maximum autonomy", particularly in economic and financial matters. Yahya then asked for specific suggestions. My advice to him was that there was nothing "final" in political thinking or policy; we had decided not to define "provincial autonomy" in 1969, but by 1970 Mujib and his followers had started a campaign of hatred, openly preaching Bengali nationalism and challenging the very existence of one Pakistan. In the changed circumstances, I added, Yahya as the country's President should firmly declare: "Thus far and no farther." He asked me to elaborate, and I then pointed out to him that it was high time that the question of provincial autonomy, which had created the most explosive situation, should no longer be kept undefined; the viability of national government must now be spelled clearly by giving the maximum possible autonomy, and then if Mujib should revolt, Yahya should put the issue in the form of a referendum to the East Pakistanis and ascertain if they wanted "genuine autonomy" or separation. I concluded that seventy-five million people couldn't be kept by force if they *really* wanted separation. But Mujib should not be allowed, like Abdul Ghaffar Khan in 1946, to mislead the Bengali Muslims. Ghaffar Khan also never said in 1946 that he wanted a separate state for the Pathans, but he demanded "autonomy" for them. Yahya listened carefully to my arguments; he always used to give serious consideration to my suggestions on constitutional issues and also on foreign affairs. He asked me to work out the details of my proposals. However, a number of factors worked against my plan.

First, Ahsan reacted sharply against any such plan; he was confident that a deal with Mujib would be made – which only betrayed his lack of understanding of political dynamics in East Pakistan. Peerzada's role was dubious; he remained on the sidelines during this crucial period. He wanted to keep his options open for a Yahya-Mujib understanding because if the rightist parties in West Pakistan, which his rival in the cabinet Major-General Sher Ali Khan was supporting, won the elections, his personal future would not be secure. Until Bhutto's conclusive victory at the polls, he would not advise Yahya anything which might offend Mujib. In the absence of the support of the provincial Governor's and the *de facto* prime minister, my plan had little chance of success as Yahya unlike Ayub could not take a bold decision without the backing of some members of the junta.

Secondly, Yahya was then busy with two important state visits – one to Washington in October and the other to Peking in November. While he was in Peking, the terrible cyclone occurred which killed a large number of people in East Pakistan. The anti-West Pakistan feelings preached by Mujib over the central government's alleged lack of sympathy for the suffering Bengalis made the situation so fluid and explosive that it was difficult for Yahya to take bold measures such as I had outlined to him in September 1970. Ahsan and Peerzada then arranged three secret meetings between Yahya and Mujib, as referred to earlier. Yahya, who habitually showed a lack of courage for any big or imaginative step, was contented with these secret parleys with Mujib, rather than challenging him for preaching against the very existence of Pakistan as a united country.

As a result of these secret parleys, Yahya asked me to prepare a constitutional draft on the relationship between the centre and the provinces. I drafted a plan for an almost confederal solution on the basis of the six points, minus the break-up of the country. My draft was so near to Mujib's ideas of autonomy (if he were interested in autonomy and not in secession) that Yahya asked me: "What is the difference between your scheme and the six points?" Yet in his final bids to save the country from dismemberment, he agreed to my plan. I give below the basic features of my formula for the centre-provinces relationship and facsimile copies of my letter to Yahya on December 11, 1970, and his handwritten reply of January 21, 1971, accepting my plan (facing pp. 142 and 143). The basic points of my plan were:

1. There should be only one list of powers for the Central Government and all other powers including residuary powers should be vested in the provinces. If any powers are to be kept by the centre for the provinces of West Pakistan, that should be enumerated in the separate list. So far as the province of East Pakistan is concerned, all powers minus the central list should be vested in that province.

2. The central list should be as short as possible, not exceeding five or six items, which should keep most essential requirements of the national government but nothing more nor less than that.

3. (*a*) No special provision for central intervention on the ground of national security, economic planning and co-ordination or uniformity should be provided. Such provision

in the constitution of 1962 was highly unpopular in the country.

(*b*) With regard to economic and financial matters, which today is the crux of the central and provincial relationship in Pakistan, the following principles may be incorporated in the constitution:

(i) Federal resources including foreign aid and foreign exchange should be distributed between the province of East Pakistan and the four provinces of West Pakistan either on the basis of population or at least on a fifty-fifty basis. But foreign aid and loans will be negotiated exclusively by the centre.

(ii) All federal expenditure, both revenue and development expenditure, should again be distributed between the province of East Pakistan and the four provinces of West Pakistan on the same principle, viz. either on the basis of population or on a fifty-fifty basis.

(iii) The taxation system in Pakistan should be such that all taxes should be levied and collected by the provinces but the contributions to the Federal Government of some of the taxes should be guaranteed in the constitution itself.

(iv) The organs of the Central Government – both legislature, executive and judiciary – should be located in the two capitals (Islamabad and Dacca) in such a way that the people of the two geographically separated wings of this country should not feel any sense of isolation. Every department dealing with central subjects must have an additional branch in the other capital. If the head office of one department is situated in Islamabad, an additional branch should be set up in East Pakistan and vice versa.

(v) Recruitment to all federal services at all levels should again be distributed between the province of East Pakistan and four provinces of West Pakistan either on population basis or on 50:50 basis.

(vi) All key posts of the Federal Government (key posts meaning posts of Joint Secretary and above in all federal departments and institutions financed by the Federal Government) should be held on rotation basis between the people of the two wings of the country.

Islamabad, dated the
11th December, 1970.

Dear Mr. President,

As per your kind instructions given during my interview with you at Dacca on 2nd December, 1970, I have now finalised the most crucial part of the Constitutional Draft viz. Relationship between the Centre and Provinces. The relationship has got three aspects — legislative, administrative and financial. This was explained elaborately in the note which I submitted to you earlier and was fully discussed during my interview with you. The relationship has been prepared as per your comments and discussion on my previous note on this subject. The original note is also sent back which may provide as a background to the final shape of the relationship as prepared.

With the completion of this part, I have practically now completed my assignment. Once you kindly approve of this important part and I have the opportunity of discussing it with you, I shall then rearrange the whole draft in proper and final form for further discussion and use.

You asked me to do this work on top priority basis and to give it to you definitely by 15th December. I am therefore submitting it today (11th December) and hope to have the opportunity of having your comments and discussion at your convenience.

With best regards,

Yours sincerely,
(G.W. Choudhury)

General Agha Muhammad Yahya Khan,
H.Pk., H.J.,
President of Pakistan, Rawalpindi.

PRESIDENT'S HOUSE

I generally agree with the changes made by you in various Clauses. See my remarks in the files.

Dr. C.K. Chaudhry

21/1/71

> In conclusion, I cannot but point out that East Pakistan has not got a fair share in various sectors of the economy such as "revenue expenditure", "development expenditure", "utilization of foreign aid", "foreign aid" or "foreign exchange". In fact, its share has been most unsatisfactory and unjust. This state of affairs is not conducive to our national unity and existence. The rise of [the] six-point [plan] and its popularity in the East is due to the fact that in the past, economic policies have been planned and executed in a way which has been detrimental to the interest of East Pakistan. This is an unpleasant fact but it has to be accepted. And if we want to ensure our national integrity and solidarity, the future political order must put an end to this sad state of affairs. We have to take imaginative and statesmanlike steps in economic and financial matters so that legitimate grievances and the interest of the geographically separated part of East Pakistan are removed. It is only by that process that we can make this nation strong. There must be some tangible arrangements to rouse feelings for national cohesion and solidarity. The new generation which has sprung up since 1947 in East Pakistan has heard and seen nothing but this state of affairs in which it has been told, and told rightly, that whereas at the time of independence the state of economic development in East Pakistan was the same as that in the West, by two decades later it had fallen far behind. We must put an end to this type of phenomenon. A constitution, however, cannot show all the details of its economic and fiscal arrangement, but what can be incorporated in a constitution is that statutory bodies can be set up which will be entrusted with the task of formulating and executing economic, fiscal and budgetary policies in such a way that these things may not be repeated.

As Mujib pledged to modify his six points, and as he also agreed to show the draft constitution which his constitutional advisers like Dr. Kamal Hossain and others were preparing, so Yahya thought that instead of challenging Mujib on the eve of elections, it was better to negotiate with him, particularly when there was hardly any difference between them if *autonomy* was the true cause of conflict.

This is the background to Yahya's adherence to the path of negotiation till Mujib presented his plan for splitting the country on March 23, 1971. Though Bhutto hailed the Pakistan Army's military action on March 25, 1971, with the words "Thank God, Pakistan is saved",[16] he changed his views when it became evident in the summer of 1971 that East Pakistan's problem could not be solved by military action; he then began to find fault with Yahya's negotiations with Mujib when the latter, as Bhutto writes, was really bent on separation and not interested in autonomy for East Pakistan. He also wrote in his *The Great Tragedy*, published only three months before the fall of Dacca: "Sheikh Mujibur Rahman manoeuvred the Government into believing that he would become more amenable after the elections, more susceptible to compromise on six-points after an election victory. . . . The Government made every effort to accommodate Mujibur Rahman and his party."[17] I agree with Bhutto's analysis of Mujib's aims and the Yahya Government's "soft" policy towards him. The latter was based on goodwill and faith in Mujib's words. But it was equally a pity that Bhutto, who was so close to Yahya, Peerzada and some other members of the junta, did not advise or offer any alternative solution. It is easy to criticize a plan based on good faith and honest intentions when it proves a failure. While most of the rightist parties in West Pakistan and all non-Awami League leaders in East Pakistan were urging Yahya to challenge Mujib before the elections, Bhutto made no constructive suggestion. He was too busy winning the election and capturing power.

Both Mujib and Bhutto expressed satisfaction with the way the Yahya régime conducted the elections, which were absolutely free from governmental pressure or interference of any kind. In one of his early post-election speeches on January 3, 1970, Mujib said: "I congratulate President Yahya Khan on the fulfilment of his promise to hold the general election."[18] In another speech Mujib repeated his praises for Yahya: "I praise Yahya Khan for fulfilling his promises and accepting some of the demands of the people."[19] Bhutto writes in *The Great Tragedy* that during his first meeting with Yahya in Karachi soon after the elections, his party "extended its co-operation to the régime without rancour in the search for a national solution".[20]

But unfortunately neither Mujib nor Bhutto showed any appreciation of Yahya's fulfilling his pledge of "fair and free" elections, which were unique in the political history of Pakistan over the previous two decades. Though Mujib and Bhutto expressed *apparent* appreciation of Yahya's role in holding the country's first election on a truly democratic basis, each adopted an uncompromising attitude towards the political settlement for which the elections were held.

Mujib's posture became more and more militant. In his post-election speeches from January to March 1971, there was no trace of any compromise or any modification of the extreme aspects of his six points. Contrary to his repeated pledge throughout 1969 and 1970, particularly that made during the three secret parleys in Dacca with Yahya just on the eve of the elections, that he would modify the extreme aspects of his six points, Mujib now declared that the six-point plan was "the property of the people of Bangladesh" and that there could be no compromise on it. In his post-election speeches Mujib made a complete *volte face*; let me quote from some of his post-election speeches. In the first of these Mujib declared: "Our people have recorded a historic verdict. . . . A constitution on the basis of the six-point formula has to be framed and *implemented in all its aspects*" [my italics]. He added: "The resounding victory of the Awami League is, in fact, the victory of . . . *Bangladesh*"[21] [my italics]; three days later, on December 13, he again declared: "I want to repeat my assurance to the people that the constitution of the country would be prepared on the basis of the six points."[22]

Then again on December 20 he repeated: "There can be no constitution except the one which is based on the six-point programme."[23] At a public meeting on January 4, Mujib made the elected members of his party swear not to modify the six points; the map of Bangladesh was displayed at this meeting.[24] After administering the oath, Mujib stated: "The future constitution . . . would be framed on the basis of six-point and eleven-point programmes (the eleven points were demands of the Awami Student League and were even more militant and uncompromising). These are no longer my party's programmes. The Awami League cannot amend it now. No one would be able to stop us framing a constitution on the six-point programme."[25]

These uncompromising statements were made when Yahya

was making serious attempts for a settlement on the future constitution. He expressed his dismay over Mujib's statements at a meeting of the cabinet early in January 1970. When I used to meet Yahya during this crucial period, I found him deeply perturbed. "How could Sheikh Sahib betray me when I have fulfilled all his demands?" he would say. But despite his anxiety, he was still hopeful, and was preparing for his dialogues with with Mujib and Bhutto.

Turning to Bhutto, one would find that in his post-election speeches he was no less uncompromising and provocative. In one of the earliest of these speeches, Bhutto declared: "No constitution could be framed, nor could any government at the centre be run without my party's co-operation." The P.P.P. (Bhutto's party) was not, he added, "prepared to occupy the opposition benches in the national assembly"; after paying "regard" for Mujib's election victory, he stated: "Majority alone does not count in national politics."[26] If Bhutto believed in democracy as he pretended, one could ask what else counted in a democratic process except the verdict of the people in favour of a majority group? In another speech on December 24, Bhutto said: "People voted for P.P.P. in great majority in West Pakistan and for Awami League in East Pakistan." "Both these parties", he added, "have to share responsibilities of the country *as the majority parties*"[27] [my italics]. He also declared that the Punjab was "the bastion of power" and as such could not be ignored in any political dialogue. It was a provocative statement at a time when the supreme need was for restraint, toleration and mutual understanding. An analysis of Bhutto's speeches during December 1970 and January 1971 reveal that he took the initiative in expounding the "two-nation theory" within Pakistan while Mujib was preparing to assume the role of father of a new nation. Bhutto hinted that Pakistan might have to recognize "two majority parties" and even "two prime ministers" in one country. An impartial reading of Bhutto's utterances, together with his active lobbying of generals like Peerzada, Omar and Gul Hasan, would lead one to conclude that if he had to make a choice between the "two P's" (Power or Pakistan) he would choose the former.[28]

Jinnah's two-nation theory seemed to be unacceptable to both Mujib and Bhutto after the country's first general election. It appeared that Pakistan could survive as a united country only under an authoritarian system (1958–71) or under a parody of the parliamentary system without a single general election for eleven years (1947–58). Democracy and the survival of Pakistan appeared to be contradictory. It was a tragic outcome to those like myself who valued and cherished the ideals and ideology of Pakistan based on broad Islamic principles and democratic forces. The vast majority of the people in Pakistan participated in a free democratic election not to see their cherished country divided but to see it march forward towards democracy and economic improvement for the poor masses, and with many other great expectations.

Both Mujib and Bhutto seemed to realize their political strength to the full. Mujib emerged as the sole leader of the Bengalis after the elections: who, after such an unparalleled victory could challenge him? It was also reliably learnt that after their defeat in the elections a large group of the pro-Moscow faction of the N.A.P. managed to infiltrate into the Awami League – not formally but for all practical purposes; it was done, as reports indicated, on directives from Moscow.[29] Mujib's Number Two in the party, Tajuddin, was also reported to have established contacts with New Delhi.[30]

Bhutto knew his strength; he had won the votes of the *jawans* (soldiers) and of the inhabitants of the "recruiting areas" for the Pakistan Army. He was now in a position to challenge Yahya if the latter should betray the "national interest" (so named by the vested interests and the ruling élite in West Pakistan) in his bids to win Mujib's co-operation. Mujib did nothing to strengthen the hands of Yahya and other Army officers, as well as the common people of West Pakistan, who were prepared to accept him as Prime Minister of Pakistan. Mujib was repeatedly urged by patriotic elements and the press in West Pakistan to visit there as the national leader of the country. I can vouch that the majority of West Pakistanis would have accepted Mujib as Prime Minister without any mental reservation. But the tragedy was that Mujib seemed uninterested in becoming Prime Minister of a united Pakistan, while Bhutto seemed bent on capturing power, whether of a united Pakistan or of a smaller Pakistan.

The situation at GHQ was also becoming complicated.

Generals like Hamid, Omar, Gul Hasan and Peerzada, who seemed always to be opposed to any real transfer of power, were now planning for a Turkish type of "military–civilian [i.e. concealed] régime". Yahya's hands were weakened by the militant and uncompromising postures of Mujib and Bhutto after the election.

So the stage was set for an imminent confrontation, and the honest and sincere efforts in the preceding two years, of Yahya, Ahsan and many others including myself to preserve the unity of the country seemed doomed.

Another factor was the personal relationship between Mujib and Bhutto. No love was lost between them, just as none was lost between Jinnah and Nehru. There was one hope for a political settlement – namely, if Mujib and Bhutto could unite and put a joint draft constitution before the assembly. In that event the most hawkish member of the junta would have had to submit to the joint demands of these two unchallenged leaders of the two wings of Pakistan. But to expect a compromise or a joint constitutional formula from Mujib and Bhutto was as absurd as it was to expect an agreed formula from Jinnah and Nehru in 1946–7.

Neither Mujib nor Bhutto could or should be compared with Jinnah and Nehru. Unlike such Congress leaders as Gandhi and Nehru or Muslim League leaders like Jinnah, neither Mujib nor Bhutto possessed any of the qualities of a leader whose aim is to achieve his objectives at a minimum cost in terms of human suffering and loss to society. In a sense both were products of Ayub Khan's authoritarian régime; both flourished on negative appeals to the illiterate voters of Pakistan, one by whipping up regional feeling against Punjabi domination and the other by whipping up militant national feeling against India. Neither had any constructive or positive approach.

Pakistan was now moving straight towards a complete deadlock and total confusion. The whole situation was desperate, and bitterly disappointing to anyone who wished the country well, yet a number of important talks were held from December 1970 to March 25, 1971, when the Army took the fatal step of resorting to arms and thereby gave the death-blow to united Pakistan.

Political Talks between December 1970 and March 1971

As soon as the results of the election were announced, Yahya sent greetings to Mujib and Bhutto. Yahya also granted an amnesty by releasing persons who had been convicted under martial law for excesses committed during the preceding eighteen months. He was anxious to begin talks with Mujib and Bhutto. Mahmoud Haroon who, more than any other member of Yahya's Cabinet, enjoyed Mujib's confidence (Mujib's close ties with the wealthy Haroon family had raised many queries and much speculation) went to Dacca with Yahya's invitation to Mujib to come to the capital of Pakistan. Mujib was already described in many quarters as the "future prime minister". Mujib, however, declined to come to the capital or to West Pakistan. This significant move was interpreted in some quarters as meaning that Mujib was not interested in becoming Prime Minister of a united Pakistan; a more charitable interpretation was that Mujib wanted to assert that henceforth it would be Dacca and not Rawalpindi where vital decisions should be made.

Yahya, therefore, had to go to Dacca, where he arrived on January 12. Yahya had expectations that Mujib would show him the Awami League draft constitution as he had pledged to do during their secret meetings on the eve of the elections. For this reason Yahya asked me to accompany him to Dacca so that he would have someone to advise him on Mujib's draft constitution. The first meeting between Yahya and Mujib took place on January 12 and lasted over three hours; no other person was present. As soon as the meeting was over, I received and answered a summons from the President's House to see Yahya. I found him bitter and frustrated. He told me: "Mujib has let me down. Those who warned me against him were right; I was wrong in trusting this person." He then gave me the substance of his discussion with Mujib in great anguish as well as anger. Mujib had refused to show him the draft constitution as he had solemnly promised before the election. He made it clear to Yahya that as leader of the majority party, he and he alone, was responsible for the new constitution; Yahya's job was to summon the Assembly immediately; he threatened Yahya with "dire consequences" if he failed to do so. For Yahya it was the greatest shock; he had taken a great risk by putting faith in Mujib's assurances and promises. His image among the army generals would be seriously affected as he had been proved to be naïve in dealing with Mujib. As already mentioned, he had had a constitutional formula prepared by me which had conceded almost all the demands of the Mujib programme. There were only two differences: Yahya agreed to have a central authority with only three subjects plus some peripheral items such as nationality, emigration, issuing of passports, etc. In the plan prepared by me, the centre's list did not have more than five or six items in all, but the real powers were three: foreign affairs, defence and currency. But since he wanted to ensure that the centre should discharge those functions properly, he demanded that while the centre would have no power of levying taxation, there should be some provisions guaranteed in the constitution so that the centre would receive a fixed percentage of certain taxes, so that it could carry on its responsibilities without being dependent on the federating units for an uncertain, if not voluntary, contribution which might even vary from time to time.

Secondly, he could not agree with the subtle distinction between political or diplomatic and economic aspects of foreign affairs, as I have earlier pointed out while analysing the six points. Yahya's compromise formula on this issue was that the state of Bangladesh would have the right to appoint its trade commissioner or economic representative abroad and also to enter into agreements with foreign countries on economic matters, provided that such economic dealings with foreign countries were "not against the fundamentals of the country's foreign policy". If, for instance, Pakistan's foreign policy demanded that there should not be any economic ties wtih a hostile country or neighbour, Bangladesh could not enter into any agreement with such country or countries. When it was argued by the Awami Leaguers that West Pakistan might not wish to have economic or trade relations with India in preference to China, Yahya's reply was that, thanks to his granting of "one man, one vote", the Bengalis would have a clear majority in the federal legislature, and the country's Prime Minister should shape its foreign policy.

There was no satisfactory answer on this from Mujib or his advisers.

The discussion between Yahya and Mujib and his party colleagues continued even after their frustrating first meeting on January 12. But it was clear that Pakistan was drifting towards a fatal confrontation.

At the time of leaving Dacca, Yahya told newsmen that he had had "useful discussions" with Mujib. He also made a significant comment: "When he [Mujib] comes and takes over, I won't be there. It is going to be his government soon."[31] I knew that there was an understanding between Yahya and Mujib that while the former would continue to be the constitutional figurehead in a parliamentary system, Mujib as the leader of the majority party would be prime minister. As he was leaving Dacca Yahya said that Mujib would be the future prime minister of the country.[32] Yahya's remark that he would not be there while Mujib took over indicated that the understanding built up between them over a period of nearly two years (1969–70), reaching its peak in November 1970 when Yahya complied with Mujib's request not to postpone the elections following the terrible cyclone, had nearly broken down.

I met Yahya on the eve of his departure from Dacca. He expressed his total frustration and bitterness over Mujib's changed attitude. He told me that he was going to see Bhutto and other West Pakistani leaders, to urge them to come to Dacca and prevail upon Mujib to see reason. When I specifically asked him: "Have you reminded Mujib about his pledges, made on the eve of elections?", Yahya's reply was made with deep anguish: "You and I are not politicians – it is difficult for me to understand their mind and ways of thinking. Let us pray and hope for the best." I knew what these words meant. I asked for his permission to go abroad for two weeks on some personal-cum-official business; he readily allowed me to go but in a rather touching way asked me not to desert him at this critical time, and I assured him of my full and loyal support to him in his endeavours to find a political solution that would prevent the break-up of the country at that crucial moment.

After the ill-fated meeting between Yahya and Mujib on January 12 and my own meeting with Yahya the same evening, I told a Bengali colleague of mine in the cabinet, Mr. Hafizuddin, about these serious developments. He had good contacts with Mujib, and is in fact a relation of his. I urged Hafizuddin to see Mujib and plead with him not to take a position of no return. Hafizuddin was equally concerned over the post-election developments. He saw Mujib and reminded him of his pledge to show Yahya the draft constitution as prepared by the Awami League. Mujib's reply to Hafizuddin was evasive; he could not deny it, but turned to Tajuddin who was also present at the meeting and Tajuddin's prompt reply, as Hafizuddin reported to me later on, was: "We did not make such a pledge, nor is there any need to show our draft constitution to anybody." It may be recalled that when the period of 120 days was fixed for completing the task of framing the constitution, it was solemnly agreed by all parties, including Mujib and his party, that the *real* discussion on the future constitution would be made and finalized *before* the assembly met; otherwise it was impossible for the assembly to produce a constitution in 120 days with so many complicated issues – because of which the two constituent assemblies in Pakistan had taken nine years (1947–56) to produce an agreed constitution.

The Larkana Dialogue

It was in this mood of gloom that Yahya went to Bhutto's home town, Larkana, to have a discussion with him. I was not present at the Larkana talks, having by this time left Pakistan for a tour abroad. Bhutto took full advantage of Yahya's frustration with Mujib. At Larkana Yahya and other prominent members of the junta – including General Hamid, whose hatred for Mujib was well known, and Peerzada, Bhutto's closest friend in the junta – enjoyed Bhutto's hospitality, and in the course of rather colourful social evenings a new and most sinister alliance seems to have developed between the military junta and Bhutto – though Yahya never believed in him. Bhutto has given his version of the discussion held in Larkana: "We discussed with the President the implications of the six points and expressed our serious misgivings about them. We nevertheless assured him that we were determined to make every effort for a viable compromise."[33] In the meantime Bhutto had a round of talks with Mujib at Dacca. He and his party arrived there on January 27. I was there to watch the outcome, if any, of the political dialogue between the two leaders who had emerged as the leaders of East and West Pakistan. There were three days of talks but, due to their lack of mutual understanding, there could hardly be any progress towards political settlement, though such talks were the most obvious course for any meaningful settlement. The election results demonstrated that neither Mujib nor Bhutto represented Pakistan as a whole; so that if an agreed constitution were to be framed, there must be some understanding between the two most representative parties in Pakistan – just as an understanding between the Congress and the Muslim League had been needed in 1946–7 for any constitutional formula that would result in the British *raj* being liquidated voluntarily. Yahya could transfer power only when the two most representative groups in the country could agree on some sort of *modus operandi* for the transfer of power from the military régime to the elected representatives. Even if they were to agree to divide Pakistan, as the Congress and the Muslim League finally agreed to divide India in 1947, there still needed to be an agreement. Yahya, true to his commitment to protect Pakistan's territorial integrity, had no mandate to preside over its dismemberment.

The Mujib–Bhutto talks, though reported in the press as having been held "in a cordial atmosphere" at the former's residence, were noted for lack of any progress. Mujib made it clear to Bhutto, as I gathered from various sources, that he was not prepared to modify the six-point plan, while Bhutto made it clear that his party could not agree to a veiled scheme of secession under the plan. Bhutto gives his version: "Mujib's strategy was to bring the national assembly to session without loss of time in order to give legal sanction to his six points – to thrust a six-point constitution on the country before full awareness of its implications could grow in West Pakistan or, for that matter, in the East wing itself. He sought to pressure the people of the country into submission, to leave no time for reflection."[34]

There is no public record of Mujib and his party's reaction to Bhutto's mission to Dacca. After the Larkana dialogue Bhutto was regarded by Mujib and his party as an "agent" of the hawkish elements of the junta who, according to him, were still unreconciled to the idea of any genuine transfer of power. Another complicating factor in a Mujib–Bhutto understanding was their divergent attitude towards India. Mujib was in favour of friendly relations with New Delhi, while Bhutto was still regarded as anti-Indian. When an elderly Bengali leader, who belonged to no political party, suggested to Mujib that Bhutto should be made deputy prime minister and foreign minister, Mujib's reaction was one of extreme disapproval and anger. Mujib was reported to be ready "to make Bhutto Agricultural Minister" in his cabinet, but Bhutto would be the last person to be given the foreign office. The elderly Bengali political leader was dismayed by this attitude, not out of love for Bhutto but for its grave implications.

Mahmood Haroon also played a significant role in ensuring that an understanding between Mujib and Bhutto, which was so vital for any political settlement, would not come about. Haroon did his best to portrait Bhutto to Mujib as "the army's man". Mujib had already been suspicious of this; he did not like the fact that Yahya and other generals had visited Bhutto's home town Larkana, and Haroon most skilfully exploited the situation.

The Contingency Plan

After the fateful Larkana talks, the army junta met formally at Rawalpindi in mid-February to discuss the political situation. It was at this meeting that the junta decided to challenge Mujib if he persisted in his uncompromising attitude, but significantly it ignored Bhutto's provocative speeches. Bhutto was now regarded by the hawkish generals like Hamid, Omar and Gul Hasan, as well as by his trusted friend Peerzada, as the defender of "the national interests" of Pakistan as interpreted by the ruling élite. It was at this meeting that the junta decided to dissolve the cabinet – whose members had already expressed their desire to be relieved after the election. But at the cabinet meeting on December 8, 1970, Yahya decided to continue with it as some of its members were useful in acting as links with Mujib, while he needed the services of some others as long as constitutional dialogue persisted. But now Yahya's hold over the junta, which had never been absolute, was declining because of his failure to modify Mujib's policy. Both Ahsan and Yahya were discredited. Ahsan wanted to be relieved and the junta decided that he should be replaced by a hawk, Lieut.-General Tikka Khan. The cabinet was also dissolved on February 17, but within forty-eight hours Yahya invited some of its members, including myself, to continue as his advisers. Instead of a council of ministers he wanted to have a council of advisers. But the Bengali members of the proposed council – with one exception, Ahsan-ul Huq – declined to continue any longer. Of the West Pakistan members of the cabinet only Cornelius decided to stay.

Because of Mujib's repeated demands and warnings, Yahya announced on February 13 that the National Assembly would meet in Dacca on March 3. Bhutto immediately raised his flag of rebellion. He declared that unless there was an understanding between Mujib and himself on the future constituent assembly, it would not be allowed to meet. He threatened "a revolution from the Khyber to Karachi".[35] Bhutto by this time knew his bargaining strength; powerful members of the junta were with him rather than with Yahya. As pointed out earlier, Yahya had a free hand in formulating his scheme for the transfer of power and holding elections, but the junta adopted a policy of "wait and see"; if Yahya were successful in maintaining the unity of the country, by whatever constitutional device, well and good, but from late January, when Yahya had had his abortive talks with Mujib, the junta was not prepared to remain as a passive spectator of political and constitutional issues. From January the process of decision-making had changed.

As already pointed out, Pakistan under Yahya had a military or inner cabinet apart from a civilian one. I had the opportunity of attending the inner cabinet while the L.F.O. was being drafted – not as a member of Yahya's civilian cabinet but rather I was a constitutional expert. I therefore had some idea of how the decision-making process operated during

Yahya's time. By and large, Yahya had a free hand in the country's day-to-day and routine administration and in external affairs, but he was always careful to have any important decision approved by his inner cabinet – even his policy statements used to be thoroughly discussed by them. Unlike Ayub, Yahya operated within a collective leadership although he retained the vital role for himself.

It is my assessment that in February Yahya, like Ahsan, might also have been replaced by Hamid; he would not perhaps have been unhappy to go. But for some reason, the junta had to carry on with Yahya. It was conscious of the adverse international reaction that would have been created by Yahya's removal or resignation, particularly in Washington and Peking, in the context of the role assigned to him by Nixon to develop ties between Washington and Peking.

So Yahya continued to play his role in an untenable situation. Following Bhutto's threat, the National Assembly, which had been scheduled to meet on March 3, was postponed indefinitely. Yahya's announcement on March 1 on the postponement of the Assembly could not have been more provocative or tragic. When I asked him about it on March 5, he looked vacant and helpless; I was convinced he had only been a signatory to it. Bhutto and Peerzada were reported to have drafted the statement. Yahya, unlike on previous occasions, did not broadcast it; it was only read out over the radio.

Before Yahya left Rawalpindi for Karachi to pursuade Bhutto to go to Dacca so that the National Assembly might not be postponed, he had already sent Peerzada, Ahsan and Yakub on the same mission to persuade Bhutto to attend the National Assembly. He gave Bhutto a solemn promise that if Mujib were to "thrust a six-point constitution" against the wishes of the majority of the West Pakistan members and if his constitutional draft would mean splitting the country, he would at once prorogue the assembly; however nothing could satisfy Bhutto. When it became evident that as a result of Bhutto's threat of boycotting the assembly, the majority of the West Pakistani assembly members would not attend the session, Yahya decided to postpone the summoning of the assembly, but he wanted to issue a statement which should cause the least provocation possible in East Pakistan. Though I was no longer a member of his Cabinet, Yahya asked me to prepare a statement in a conciliatory vein. I immediately began to draft the proposed statement, which ran as follows:

> In view of the complete deadlock between the two principal parties representing East and West Pakistan respectively, I am constrained to postpone the meeting of the National Assembly on March 3, 1970. I would however wish to make it absolutely clear that the postponement will not exceed two to three weeks and during this short period, I shall make all endeavours to bring rapprochement between the elected representatives of the two regions of our country. As you will recall, I have often said in the past and I want to reaffirm that I have no desire to impose a constitution either on East or on West Pakistan against the wishes of the people. A true federal constitution, to which the political parties and my régime are all committed, cannot be framed without the consensus of various federating units. I shall be the happiest person when a consensus on a federal union is arrived at, and on my part I assure my nation that I shall spare no efforts to achieve this supreme goal.
>
> I sincerely hope and appeal to my brethren in East Pakistan to appreciate the gravity of the situation and allow mc this short period of two or three weeks to work for an agreed formula. *Insha Allah* [by the Grace of God] we shall overcome this difficulty. Let us remember Quaid-e-Azam's immortal saying "Pakistan has come to stay"; let us all dedicatc ourselves to the fulfilment of the desire of the Father of the Nation.

I personally handed over the draft of the statement at Islamabad airport as Yahya was leaving for Karachi. He subsequently gave it to Peerzada, who, in alliance with Bhutto, torpedoed it. I still feel regret that I did not accompany Yahya to Karachi. My reluctance was due to the fact that I was no longer a member of the cabinet; I also expressed my inability to accept his offer of being an "adviser". By accompanying Yahya to Karachi, I would have caused unnecessary speculation about my links with Yahya. But I now realize that Yahya's great weakness was his fickle-mindedness; he approved my draft, but in my absence, when Bhutto and Peerzada presented another draft, Yahya, true to his weak personality, accepted the provocative one. Though I cannot provide documentary evidence of this, I heard from the personal staff of the President, including his Military Secretary, that Yahya was most reluctant to sign the statement prepared by Peerzada in collusion with Bhutto. But the pressures were strong and Yahya yielded.

Dacca Revolts

As soon as the postponement of the Assembly was Announced over the radio, the reaction in Dacca was violent. Mujib started what he termed "non-violent non-co-operation", but it was not the Gandhian type of non-violent non-co-operation, nor was the Pakistan ruling junta's reaction marked by any moderation as was that of the British authorities. Mujib started an open revolt which virtually amounted to a unilateral declaration of independence for Bangladesh, and what was almost a parallel government began to function under Mujib's instructions. Between 3 and 25 March the central Government's writ did not run in East Pakistan.

But even at this stage Yahya and Mujib were still talking to each other by long-distance telephone. On the eve of Mujib's public meeting on March 7, when many people thought that he would finally announce the independence of Bangladesh, Yahya had lengthy talks with Mujib over the phone. The tone was still cordial; both still seemed eager to negotiate. Mujib invited Yahya to come to Dacca and see the explosive situation for himself, while Yahya appealed to Mujib not to take a step from which there would be no return. I was present in Yahya's office when the telephone call came. I wanted to leave but Yahya indicated that I should stay.

Mujib did not declare independence on March 7 but he laid down four conditions to be met before he could consider participating in the National Assembly, which Yahya decided on March 6 to summon at Dacca on March 25 without any conditions. But Mujib would not now attend the Assembly the postponement of which had created a most explosive situation from March 1 onwards. Mujib's four conditions were: immediate withdrawal of martial law; the Army's return to barracks; a judicial inquiry into the loss of life caused by the Army's action; and immediate transfer of power, i.e. before the Assembly met or could frame a constitution.

REFERENCES

1. See *The Partition of India: Policies and Perspectives, 1938–1947*, ed. C. H. Philips and Mary D. Wainwright, London, 1970.
2. This was the constant theme of the Soviet writings on Pakistan from 1947 to 1965. See *Current Digest of the Soviet Press* and *The Central Asian Review*.
3. Percival Griffiths, *The British Impact on India*, London, 1952, and *The Economist*, May 17, 1947.
4. See my "Bangladesh: why it Happened", *International Affairs* (London), April 1972.
5. Ibid.
6. *Six-Point Formula: our Right to Live* by Sheikh Mujibur Rahman, Dacca, 1966.
7. Ibid., p. 3.
8. See *The Legal Framework Order, 1970*, Government of Pakistan, Karachi, n.d.
9. See *Six-Point Formula*, op. cit., pp. 5–9.
10. Ibid.
11. See Abdul Kalam Azad, *India wins Freedom*, London, 1959.
12. K. C. Wheare, *Federal Government* (4th ed.), London, 1963, p. 94.
13. See *Six-Point Formula*, op. cit., and his various speeches during the election of 1970.
14. Ibid., p. 12.
15. I obtained the copy of the preliminary draft constitution of the Awami League from a former colleague of mine at Dacca University who had close links with the small group headed by Kamal Hossain to prepare the draft.
16. *Dawn*, Karachi, March 27, 1971.
17. Z. A. Bhutto, *The Great Tragedy*, Karachi, September 1971, p. 13.
18. *Bangladesh, my Bangladesh: Selected Speeches and Statements* by Sheikh Mujibur Rahman, New York, 1972, p. 39.
19. Ibid., p. 55.
20. Z. A. Bhutto, *The Great Tragedy*, op. cit., p. 62.
21. *Bangladesh, my Bangladesh*, op. cit., pp. 20–1.
22. Ibid., p. 24.
23. Ibid., pp. 22–7.
24. Ibid., pp. 35–6.
25. Ibid., p. 36.
26. *Pakistan Times*, Lahore, December 22, 1970.
27. *Dawn*, Karachi, December 25, 1970.
28. See G. W. Choudhury, "The Last Days of Pakistan: A Personal Account" in *International Affairs*, April 1973.
29. Based on unpublished papers of the Government of Pakistan.
30. Tajuddin became Prime Minister of the exile government of Bangladesh in India from March 26, 1971.
31. *Dawn*, Karachi, January 15, 1973.
32. Ibid,

33. Z. A. Bhutto, *The Great Tragedy*, op. cit., p. 20.
34. Ibid., pp. 22–3.
35. See Z. A. Bhutto's statement at press conference in Peshawar on February 15, 1971, *Dawn*, Karachi, February 16, 1971.

7

THE DACCA DIALOGUE

March 16–24, 1971

Yahya's trip to Dacca on March 15, 1971, and his final bids to save the unity of Pakistan were something like giving oxygen to a dying patient when the doctors have declared him a lost case. Yet the crucial talks began while Mujib had declared the unilateral independence of Bangladesh and invited President Yahya to visit Dacca as the "guest of Bangladesh"! On the day of Yahya's arrival in Dacca, March 15, Mujib issued a highly provocative and uncompromising statement: "The heroic struggle of the people marches forward. . . . The people of Bangladesh, civil servants, office and factory workers, peasants and students, have demonstrated in no uncertain terms that they would die rather than surrender. . . . The spirit of Freedom in Bangladesh cannot be extinguished. . . . The struggle shall, therefore, continue with renewed vigour until our goal of emancipation is realized."[1]

Mujib also issued as many as thirty-one "Directives" as to how "Bangladesh shall be governed": all government and semi-government offices would remain closed: no communications with West Pakistan, inter-wing telex, telephone and wireless communications would be allowed. "The sense of a separate state", a foreigner reported to his head office abroad, "began to take quite unambiguous shape. . . . It was clear that in all but military ways Sheikh Mujib was running East Pakistan."[2] Foreign journalists were also turning in similar reports. For instance, *The Daily Telegraph* (London) reported on March 9, 1971, that "Sheikh Mujibur Rahman appears to have declared the independence of East Pakistan", while on the same day the paper in its editorial wrote: "Already we hear the putative name of the separate state that East Pakistan could become – Bangladesh, Bengali land. The flag has been devised." Similar reports appeared in *The Economist* (March 13, 1971) and *Time* magazine (March 15, 1971): "Pakistan as it stands today is finished."

In the mean time, India had already banned all flights of Pakistani planes between East and West Pakistan as of February 1971, because of an alleged hijacking of an Indian plane by "Pakistanis" at Lahore. Pakistan was frantically making efforts through the help of friendly countries, including the United States and Great Britain – the Soviet Union was also approached – to dissuade India from taking this extreme measure at a time when East–West Pakistani contacts were more vital than ever. But India would not listen to any counsels of restraint or offers of mediation by the U.N. Secretary-General. A judicial inquiry conducted subsequently by the Pakistan Government revealed that the hijackers were Indian agents from the Indian-occupied part of Kashmir. Mujib indirectly endorsed the Indian action by terming it as "a conspiracy by the Pakistan Government to postpone the transfer of power". This was an unfortunate remark since Yahya was at that time sincerely working for a political settlement. Mujib's remarks about India banning Pakistani planes from flying to East Pakistan had only deepened the suspicion of those members of the military junta who had always considered Mujib to be an "Indian agent". Bhutto's performance at the time of the alleged hijacking was also ludicrous: he described the allegedly "Pakistani" hijackers as "national heroes"! Could there be clearer evidence of the bankruptcy of wisdom on the part of the two elected leaders of East and West Pakistan than such a reaction to a serious threat by the Indian Government to the national security and viability of Pakistan?

Bhutto's reaction to Mujib's proposal for handing over power before the National Assembly could meet or frame a constitution was equally distressing and shocking. In a statement on March 14, when Yahya was on his way to Dacca to make his final bid to Mujib, Bhutto declared: "If power were to be transferred to the people before any constitutional settlement as demanded by Sheikh Mujibur Rahman, it should be transferred to *the majority party in East Pakistan and the majority party here* [West Pakistan – my italics]."[3] In a subsequent statement on March 15, Bhutto went one step further by declaring that "in the situation faced by Pakistan, having a geographical distance between the two parts, *the rule of the majority did not apply*" [my italics].

So Yahya landed in Dacca on March 15, at a time when Mujib had almost declared the independence of Bangladesh and the majority party leader in West Pakistan, Bhutto, also seemed to favour "two governments", or a splitting up of the country. It was the smaller parties in West Pakistan and the Pakistani Government, headed by Yahya Khan, who still talked of "protecting" the territorial integrity of Pakistan. Bhutto was requested by Yahya to go to Dacca but declined initially on the grounds that after Mujib's virtual declaration of independence, there was no point in making the journey. He now seemed more interested in getting power than in the unity of Pakistan. For him a twenty-one-gun salute was more attractive than going to Dacca to find a solution for a united Pakistan.

Yahya asked me to go to Dacca and to take part in the final political dialogue, first as an official adviser and then as a private citizen. I declined both offers because there seemed to me hardly any chance for a compromise and the talks were likely to be a futile exercise. While Yahya sincerely urged me to go to Dacca, two important members of the junta "advised" me as my "well-wishers" not to burn my fingers in such a futile exercise. Since Mujib began his movement in March, I had given up all hope of a settlement. My foreigner friend whose report I quoted earlier referred to my agony: "That evening [March 2] the man who had been the chief political adviser to the President, a Bengali, had dinner with my wife and me. He and his wife were in great distress. . . ." For me it was a terrible shock to see the plan for the transfer of power – in which I had sincerely tried to accommodate all the legitimate demands and aspiration of the Bengalis while at the same time protecting the unity of Pakistan – being torn to pieces by Mujib and Bhutto, playing their unscrupulous roles the former being also under some foreign influences, and to see, in unmistakable terms, the ending of my cherished homeland.

I had already wound up my affairs in Islamabad after the dissolution of the cabinet on February 17, and was planning to go to London for an academic assignment at the Royal Institute of International Affairs. But I did not wish to leave Pakistan before the outcome of the Dacca dialogue had become known. I stayed behind in Karachi on my way to London to watch carefully the last phase of the drama which marked the end of united Pakistan. I also assured Yahya that if the situation were to improve so that there was any chance of a political settlement, I would immediately dash to Dacca to contribute my little part in helping his efforts to protect the unity of the country – but such a prospect hardly seemed likely.

The two sides were also reported to be preparing their contingency plans for the imminent confrontation. The Pakistani Army was reinforced in East Pakistan by being flown over a circuitous sea route of 3,000 miles because of India's continued ban on all flights between East and West Pakistan. India also put pressure on Ceylon not to allow Colombo airport to be used for Pakistani forces, but without success. Mujib was also making his plan. He appointed Colonel Usmani as Commander of "the Revolutionary forces". A few other retired Bengali officers of the Pakistani Army joined Usmani in organizing an armed uprising. Three weeks of *de facto* independence of "Bangladesh" provided Mujib with unique opportunities for challenging the central Government. He had absolute control over radio, television and the press, which were asked to publish his edicts. The East Bengal Regiment and the East Pakistan Rifles, as well as the police force of the provincial Government in East Pakistan, were all united in showing their allegiance to Mujib and not to the central Government.

When Yahya arrived in Dacca on March 15 he was virtually a "foreign guest" of Bangladesh. Yet, in spite of everything, the political dialogues began.

The first meeting between Yahya and Mujib took place on March 16. Mujib arrived at the President's House at 11 a.m. in a car flying a black flag to mourn the death of those killed during the preceding two weeks. His car also had a symbol of Bangladesh pasted onto it. During the meeting Mujib put forward his four points relating to the immediate lifting of martial law and the transfer of power. Prospects of framing a constitution on the basis of Yahya's transfer of power plan as formulated in 1969–70 had ceased to exist. The choice before the military régime was between recognizing the *de facto* independent status of Bangladesh and challenging Mujib; or, expressed another way, between presiding over the dismemberment of the country and embarking on a military venture which would not only be terribly costly in terms of human lives but would also be uncertain in ultimate consequences. This was the dilemma before Yahya.

Of course, there were hawkish generals, like Hamid and a few others, who were confident of "fixing" the whole situation in, as they said, seventy-two hours. The calm with which the imposition of martial law had been accepted in 1969 gave these hawkish generals a false sense of confidence. They did not realize that the Bengalis had accepted martial law so calmly in 1969 because there were behind-the-scenes parleys between political leaders and the new military régime, with the promise of an election and transfer of power. By March 1971 the whole situation was changed. The year-long election campaign enabled Mujib and his party to preach the gospel of Bangladesh in homes all over East Pakistan; Bengali nationalism was no longer dormant but had become highly articulate and militant.

Yahya made earnest pleas to Mujib, as I learned from him subsequently, to avoid the path of confrontation. Yahya and others who accompanied him to Dacca for the talks were rather surprised to see Mujib shaky and nervous. Mujib, who has never had the reputation of being the bravest or the most intelligent of politicians, was in a situation which probably would lead him nowhere – this was his own assessment at the time in spite of his big talk and militant press statements.

The result was that even in this hopeless and dismal situation, Yahya and Mujib were still talking in terms of a political settlement, while Yahya's militant army generals were getting ready for a confrontation and Mujib's militant supporters were similarly opposed to any compromise. Yet by March 20 – i.e. four days after Yahya's arrival in Dacca – the press was reporting that an agreement had been reached on a compromise constitutional formula incorporating most of the fundamentals of Mujib's six points. A formula had reportedly been presented and agreed upon by Yahya and Mujib, providing for the immediate lifting of martial law and the transfer of power. A draft proclamation effecting an immediate transfer of power was ready; it provided for the formation of provincial and central cabinets from among the elected representatives. The National Assembly would be split into two committees to formulate special provisions and requirements of East and West Pakistan to be incorporated into the future constitution. The National Assembly would then be summoned to frame a constitution for Pakistan.[4]

The White Paper, published by the Government of Pakistan, gave only a summary of the draft proclamation;[5] I saw its full text during my private visits to Islamabad and Dacca in May 1971. The full text, as I discovered from the minutes of the Dacca dialogues, revealed a rather different picture in that it allowed for much more compromise than was conveyed by the White Paper. It accepted the relationship between the central Government and the "State of Bangladesh" (the nomenclature was also now accepted) on the basis of the formula which I had prepared for Yahya in January 1971, and which was virtually the six points minus the dismemberment of Pakistan. When I inquired why the White Paper did not publish the full account, the answer I received from Peerzada was that "a proclamation was made under duress" – implying that the Army was no longer prepared to grant those concessions after it had "crushed" the secession movement. What a sad commentary on the junta's wisdom!

Returning to the Dacca dialogues, Yahya and Mujib, together with their aides, were examining the proposed proclamation in a series of daily meetings. The dialogues were on two levels: between Yahya and Mujib and between technical experts. Yahya's team was led by Justice Cornelius and General Peerzada; M. M. Ahmad, Deputy Chairman of the Planning Commission, was also associated with the talks inasmuch as financial and economic matters figured prominently in the question of the relationship between the national Government and the new state (province) of Bangladesh. A legal expert, Colonel Hasan of the Chief Martial Law Office at Rawalpindi, was the fourth member of the Yahya team. Nobody in this team had any deep understanding of the political dynamics or the external forces working in East Pakistan. Most of the prominent members of the junta (Hamid, Gul Hasan, Omar, Mitha) were present at Dacca. They had regular meetings among themselves at the military headquarters in Dacca and with Yahya. Colonel Hasan told me how, while Yahya was making concession after concession to make Mujib agreeable to a political settlement, the junta warned him of the "dire consequences" of "weakening" the national Government. There has always been a tendency among the Pakistani Army generals to believe that they alone could protect the *Izzat* and *Gharat* (honour and self-respect) of the nation.[6] Since the early 1950s, the Pakistani Army under Ayub seemed to regard itself as the sole guardian of the "national interest"; it was also prejudiced against the politicians of both East and West Pakistan.

There were, however, exceptions. Many army officers in 1969–70 were genuinely anxious for a satisfactory settlement of the East–West Pakistan issue. The majority of the army as well as of the common people in West Pakistan would have accepted Mujib as Pakistan's prime minister provided he was willing to keep the country united. Similarly, the vast majority of the Bengali Muslims were not prepared to see Pakistan dismembered and their homeland become again a target of domination by the *Bhadralok* (élite) from Calcutta. They were interested in having genuine regional autonomy. In fact, their basic demand was for the improvement of their economic lot. Mujib captured their imagination because he promised them a "golden Bengal" if they would only vote for his six points – not because he favoured the splitting of their cherished homeland into two parts and the setting up of a country whose geopolitical realities would make it a client-state of New Delhi. But who cared for the "silent majority", either in East or West Pakistan? The fate of this country of 120 million people was instead in the hands of the vested interest groups – the Western big business and senior civil servants, who had always dominated the political scene in Pakistan – and two ambitious politicians.

Mujib's negotiating team consisted of the hard-liner in his party, Tajuddin Ahmad, and other top Awami Leaguers – Nazrul Islam, Mustaq Ahmad, Qamaruzzaman, and Mansoor

Ali. The real constitutional expert on Mujib's team was Dr. Kamal Hossain, who became Bangladesh's first Minister of Law and drafted the country's constitution in 1972. A number of Bengali economists were helping the team but they were not participating directly in the dialogues. These economists, aided by some foreign economists financed by the Ford Foundation, were the loudest in making extreme demands, and they were, to a large extent, responsible for the failure of the Dacca dialogue.

Notwithstanding the highly explosive situation outside the President's House at Dacca and the provocative press statements, militant rallies, meetings, etc., the dialogues continued from March 16 to 20 rather quietly, and it caused great surprise in many quarters that there seemed to be some "progress" – although it was hard to believe at that stage that a political settlement could still be reached. The draft proclamation as presented by Yahya was seriously considered. In private discussions, Yahya and Mujib seemed to be nearing a "settlement" – at least, that was my impression in May 1971 reading the minutes of the Dacca dialogues up to March 20. Meanwhile, the leaders of smaller groups from West Pakistan arrived in Dacca to help the success of the talks.

On the evening of March 18, while I was in Karachi in transit to London, I received an unexpected but most pleasant signal from Yahya's offices in Dacca that there were "good prospects" of a political settlement and that the President might need my services in finalizing the agreed constitutional formula. I was, therefore, advised not to leave for London but rather to be prepared to go to Dacca. I could hardly believe in this "green signal" as other developments both inside East Pakistan and outside the country were working against such prospects. All India Radio stepped up its propaganda in favour of Bangladesh. Some of the foreign diplomats were hinting at already established links between Mujib's headquarters in Dacca and the Indian authorities. The Pakistani intelligence services had received many such reports.

By this time Mujib had sized up U.S. policy towards the political situation in Pakistan. As I have already mentioned, the U.S. Consul General in Dacca, Mr. Archer Blood, had given Mujib a false sense of optimism about possible "support" from Washington for his confrontation with the Pakistani central authorities. The U.S. Ambassador, Mr. J. Farland, had a meeting with Mujib in Dacca in March and told him, in unmistakable terms, not to expect any "support" for what the U.S. Government considered an "internal problem of Pakistan". Mujib was bewildered by the U.S. Ambassador's remarks, as the latter told me subsequently in London. Mujib's real sources of support (New Delhi and, via New Delhi, Moscow) were, however, certain.

On March 21 Mr. Bhutto and his aides also arrived in Dacca. Bhutto, who had earlier declined to to to Dacca when Yahya had urged him to talk to Mujib, now suddenly hurried there amid unexpected rumours of a "settlement" between Yahya and Mujib. Bhutto's presence was, no doubt, needed as he was the leader of the majority party in West Pakistan: however, it did not contribute to any settlement but rather created further complications. Bhutto and his aides were given copies of Yahya's constitutional draft proclamation, and raised a number of objections to it. One argument put forward by Bhutto and subsequently echoed by Yahya after the failure of the Dacca dialogue was that if the transfer of power was effected and martial law was lifted without the approval of the National Assembly, it would create a legal vacuum and the proclamation would be "without legal validity". What they conveniently forgot was that when Ayub in 1962 had introduced a constitution and lifted martial law by a proclamation, there had been no question of "legal validity".

Though Mujib was opposed to meeting Bhutto, Yahya was successful in arranging a tripartite conference among them; so the three principal parties (Yahya, Mujib and Bhutto) met on March 22. However, on the day before the proposed meeting a most discouraging development took place. Mujib, accompanied by Tajuddin, on his own initiative sought an unscheduled meeting with Yahya. At that crucial meeting Mujib had Tajuddin inform Yahya that the Awami League could not agree to the setting up of any "central or national cabinet". Instead, it was argued, the Awami League wanted power to be transferred to the two provinces or regions of East and West Pakistan. This meant that they were formally asking for the country to be split into Bangladesh and West Pakistan.

Yahya was completely shocked by this demand to dismember the country, and he pleaded and urged Mujib to reconsider. Yahya reminded Mujib of his pledge to the nation in 1969 that his intent after coming to power would be the transfer of power to the elected representatives of the people and not the dismemberment of the country. Yahya told Mujib in unmistakable terms that he could not preside over the liquidation of his country and that Mujib's threat to the territorial integrity of the country would not remain challenged.

Zero hour was rapidly approaching and the rumours of a settlement that had been circulating in the previous four or five days were fading away. Instead, the grim shadow of civil war loomed near when the tripartite talks began at the President's House on March 22. Bhutto gave the following version of his March 22 meetings with Mujib: "He suggested that I should become the Prime Minister of West Pakistan and he would look after East Pakistan. According to him, this was the only way out of the impasse."[7] Bhutto added that he told Yahya of his reaction to Mujib's proposals: "I could not be a party to the proposed scheme as it inevitably meant two Pakistans."[8] Nobody who cherished any hope of a united Pakistan could agree to Mujib's plan for dividing the country.

According to the minutes of the talks on March 22, no progress was made at all. The Awami League had expressed its unwillingness to accept Yahya's draft proclamation, and promised to prepare a counter draft proclamation, but it was not presented at the meeting on March 22. It seemed that what Mujib proposed to Yahya and Bhutto on March 21 and 22 in private conversations, which amounted to splitting the country, would now be presented in a more subtle document so that the onus for the failure of the Dacca dialogue and its dire consequences would not fall on the Awami Leaguers. So Dr. Kamal Hossain was now engaged with his economic advisers in putting the final touches to the plan for separation in a camouflaged form. The same technique of a veiled scheme of secession, which the constitutional experts and economists of the Awami League had been preparing since 1970, would now be formally announced to the people. Yet even at that stage, they were cautious not to announce formally an unqualified plan for the division of the country. Their technique seemed to be to speak in terms of a "Confederation of Pakistan", rather than the Federal Union which the six points had pledged to the people, while in reality their plan was the division of the country – a plan which both Mujib and the Awami League knew to be unacceptable to the Army, thus making a confrontation inevitable.

March 23

March 23 has for long been a great day for the Muslims of the Indian subcontinent. It was on this day in 1940 that Quaid-i-Azam Mohammed Ali Jinnah, the founder of the future state of Pakistan, proclaimed to the world that the ultimate goal of Muslim nationalists in India was a separate state of their own. On the creation of Pakistan in 1947, March 23 was declared a "national day" and is still observed with due solemnity and dignity just as January 26 is observed in India. But in Dacca on March 23, 1971, it was observed as "Resistance day". No Pakistani flag was allowed to be hoisted, even on public buildings, let alone private houses; the two lonely flags that were hoisted were those at the President's House where Yahya was staying and at the Provincial Government House; of course, it was also flown in the cantonment areas in Dacca. Not only was the Pakistani flag not hoisted, it was everywhere burned and insulted, and the flag of Bangladesh flew everywhere. Mujib took the salute at a march-past composed of Bengali paramilitary units at his residence; the flag of Bangladesh was hoisted with great pomp and grandeur as if the new nation of Bangladesh were already established. Mujib's public statements were equally unfortunate and provocative. At a time when vital negotiations were going on, his actions and speeches only confirmed the fears of those who had earlier expressed doubts that once the election was over, Mujib would establish Bangladesh and not become Prime Minister of Pakistan, even if genuine autonomy on the basis of the six points were granted. March 23, 1971, was a truly tragic day for the history of united Pakistan. When the Chinese and Iranian consulates tried to hoist the Pakistani flag they became targets of mob violence.

Mujib's Final Plan

It was also on March 23, 1971, that Mujib finally provided his own draft constitution, rejecting the one offered by Yahya which granted full autonomy on the basis of the six points minus dismemberment of the country. Mujib's new proposal was presented by Dr. Kamal Hossain to Yahya's aides at 11.45 a.m. at a meeting held at the President's House. This date thus marked the virtual ending of a united Pakistan.

The worst fears about Mujib's six points as well as the doubts about his repeated pledges to modify the plan were now proved to be justified. The text of the new Mujib plan can be studied in the White Paper published by the Government of Pakistan on August 5, 1971. I read the original copy submitted by the Awami League negotiating team on March 23. The text was prepared by Dr. Kamal Hossain and it ran into twenty-six typed pages and had the signatures of the Awami League aides including Tajuddin, who became the Acting Prime Minister of the Bangladesh government in exile set up on Indian territory after the failure of the Dacca dialogue. It began with a preamble and had eighteen articles with many sub-clauses and a lengthy schedule. The plan both dealt with interim arrangements that were demanded immediately and proposed a procedure for framing the "two constitutions" by two sovereign "constitutional conventions" for the so-called "Confederation of Pakistan".

By the interim arrangement, the powers of the central government with regard to the "State of Bangladesh" would be confined to "defence", "foreign affairs excluding foreign trade and aid", currency, and a few peripheral items such as citizenship, public debt of the centre, standards and weights and measures, property of the centre, co-ordination of international and inter-wing communications, etc. The six-point formula of a strictly three-power central government was proposed. As I have already pointed out, Yahya was willing to agree to a central government having only three powers with regard to East Pakistan or Bangladesh. But the real issue was that the Mujib plan gave the centre these three powers on paper only and not in reality.

Let me take each of these items. In all previous constitutions of Pakistan "defence" had been adequately defined so as to cover ancillary powers connected with the defence of the country, such as connected industries, the manufacture of arms, jurisdiction of cantonment areas, etc. But under Mujib's plan, no such powers connected with defence were allowed. The meaning and connotation of defence as given in the Mujib plan were vague and narrow.

More important, while the centre was given the responsibility of "defence", however narrowly and restrictively defined, it was not given any independent financial resources to carry out its responsibilities and obligations. The financial relationship between the centre and Bangladesh as proposed in the Mujib plan was as follows:

> All duties and taxes which were prior to the commencing day (i.e. the day on which the proclamation comes into force) levied and collected within the State of Bangladesh by or under the authority of the Central Legislature shall be collected by the Government of Bangladesh and after adjustment against all Central Government financial allocations to and direct expedition in the State of Bangladesh as provided in the Central budget of 1970–1, the residue remaining shall be made over by the Government of Bangladesh to the Central Government; if upon such adjustment, an amount is found to be due to the State of Bangladesh from the Central Government, the Central Government shall make over such amount to the Government of Bangladesh.

The implications of the proposed financial arrangement were that the central Government would have no power of taxation or any source of revenue. The contribution of Bangladesh to the central Government's expenditures were made uncertain and vague. In fact, while the central Government was denied any financial powers or resources as far as Bangladesh was concerned, it might be liable to pay "dues" to Bangladesh on the basis of the Yahya Government's budget of 1970–1 under which generous allocations had been made for East Pakistan, if the Bangladesh Government should decide that these were due to it from the centre. The Mujib plan seemed to seek both advantages: absolute control over financial resources and at the same time the centre's grant to Bangladesh. Yahya and his aides proposed that either the central Government should retain authority to levy taxes to the extent needed to meet its obligations in defence and foreign affairs, or Bangladesh could levy and collect all taxes, with the centre assured of a "fixed percentage" of contributions towards the central Government's expenditures.[9] But none of these constructive suggestions was acceptable to the Awami League, whose plan was to make the central Government of Pakistan as dependent on Bangladesh in financial matters as the United Nations is dependent on its members for voluntary contributions, though in the case of the U.N. the member-countries' contributions are at least fixed, even though they are voluntary.

Turning to foreign affairs, the Mujib plan made an untenable distinction between the diplomatic and the economic aspects. I have already explained how absurd this distinction was; it meant giving the centre something with one hand and taking it away with the other. In order to assure the Awami Leaguers that the Bengalis would no longer be subject to any control from the central authority in their economic and financial matters, including foreign aid and foreign trade, Yahya proposed that foreign trade and aid should be negotiated by the centre for the whole country but with a constitutional guarantee for "a predetermined share in percentages for Bangladesh on the basis of population or for some years even a higher figure". Once the aid had been negotiated by the central Government, including representatives from Bangladesh, the Government of Bangladesh would be free to negotiate projects "directly, on the basis of its predetermined share, with the foreign countries and international agencies like the World Bank".[10] It was further proposed by Yahya and his negotiating team that both the posts of Minister and Secretary for the portfolio of External Trade and Aid would be in the hands of the Bengalis for the next five to ten years, so as to mollify the Bengali fears that their economic rights and interests were not being properly safeguarded.[11] Again, none of these proposals was acceptable to the Awami Leaguers: if they were as interested in regional autonomy as they claimed ever since Yahya's formulation of his plan for the transfer of power in 1969, there was no reason why these suggestions should not have been accepted. Their personal attitude during the Dacca dialogue was adamantly unresponsive to any suggestion regarding the modification of their plan.

The Mujib plan placed inter-wing trade, i.e. the trade between East and West Pakistan, on the same level as foreign trade. Within "one country" the two regions would have trade transactions as if they were two separate countries. This too was untenable. The Yahya team suggested that while Bangladesh should be the master of its economic policies and programme, there should at least be some inter-wing council for any common matters relating to the economy of the country as a whole; but nothing of this sort was acceptable to the Awami League. Regional trade under the Mujib plan would be transacted, if at all, in the same manner as foreign trade; Bangladesh and West Pakistan would have separate barter deals and trade agreements with foreign countries as well as between themselves, if they so wished. Thus under the Mujib plan Bangladesh might have closer trade and economic relations with India, for instance, than with the other unit of the so-called "Confederation of Pakistan". Similarly, Bangladesh and West Pakistan would have the power to borrow abroad independently of any control by or even co-ordination with the national Government. When Yahya and his team pointed out that the charter of an international organization like the World Bank provides that it can only lend on the guarantee of a member country and not of its constituent units, the Awami Leaguers replied: "We are quite competent to look after our economic policies and problems."[12]

The Mujib plan demanded complete separation of economic planning. This had been accepted by Yahya long before: when he asked me to prepare a formula for the relationship between the centre and the provinces, it was already conceded that East Pakistan would have absolute and unfettered control over its economic planning. What was significant was that even in a confederation there are provisions for co-ordination and co-operation among the units in economic matters, but the Awami League would have no such provisions even for voluntary co-operation or co-ordination such as exists, for instance, between Pakistan, Iran and Turkey under their Regional Co-operation for Development (RCD) Plan.

The Mujib plan also demanded a separate central bank

for Bangladesh – the "Reserve Bank of Bangladesh". Under Article 16 of the Mujib plan, "the State Bank of Pakistan at Dacca shall be redesignated as the Reserve Bank of Bangladesh, and all branches of the State Bank of Pakistan in Bangladesh shall become branches of the Reserve Bank of Bangladesh. . . . The Reserve Bank of Bangladesh and its branches shall be under the legislative control of the State Legislature of Bangladesh."[13] The proposal for an entirely independent central bank for Bangladesh had far-reaching implications, as it would unmistakably mark the separate entity of the state of Bangladesh from the rest of Pakistan.

In fact, the Mujib plan, as given to Yahya on March 23, with Tajuddin's demand that it be issued in the form of a proclamation "within forty-eight hours",[14] was nothing but an unqualified scheme for splitting the country into two separate entities, Bangladesh and West Pakistan. History has not yet furnished an example of a form of government – federal or confederal – where a central authority can discharge its fundamental obligations to protect the territorial integrity or carry on its normal duties as in the plan presented by Mujib. Under his plan, the central authority would have had no independent financial resources, either direct taxation or a guaranteed financial contribution from the units; no effective control over foreign affairs because of the artificial and absurd distinction between the economic and political aspects of external relations. The central authority would also have had no control over the country's monetary policy, banking, foreign trade, external borrowings, fiscal policy or – for that matter – in any important sphere.

The Mujib plan for the interim government demanded the full implementation of the secession scheme, which had always been veiled in his six points. Now, contrary to the pledges he had made not only to Yahya but also to the Bengalis during the 1970 elections, Mujib proceeded to divide the country under a deceptive plan for the "Confederation of Pakistan", which would not have been workable even for a day. Yahya was not wrong when he remarked that "through this plan they expected to establish a separate state of Bangladesh. That, needless to say, would have been the end of Pakistan as created by the Father of the Nation."[15] But Yahya failed to see that when he made these remarks on June 28, 1971, Pakistan as it had been established in 1947 was already dead.

Turning to the process of drawing up the constitution for the so-called "Confederation of Pakistan", the Mujib plan would have split the National Assembly as elected in December 1970 for the country as a whole into two separate "constituent conventions", just as the original Constituent Assembly of India had been divided into two assemblies under the Mountbatten plan of June 3, 1947, when the British Government, the Congress, and the Muslim League jointly agreed to the partition of India. The two constituent conventions – one for Bangladesh and the other for West Pakistan – would be free to frame any form of constitution, acting as two sovereign bodies. The five principles which were spelled out in the Legal Framework Order of 1970, in consultation with and with the approval of Mujib, as the basic and minimum requirements of a united Pakistan would no longer be binding on the two constituent conventions. Under the Mujib plan, the President would be required to authenticate the proposed constitution as framed by the two constituent conventions, no matter whether the proposed constitution divided the country or not. Under Article 17, sub-clause 7, of the Mujib plan, it was laid down that even if the President would not sign or authenticate the proposed constitution, "in any event upon the expiration of seven days" from the date of such presentation of the constitution, it "shall be deemed to have been authenticated".[16] The members of the National Assembly who were elected under the Legal Framework Order of 1970 were required to take an oath of allegiance to Pakistan: "I . . . do hereby swear (or affirm) that I will keep true faith and allegiance to Pakistan."[17] Even this was not acceptable to Mujib. His plan demanded that members of the two constituent conventions take an oath in the following form: "I, A. B., do solemnly swear/affirm that I will be faithful and keep true allegiance to the constitution of Pakistan as by law established."[18] This was also significant in understanding the *modus operandi* of Mujib and his advisers; they were not even prepared to pay allegiance to Pakistan. This demonstrated clearly that the Awami League did not believe in the unity of Pakistan, although Mujib told the Muslim voters in 1970 that he would never destroy Pakistan: "Pakistan has come to stay."[19]

There was a final meeting between Yahya's team and the Awami Leaguers on March 24 at 6 p.m., but no further meeting took place between Yahya and Mujib after their meeting on March 22. In fact, March 23 virtually marked the end of the Dacca dialogues and also of united Pakistan. After the incidents of March 23, when the Awami Leaguers did not even allow the Pakistani flag to fly on the National Day, and after the Awami League presented its final plan, the Army decided to take military action to challenge Mujib and plunge the country into a most tragic civil war, which I shall describe in the next chapter.

In the meantime, all West Pakistani leaders not belonging to Bhutto's party had meetings with Mujib and tried to persude him to avoid the path of confrontation, but without success. They also met Yahya; Bhutto and his team had meetings with him on March 24. By that time, they could only discuss the post mortem of the Dacca dialogues.

Outside the President's House at Dacca, the movement for Bangladesh was going full steam ahead. Mujib and Tajuddin made declarations to the effect that they had nothing new to announce. Mujib said on March 24: "Our demands are just and clear and they have to be accepted." He warned against any attempt to impose a decision on the people of Bangladesh, saying that "we would not tolerate it".[20] In a subsequent press statement on March 25, Mujib called for a general strike on March 27 against the Army's actions in certain places in East Pakistan or Bangladesh. This was his last press statement before the Army began its military operations on the night of March 25–26, which ended in the formal dismembering of Pakistan on December 16, 1971, when Dacca fell to the Indian Army.

Yahya left Dacca at an undisclosed hour sometime on March 25. The Pakistan Government in its White Paper gave details of what it termed as "an armed rebellion" to be launched in the early hours of March 26. Nobody can vouch for the authenticity of the account given in the White Paper; in many quarters it was interpreted as a justification for the military measures taken by the Pakistani Army at midnight on March 25. One might not believe the details of the so-called "operational plan" as given in the White Paper; there were obviously some exaggerations. But it was obvious from the stiff resistance faced by the Pakistani Army when it launched its military operation that some sort of resistance plan had been organized by the Awami League with the help of the East Bengal Regiment, the East Pakistani Rifles, and the police forces in East Pakistan. In fact, the major part of East Pakistan or Bangladesh was under the control of "rebel" or "liberation" forces throughout the month of April and in some areas in early May, so that the Pakistani Army "occupied" or "liberated" the various areas under the control of opposition forces. Obviously such resistance could not have been spontaneous or unorganized.

Thus it was evident, as pointed out already, that both sides, while engaged in political dialogue, were simultaneously preparing for the fatal confrontation.

REFERENCES

1. *Bangladesh Documents*, op. cit., vol. I, pp. 247–8.
2. Two years after the creation of Bangladesh, my foreign friend showed me his report, "Notes on Events in East Pakistan, March 2–16, 1971", sent from Dacca on March 5, 1971.
3. *Bangladesh Documents*, op. cit., vol. I, p. 234.
4. *The White Paper on the Crisis of East Pakistan* (Islamabad), Government of Pakistan, August 5, 1971, pp. 39–60.
5. Ibid., pp. 19–20.
6. Fazal Muqueem Khan, *The Story of the Pakistan Army*, Karachi, 1963, p. 63.
7. Z. A. Bhutto, *The Great Tragedy*, op. cit., p. 43.
8. Ibid., p. 45.
9. Based on the unpublished minutes of the Dacca dialogues in March 1971.
10. Ibid.
11. Ibid.
12. Ibid.
13. See the text of the Mujib plan in the White Paper, op. cit., pp. 47–59.
14. Based on unpublished minutes of the Dacca dialogues in March 1971.
15. See the text of Yahya's speech on June 28, 1971, in *Dawn*, June 29, 1971.
16. See the text of the Mujib plan in the White Paper, op. cit.
17. See the Legal Framework Order, 1970, op. cit., p. 8.
18. See the text of the Mujib plan in the White Paper, op. cit.
19. See Mujib's election speeches in *Bangladesh Documents*, op. cit., Vol. I., pp. 82–7 and pp. 95–127.
20. Ibid., p. 266.

8

THE CIVIL WAR

The Dacca dialogues had failed. For this the Pakistan Government headed by Yahya and Bhutto and his party put the entire blame on Mujib. Yahya denounced Mujib as a "traitor" and banned the Awami League. In a broadcast he said: "The proclamation that he [Mujib] proposed was nothing but a trap. He knew that it would not have been worth the paper it was written on. . . . . His obstinacy, obduracy and absolute refusal to talk sense can lead to but one conclusion – the man and his party are enemies of Pakistan and they want East Pakistan to break away completely from the country. He has attacked the solidarity and integrity of this country – this crime will not go unpunished."[1] Tajuddin Ahmad, Acting Prime Minister of the Bangladesh government-in-exile in India, on the other hand stated: "It is now clear that Yahya and his generals never had the slightest intention of solving Pakistan's political crisis but were only interested in buying time to permit the reinforcement of their military machine within Bangladesh. Yahya's visit to Dacca was a mere cover for his plan of genocide. . . . In an act of treachery unparalleled in contemporary history a programme of calculated genocide was unleashed on the peaceful and unsuspecting population of Dacca by midnight of 25 March."[2] The third party to the talks, Z. A. Bhutto, wrote: "Foreign pressure was partly responsible for the position eventually taken by him [Mujib]. It seems that India wanted him to call the Army's bluff and strike before it was too late. Perhaps India was getting worried about the turns of events . . . desperately wanted Mujibur Rahman to wrench Bangladesh out of Pakistan . . . or did India have an inkling of new initiatives in Sino-American relations?"[3] None of these three statements is wholly true, but they cannot be dismissed altogether. None of the three parties could be totally exonerated for their part in the failure of the Dacca dialogues. The post mortem on Pakistan began long ago[4] and many interpretations have already been offered for the failure of the Dacca dialogues. The process of retrospection may well continue for many years to come.

But one thing is certain. The Pakistan Army's brutal actions, which began on the midnight of March 25, 1971, can never be condoned or justified in any way. The Army's murderous campaign in which many thousands of innocent people including women, the old and sick, and even children, were brutally murdered while millions fled from their homes to take shelter either in remote places or in India, constituted a measureless tragedy. The miscalculation on which it was based is beyond understanding, just as the results in human suffering were beyond description.

The exact figures of death and destruction will probably never be known accurately – Mujib has talked of "three million killed", while the Pakistan Government tried to estimate the figures in thousands only. But Mujib was right when he said that few nations had had to make such colossal sacrifices in human life and suffering as the Bengalis in "an epic liberation struggle" – though he himself had no part in the sufferings; he made a cowardly surrender to the Army, leaving the people to their terrible fate.

Unlike some other tragedies in Afro-Asian countries, the Bangladesh tragedy was given the publicity it deserved which went a long way to arouse world-wide sympathy and support for the suffering people of Bangladesh. The whole world was shocked by the Pakistan Army's brutal assault. The foreign press, particularly in the United Kingdom and the United States, did a service to humanity by giving prominence to the atrocities perpetrated on the Bengalis.

What factors compelled the Pakistan generals to embark on such a suicidal course? There was, undoubtedly, a serious threat to the territorial integrity of the country – not least from outside forces. But was the course adopted by the Pakistan Army appropriate – not to speak of justice or moral issues – to "protect the territorial integrity of the country"? The Army could have punished the leaders and groups of people who might have been guilty of attempting to bring about the armed secession of East Pakistan with the help of a hostile neighbour. But could there be any justification or rationale for the killing of thousands of innocent villagers who had not the slightest idea of the issues involved in the political dialogues, either before or after the elections in December 1971? These people had neither wanted secession nor been a party to any conspiracy. Why were children killed in the presence of their parents and women raped in the presence of fathers or husbands? Villages were burnt wholesale as a part of what was termed by the military Governor, Tikka Khan "butcher of the Bengalis" and as such destroyer of Pakistan – as part of a policy of collective punitive measures. The most pertinent question is whether the Pakistan Army would have taken such cruel measures *in West Pakistan* if Bhutto had taken the same position as Mujib on March 23, 1971. Had not Bhutto been largely responsible for the deadlock in the political negotiations after the election by forcing the adjournment of the national assembly scheduled to meet on March 3, 1971? Why then did Bhutto's actions remain unpunished? Was it due to the fact that he represented the recruiting areas of the Pakistan Army and received the votes of the *jawans* in the 1970 election? Did not the Pakistan Army's action betray a deep-rooted ethnic

hatred on the part of the Punjabis against the Bengalis? In any case the Pakistan Army, which had been maintained at a high cost by the people of Pakistan including the Bengalis to defend their homeland, fell stupidly into the deep conspiracy hatched by both internal and external forces to finish off Pakistan as a united country. Not even the most militant member of the Indian Hindu Mahasabha, or any other Indian elements which always preached the gospel of *Akhand Bharat* (united India) and the undoing of the 1947 partition, could have done the job of finishing united Pakistan as quickly as the actions of the Pakistan Army while trying to protect the country's territorial integrity. Could there have been greater folly or miscalculation?

On March 29, before I left Karachi for London with my family, I sought and had a meeting with Yahya. I asked him why he had resorted to such measures after two years of what I still believe to be sincere and honest efforts to transfer power to the elected representatives of the people. He gave me his version of the Dacca dialogues, which was the same as was given in his speech of March 26. After listening carefully to his account I further asked him why he had not resigned when his plan for the transfer of power had proved a failure, just as Ayub quitted when his constitution and Basic Democracies had also proved failures? Yahya gave a lengthy reply saying that the two situations were not similar; in March 1969 when Ayub resigned there was no threat to the existence of the country, while in March 1971 when Yahya ordered the Army action in East Pakistan, he, according to his interpretation, was carrying out his obligations not only as President of the country and also as chief of the armed forces. He reminded me of his oath of office to protect the country's independence and territorial integrity. Legally his argument may have been valid but morally it was not.

I further asked Yahya why he did not call for a referendum when the political talks failed, and why he had not taken the Bengalis into his confidence and told them the whole truth. As already mentioned, I suggested a referendum in August – September 1970. Yahya's answers were incoherent and vague. I realized that he had lost the control over the decision-making process. From March 15 to 22 the Army, as a member of the Dipomatic Corps stationed in Dacca wrote in his notes, was willing to make big concessions to Mujib and virtually to accept his six-point plan, but when Yahya's own draft constitutional formula failed to get Mujib's approval and Mujib presented his separation plan on March 23, Yahya lost all his initiative and so on March 24 the generals decided to take action. Only the exact hour of their operation was yet to be fixed.

From Ballot to Bullet

General Tikka, who became Commander-in-Chief of the "New" Pakistan under Bhutto, was appointed to carry out the military operations in East Bengal. In an unpublished interview with the influential Egyptian journalist Muhammad Hasanain Haykal, Tikka summed the military situation in East Bengal when he arrived in Dacca in the first week of March 1971:

> When I turned to the military aspect, I found we were like blind men in the Eastern region [Bangladesh]. The officials of the special branch, the police and the intelligence came to tell me that the people refused to co-operate or give information to their men. We were in complete darkness regarding what was happening except where we had troops. This was intolerable. It has never occurred before and it is impermissible. . . . This man [Mujib] incited mutiny and a boycott of my troops.[6]

Tikka, as Haykal rightly pointed out, did not know that he was facing an all-out popular revolution. He did not know that this revolution arose from deep-rooted national aspirations which were supported by good reasons. Tikka then narrated how the political negotiations had not led to any result and he was ordered by Yahya on March 24 to be prepared to impose security and order – "I received the order to intervene on March 24 on the understanding that I would begin action at dawn on March 25."[7]

The whole population of Dacca was awakened at 1.30 a.m. on March 26 by massive machine-gun firing. Dacca University and the headquarters of the police in Motijeel and of the East Pakistan Rifles in Pilkanna were the major areas from which machine-gun fire was heard; heavy explosions were frequent and it appeared that 105-mm. recoil less rifles were being used. Flares were also being fired and large fires were burning in many parts of the city. Iqbal and Jaganath Halls – the two largest dormitories of Dacca University – were almost completely gutted and many students were killed. The East Pakistan Rifles and the police put up a brave resistance though they were overwhelmed by the Army's massive use of guns and tanks. The official historian of the Pakistan Army, Major-General (retd.) Fazal Muqeem Khan, described with apparent pride the "heroic" performances of the Pakistan Army when, at midnight on March 25–26 "after due warning [which is not correct], the army had to use rocket launchers to break open some rooms of the halls [Dacca University]. From the sound of fire during that fateful night in Dacca, it appeared as if there was *an actual war on with modern weapons*" [my italics].[8] This was not an "exaggerated account" by foreign correspondents who, according to a so-called "liberal" West Pakistani author, "were fed" by the Indians with the "wildest of stories about 'genocide' and 'pogrom' ".[9] All foreign correspondents in Dacca were forced to leave and were taken by the Army to the airport in an undignified manner, searched thoroughly and put on a plane. Three correspondents, however, were left behind inadvertently – Arnold Zeitlin, Michel Laurent and Simon Dring. They were the first to carry the stories of the Army's operation in Dacca on the midnight of March 25–26. One of them, Simon Dring of *The Daily Telegraph*, published an account entitled "How Dacca paid for a united Pakistan", one of the earliest stories to be published in the Western press—March 30, 1971. His accounts of the Army's raid on the campus of Dacca University was vivid and shocking:

> Led by the American-supplied M-24 World War II tanks, one column of troops sped to Dacca University shortly after midnight. Troops took over the British Council library (situated within the campus) and used it as a fire base from which to shell nearby dormitory areas. Caught completely by surprise, some 200 students were killed in Iqbal Hall, headquarters of the militant anti-government students' union, I was told. Two days later bodies were still smouldering in burnt out rooms, others were scattered outside, more floated in a nearby lake. . . . At another hall, reportedly, soldiers buried the dead in a hastily dug mass grave which was then bull-dozed over by tanks. People living near the University were caught in the fire too, and 200 yards of shanty houses running alongside a railway line were destroyed.[10]

There were many such accounts either from eye-witnesses or persons whose integrity could not be challenged. An authentic report was given by Mr. Hendrick van der Heijden, a member of the International Bank for Reconstruction and Development mission that visited East Bengal in June 1971. The report was obtained by *The New York Times* and reproduced in *The Times* of London on July 14, 1971. This report and *The Times*' editorial comments on it on the same day deserve the attention of anyone who wishes to appreciate the magnitude of the Army's atrocities in East Bengal during the civil war.

After the dreadful night of March 25–26, the curfew was lifted on March 27 for three hours from 9 a.m. until noon.

Thousands of people were now streaming across the open fields to take shelter in remote places, and even as they fled the Army did not hesitate to kill them. At noon there was again firing from machine-guns on the ground and from many C-130s and circling aircraft and helicopters, the aim being to create a general panic among the whole population.

The Resistance

While the Army was successful in bringing the peace of the graveyard to Dacca city, its position in the rest of East Bengal was untenable. Its situation was most desperate in the major seaport of East Bengal, Chittagong, where the second-in-command of the East Bengal Regiment, Major Ziaur Rahman, after killing the West Pakistani commanding officer, announced the formation of the provisional government of Bangladesh from Chittagong Radio Station on March 26. The Bangladesh Government, however, says now that Mujib, before his arrest, had made a declaration of independence at midnight on March 25. It was as follows: "This may be my last message. From today Bangladesh is independent. I call upon the people of Bangladesh, wherever you might be and with whatever you have, to resist the army of occupation to the last. Your fight must go on until the last soldier of the Pakistan occupation army is expelled from the soil of Bangladesh and final victory is achieved."[11] Yet another declaration of independence was issued by Tajuddin Ahmad, Prime Minister of the exile government in India, on April 17, 1971, when after proclaiming Bangladesh as a sovereign Republic, he said: "Pakistan is now dead and buried under a mountain of corpses."[12] From all the available evidence it appears that Mujib never made any proclamation of independence; it was Major Ziaur Rahman who acted on his own initiative and was the first to announce it from Chittagong Radio Station at midnight on March 25–26. The "mutiny" of the East Pakistan Rifles and the police, and particularly of the East Bengal Regiment, "came as a great shock",[13] as Fazal Muqueem says, but how could one expect the Bengali personnel of the armed forces, the paramilitary force and the police to be passive spectators while their own people were being massacred?

The so-called "mutiny" was a natural consequence of the Army's operations. It is, however, correct to say that just as the Army was preparing for confrontation, so also the Bengali armed personnel were preparing on the lines of their contingency plan under the command of Colonel Osmani, who later became commander-in-chief of the resistance forces – the *Mukti Bahini* or liberation army. It was not until the end of April that the Pakistan Army was able to regain control of the various districts and areas of East Bengal. By May 1971 the Army had apparently crushed the movement, although the Army's situation was never stable or secure.

Indian Involvement

After this apparent defeat, the Bengali resistance forces then crossed over to India, where they could obtain arms and ammunition as well as sanctuary – the Pakistan Army would not dare to cross the Indian border, and thus giving sanctuary to the *Mukti Bahini* was the first significant move by India in her involvement in the crisis. Without India's arms and sanctuary, Bangladesh might have remained a distant dream of the Bengali nationalists for many years to come. Just as the Pakistan Army's brutal atrocities can never be condoned, similarly India's role, which I discuss in the next chapter, was contrary to all the basic principles of the U.N. Charter and international law.

Turning to the internal scene in the emerging Bangladesh and West Pakistan, the temporary "victory" by the Pakistan Army over the Bengali resistance forces gave the military junta in Islamabad a sense of optimism. But instead of using the time gained for developing a constructive and imaginative approach to the crisis, the Army generals in West Pakistan allowed themselves to be fooled. The military régime imposed a strict censorship of all news about "East Pakistan". Not only the public in West Pakistan but even the ruling élite seemed to believe that the uprising in East Bengal was merely the product of "Indian agents" and a few "miscreants". It was widely believed in West Pakistan that the *people* of "East Pakistan" were not behind the movement. Of course, the Bengali Muslims, as I have already pointed out, did not like to see Pakistan destroyed,

ticularly by the Indian forces. But the Army's atrocities t the Bengalis – whether Awami Leaguers or nationalists – with no choice. The Army's actions, particularly Tikka's and subsequently Niazi's policy of "collective punitive actions", under which village after village was burnt and destroyed, turned the entire population of East Bengal against the Pakistan Government. It was therefore no wonder that people in such a desperate situation were prepared to embrace even the devil to escape from total annihilation. Nothing could be further from the truth than Fazal Muqueem's statement: "The Muslim population, particularly in the rural areas, had welcomed the troops and were coming forward in large numbers to help them."[14] In fact, the people were living in dread – their young men's lives were not secure and their women were not safe. How could they welcome the troops who were intent on subjugating them?

May–July 1971

"The revolt in East Pakistan had been completely crushed by the end of May."[15] Thus asserted Fazal Muqueem, and all the publicity organs of the Government of Pakistan began to tell the same story. The White Paper published by the Pakistan Government in August 1971 contained false assertions to the same effect. But those living outside the jurisdiction of the "iron curtain" imposed by the Pakistan Government's press censorship had no illusion about the real situation. The Bangladesh crisis was deepening and becoming more complex, due both to the Army's continued atrocities and to the lack of any positive steps by the Pakistani Government, and indeed to India's growing involvement in the crisis.

I had left Pakistan within a week of the Army's military action and came with my family to London to begin a research assignment at Chatham House. However, no Bengali at that time could have concentrated his full attention on research. My family and I spent most of our time reading the British newspapers and listening to the news on radio and television. It was the most agonizing period of my life – Bengalis were being killed mercilessly; Pakistan was nearing its destruction, which meant too that the Indians were nearing the realization of their long-cherished dream. In a letter on April 13 from London, I wrote to Yahya urging him passionately to stop the forces of terror and destruction let loose by the Army's action. His reply was, in a sense, pathetic; he repeated what he had told me at our farewell meeting in Karachi on March 29. He now seemed to have realized Bhutto's insincerity but he had never been a serious administrator, and he now seemed to have lost all control. Among the large community of Asian immigrants in London, there were all sorts of stories and rumours. At one stage, it was circulated there that the generals had realized the futility of their military adventures in East Pakistan. The number of Pakistani soldiers, including officers, killed in the military operations in East Bengal was rising; Pakistan's economic situation was desperate. All foreign loans and aid for development had been stopped. The United States had announced a ban on military supplies to Pakistan, only those items "already in the pipeline" being allowed. Any sensible régime would have tried seriously to get out of the impasse; it was difficult for me to believe that the junta had not yet realized the blind alley into which their military operations had led them. Was there nobody in West Pakistan to see and tell them the truth?

In the latter part of May I decided to go to both West Pakistan and Dacca to see the situation for myself. In the preceding two years, from April 1969 to February 1971, I had been an active participant in the political process in Pakistan; it was thus almost impossible for me to be in London while my country was disintegrating; near relations and dear friends were involved. So I decided to make the trip although it caused unjustified comments in certain quarters that I was still involved in Pakistan's quest for a constitution. First, no political realist could expect a "constitutional formula" for both East and West Pakistan in the summer of 1971. Secondly, I had already declined Yahya's invitation to become an adviser, and accepted an academic assignment in London. My trip was solely to watch the latest developments both in West Pakistan and in Dacca. I had no illusions about the situation; the Pakistan press censorship had not been able to reach me in London.

I landed at Karachi on May 16. Yahya was there on a tour,

so I met him the next day. I told him my reaction to the Army's atrocities. He tried to convince me, at one stage, that all that I had read in the British and American newspapers was incorrect but I told him that I was going to Dacca to see the real situation for myself. I asked him why, as President of the country, he never cared to visit "East Pakistan" after a situation had developed which was causing worldwide concern; he replied that he would visit Dacca as soon as he could finalize "a programme to offer the Bengalis". It was truly a pity that the country's President could not even now make up his mind about the "next steps".

I went to Dacca, and it was the worst experience of my life. Everywhere I went, I heard the same story: one person had lost a son; another a husband; many villages were burnt. The people who did not agree with Mujib's secession plan told how they too had been victims of indiscriminate and stupid acts by the Army. Many people, including my close relatives and friends, could hardly express themselves without tears in their eyes. They urged me to tell Yahya to come to Dacca and to see for himself the damage his Army had done. They repeatedly asked me: "Is there no way for our survival?" They knew of my close involvement with political developments from April/May 1969 and that I had been close to Yahya while he was formulating his plan for the transfer of power. But what answer could I give? I returned from Dacca bewildered and with a heavy heart. I wrote a lengthy report giving authentic accounts of the many cruel acts of the Army including the raping of women.

My next meeting with Yahya took place in Rawalpindi – in the same house and in the same room where I had spent many hours with him in 1969–70 with great expectations of a political solution to the growing East–West Pakistan conflict. Yahya's first question was what I had seen in Dacca. My prompt reply was that no single foreign newspaper had exaggerated. On the contrary, the people's agony, suffering and humiliation had not been fully exposed. I also told him that it was not only the number of deaths but the manner in which innocent persons had been killed and women raped that had destroyed our cherished homeland for which the Muslims of the subcontinent had sacrified so many thousands of lives in 1947. I knew from past experience that it was no use giving Yahya a lengthy report such as I had prepared while in Dacca. So I begn to read extracts from my notes – all factual data. He looked vacant and seemed unable to talk to me. He knew my devotion to the concept of a united Pakistan and he also knew that I had never supported Mujib's veiled secessionist plan. He could not, therefore, dismiss my account as that of a "typical secessionist under the influence of India" – the last thing I wanted to see was the destruction of Pakistan with the help of the Indian armed forces. Our meeting ended in a confused way. Yahya asked me to see him again before I returned to London.

Then I began a round of visits to a number of other members of the ruling élite. It was a shocking experience to see their attitude: "The rebels must be crushed; then we can talk of any political settlement." It was also agonizing for me to see the calmness of life in the federal capital as if nothing had happened. There was only concern over India's involvement in the crisis but none for the suffering humanity in East Pakistan.

It is, however, true that some of the Army officers who had been in East Bengal from March 25 or had taken part in the military operations seemed to realize that Pakistan was finished. They also were aware of India's growing involvement. Some of the "fat" generals holding high positions in the administration, who had been accustomed to a life of luxury since the country's first military coup in 1958, seemed to be completely out of contact with the military aspects of the situation. They professed "confidence" in facing simultaneously both the Indian threat and the secessionist challenge from East Bengal. This group of seemingly degenerate generals thought they had crushed the national uprising in Bangladesh. They did not or could not fully realize the international implications of the crisis, particularly the direct involvement of India and indirect involvement of the Soviet Union. A group of the junta headed by Hamid, Peerzada and Omar, thought that the problems of "East Pakistan" had been solved for ever by force. So why make any more concessions to the Bengalis? Justice Cornelius was asked to prepare a constitution giving "autonomy" to East Pakistan but "within limits", so that in future there might not be any repetition of Yahya's mistakes of 1969–70, when Mujib was assured, according to the opinion of this group, an "undue quantum of autonomy" bordering on secession. So the constitutional draft prepared by the Cornelius committee, which used to meet under the chairmanship of the Rasputin of the régime, Peerzada, was worse than Ayub's constitution of 1962.

Before I left Islamabad for London, I had my third meeting with Yahya and asked him bluntly if he shared the views of some of his generals, who seemed to think that the crisis was over and that the constitution being prepared by Cornelius would be acceptable to the Bengalis, when they had already opted for independence. This time, Yahya told me his views frankly. The Cornelius constitution, he revealed to me, was being prepared to deal with Bhutto who had been demanding that his party should be given effective power, being the second largest group in the national assembly – the largest party, the Awami League, having been outlawed. Yahya was not willing to yield to Bhutto's pressure, as to do so would constitute another provocation to the Bengalis by giving power to a party which had not even dared to put up a candidate in East Pakistan in the 1970 election. Moreover, Bhutto was the most hated person in East Bengal as the Bengalis believed, not without justification, that he, in collaboration with the hawkish generals, had precipated the crisis. Yet Yahya could not challenge Bhutto, who now began to behave as if he were already the country's Prime Minister; furthermore, a number of generals like Peerzada, Gul Hasan and Omar were in league with Bhutto. Yahya showed me his correspondence with Nixon and the Chinese leaders, who were keenly hoping that a political settlement with the Bengalis might be possible on the basis of a "brotherly parting of the ways" if no solution that involved living together with the West Pakistanis were acceptable to them. I came away from my third meeting with Yahya with the impression that the initiative was no longer in his hands or even within the control of the Pakistan Government. Outside forces were determining the final course of events. Yahya had not yet realized the full implications of the grave international factors connected with the Bangladesh crisis. And up till June 1971 the Pakistani ruling élite was unable to grasp the full implications of the civil war, and "to count", as Haykal put it, "without mistake all the parties participating in the struggle over Bangladesh, their aims and their ability to intervene in this struggle. . . . The Pakistani régime could not see beyond its feet. This was one of the main causes of the tragedy."[16] This was a correct assessment of the Pakistani régime caught in a desperately dangerous civil war.

I returned to London in June with no clear idea as to how the crisis would be solved. In Dacca the situation was desperate; the people could never be sure that they would live through the next twenty-four hours – a reign of terror prevailed everywhere. East Bengal seemed on the verge of total collapse, while in West Pakistan the ruling élite still lived in a world of illusion, talking of "granting autonomy" to the Bengalis – now the autonomy was trimmed down from "maximum" to "reasonable".

Soon, in July–August 1971, the situation was to take a dramatic turn and the sense of "victory" among the Pakistani generals vanished. Grim realities seemed to have prevailed.

Towards the Final Phase

Fears were expressed that during the rainy months of the monsoon period (June–July), the Pakistan Army would be unable to face the challenge of the resistance forces, who were now getting better equipment and training in India. But the Pakistan Army, against heavy odds, brought the situation under control by July. The *Mukti Bahini* (Liberation forces) were almost eliminated.

But once the monsoon season was over and the failure of the *Mukti Bahini* was evident to the Indian authorities, the Indian Government, which had now prepared new excuses for interfering in the crisis because of the influx of refugees from East Bengal, was planning direct military involvement. The Indian Government had been fighting the Bangladesh war by proxy from the beginning. But it was now realized that the *Mukti Bahini* could not deliver the goods, no matter how much indirect help and assistance the Indian Government might give. The influx into India of refugees, mostly Hindus – the exact number of refugees was never known: India claimed "ten million" while Pakistan gave a figure of two million, both of which were incorrect – provided the Indian Government with a "strong argument" to take "some actions" to solve the crisis. India seemed to have only one solution: the total humiliation of Pakistan through the dismemberment of the country.

By July the Pakistan Government had received reliable reports from a friendly great power to the effect that the Indians had begun to prepare for a military confrontation.[17] The most immediate factor was Henry Kissinger's secret trip to Peking via Rawalpindi. Further, Kissinger was reported to have told the Indian ambassador in Washington after his visit to Peking that China would "intervene" if India attacked Pakistan, and the United States might not come to India's help as it had done in 1962 and 1965, when it had warned China against intervention.[18] This caused consternation in India, as her plan to dismember Pakistan by direct military intervention was placed in grave danger by the so-called "Sino-U.S. detente". Sirir Gupta of Nehru University, New Delhi, wrote: "However great the reluctance of the Indian optimists to admit it, the fact is that the Sino-U.S. *rapprochement* has altered the international context in which India has to conduct its local struggles and that on the specific issue of Bangladesh, the entire weight of this development can be thrown against our country."[19]

This led India to sign the treaty with the Soviet Union which had been in preparation for more than two years – since Brezhnev had spelt out his scheme for a collective Asian security system. Though termed the treaty of "peace, friendship and co-operation", a closer scrutiny of the text leaves no doubt as to its military emphasis – it was a disguised military pact. Once the Indians got the umbrella of protection by a super-power against any potential Chinese threat in her military adventures against Pakistan to "solve" the Bangladesh crisis, their war preparations began in earnest. Simultaneously the trained Indians joined the *Mukti Bahini* in military operations in East Bengal. The destruction of bridges and sinking of Pakistani ships at the port of Chittagong could not have been done by the inexperienced *Mukti Bahini*. There was evidence of growing involvement by trained personnel of the Indian armed forces in these destructive activities in East Bengal.

What was the reaction in Rawalpindi to the growing Indian involvement? There were reports, some based on sources which could hardly be disregarded, that the military régime in Pakistan had now realized the futility of their military actions in East Bengal and were genuinely worried about an immediate Indo-Pakistan war in which Pakistan was bound to lose – first, because of the military balance of power in the subcontinent, and secondly due to the Russians' palpable backing of India. Further, as a result of the Indo-Soviet treaty, the hope of help from Peking was also becoming uncertain, though Yahya and the junta expected it from both Peking and Washington. At all events, the gravity of the situation was now fully realized.

In the meantime, President Nixon and the Chinese Government advised Yahya to find a political solution to the crisis. The White House, with the assistance of Senator Barry Goldwater, revealed subsequently what the United States had been doing privately over the nine months of civil war in Pakistan to solve the crisis by means of a political settlement, rather than by military operations. A "background" news conference with Henry Kissinger on December 7, 1971, which Goldwater put into the Congressional Record on December 9, established that the U.S. Government had been working "to induce political compromise in Pakistan and military restraint in India".[20]

Before I discuss the Nixon plan for the solution of the Bangladesh crisis and Yahya's willingness to accept it, let me turn to a number of developments. As the situation for Pakistan worsened, the political scene in Rawalpindi became more and more confused. In August I received an authentic report that Yahya was making frantic moves to get himself out of the impasse. A dialogue had begun with Mujib, as well as with the exile government of Bangladesh in Calcutta with the help of the American officials there. The dialogue with Mujib was carried on through his lawyer, A. K. Brohi. In the meantime there began a "trial" of Mujib by a military tribunal, and Brohi was allowed to act as Mujib's defence counsel. In fact, the "trial" was never a serious one. Thanks to pressure from the White House, the safety of Mujib's life was guaranteed.

In fact, even before Mujib surrendered to the Pakistan Army in March, there was a secret deal, again through the good offices of the American officials, ensuring that Mujib's life would be protected. Whereas the Pakistan Army was out to eliminate other top Awami Leaguers, including Tajuddin, and their families, Mujib and his family were treated in a strangely pleasant way by the Army. The fabricated story of digging a "graveyard" for Mujib on the floor of his cell in the prison has been exposed by the journalist, Oriana Fallaci, in her *Mujib in Power: a Portrait.*[21] It is, however, true that some hawkish generals, in collaboration with Bhutto, would have preferred to execute Mujib if it had been feasible but Nixon's strong pressure made such a venture impossible. Yahya had no such plan. He was rather relieved to receive Nixon's letters on this matter which strengthened his hand in restraining the hawks.[22]

In August when I became convinced that Yahya was searching frantically for a political solution of the crisis, and I knew that some political dialogue had again started, I made my second trip from London to West Pakistan and Dacca. The scene in Islamabad, where I landed on August 23, 1971, was bewildering. Cornelius was still busy finalizing his constitution. A group of "experts" from Bhutto's party had regular sessions with Cornelius and his aides – a group of civil officials headed by the all-powerful Peerzada. Peerzada and Cornelius seemed "satisfied" with the "quantum of provincial autonomy" to be given to the people of "East Pakistan" – which was no longer a reality. A significant feature of the proposed constitution was the provision for a "Bengali Vice-President" who would exercise provincial autonomy sitting in Dacca. Peerzada explained to me that this was a "big concession" to the Bengalis! It was difficult to control one's laughter at the stupid exercise. It seemed that the process of constitution-making in Pakistan was endless – it had begun when the country obtained independence on August 14, 1947, and it was still continuing when Dacca fell on December 16, 1971. How could either Bhutto or Peerzada still believe that a constitution framed by a few West Pakistani civil and military officials sitting in Rawalpindi would be acceptable to the Bengalis, who had proclaimed their national goal of an independent state?

However, the "inside" scene was quite different and perfectly realistic. The whole situation had changed since my previous visit in May–June. Yahya was like a man in a trance. The other members of the junta – Hamid, Gul Hasan, Omar (who was busy organizing a musical performance for his son's marriage at which Yahya was to be the chief guest) and even Peerzada were in the deepest gloom. The chief of Inter-Services Intelligence (I.S.I.D.), Major-General Gillani, an intelligent and honest officer, and his able predecessor General Akbar, both told me about the imminent Indo-Pakistan war on Bangladesh and its grave implications.

I had a casual meeting with Yahya after my arrival in Islamabad, and asked him about the Cornelius constitution. Before giving any answer he asked me for my own comments. My reply was that it would be the final nail in the coffin of Pakistan. Without contradicting, Yahya asked me to see him on September 6, which had been observed as "Defence Day" since the 1965 Indo-Pakistan war, and as such was a public holiday. He asked me to see him alone on that day in the morning: it was my last serious meeting with him, and lasted three hours. I paid him a courtesy farewell call on September 22.

The following was the substance of my interview with Yahya on September 6. There could be no military solution to the crisis. Mujib must be released, and talks must begin with him and his exile government in Calcutta. The Americans, with his knowledge and approval, had already started talks with the exile government, and the Americans were also being given facilities to negotiate with Mujib through his lawyer, A. K. Brohi. When I asked what would be the basis of the political settlement, he told me that he was not sure yet of its final shape or outcome. All that interested him was to keep the green and white crescent flag intact if possible, but if seventy-five million Bengalis would not have it, "let there be two Muslim states in the subcontinent" – he made this comment with great anguish. To my query about the procedure of political dialogue, Yahya's answer was that Mujib would be released as soon as the Assembly met and passed a resolution asking him to do so. This was a face-saving device after he had denounced Mujib as a "traitor". Yahya then told me that he was relying heavily on Nixon for the success of this final attempt; the help of the

Shah of Iran was also referred to. When I asked what were the prospects, his reply was that two persons were creating great obstacles – "that deceitful woman" (Mrs. Gandhi) and "that inordinately ambitious man" (Bhutto). He confessed that his first major mistake was his unqualified faith in Mujib's word and pledges before the election in December 1970, and that when he had turned to Bhutto, he had been let down in that quarter as well. I found him no less bitter towards Bhutto than towards Mujib: he said that Bhutto, no less than Mujib, was determined to destroy united Pakistan, and for petty personal motives.

After my talks with Yahya, other generals, top civil servants, Bhutto, Justice Cornelius and many others, I visited Dacca and had discussions with many people there including supporters of the Awami League. In London later I talked with people closely connected with the Bangladesh mission there and finally had a lengthy discussion in London early in 1972 with the American Ambassador in Islamabad, Mr. Farland. From all these I gathered that a serious move was made by President Nixon to avert a war in the subcontinent, but by the time it was made (September–October 1971) the Indian Government had decided to "liberate" Bangladesh.

Yahya was extremely responsive to Nixon's gestures and attempts. The Chinese would also have been happy to see the success of Nixon's mediatory efforts rather than the military victory of the Indians backed by the Russians. The exile government of Bangladesh in Calcutta was favourably disposed to a political settlement under Nixon's initiative, except for Mr. Tajuddin, the acting Prime Minister. The then acting Foreign Minister, Mostaque Ahmad, and Foreign Secretary, Mr. Alam, eagerly supported the American-sponsored moves.[23] Both were removed from the Ministry of Foreign Affairs after the creation of Bangladesh.

Yahya made an earnest appeal to the Indian Prime Minister, Mrs. Gandhi, to avoid war. When the newly-appointed Indian ambassador, Jai Kumar Atal, presented his credentials to him in mid-November, Yahya gave him a secret five-point peace plan in which – he agreed to release Mujib and to arrange a referendum to determine whether or not the Bengalis wanted an independent state of their own or to stay in a united

Pakistan. The other points of the peace plan included the immediate formation of an all-party government in Pakistan as an interim measure; and an arrangement to return the refugees from India under U.N. supervision and protection.[24] Could there have been a more constructive and liberal offer than this? It virtually accepted the independence of Bangladesh which, it was proposed, should be established by a referendum rather than by the invasion of East Bengal by Indian troops.

The Indian ambassador, immediately after presenting his credentials, flew back to New Delhi. His sudden dash back to India raised many last-minute hopes that another Indo-Pakistan war would be avoided. But all hopes were dashed to ground when the ambassador came back to Islamabad with the report that Yahya's peace plan was unacceptable to Mrs. Gandhi on the ground that the 1970 election had already been a referendum for the Bengalis, and that there was no need for a new one. But how was peace obtained in Vietnam? Was it not based on an accepted method of ascertaining the wishes of the Vietnamese people? But who cares for international peace or voices of restraint in a country which is guided by narrow selfish interests and backed by a super-power intent that it should pursue those narrow interests? How could India honestly maintain that the people of East Bengal had opted for independence in the 1970 election? That election (see Chapter 5) was held on the basis of a united Pakistan, and Mujib repeatedly told the Bengalis that he was fighting it for regional autonomy in a "true federal union". Secession was not the issue. Unless Mujib already had a secret deal with New Delhi whereby, once the election was won, India would back him in his hitherto veiled plan to dismember Pakistan, it was dishonest to say that the 1970 election had already provided the Bengalis with a referendum to declare independence. It is little wonder that even liberal Western papers like the *Washington Post* and *The Guardian*, which had condemned the Pakistan Army's actions in the preceding nine months, criticized India severely in November and December 1971 for provoking a war in the subcontinent. "The Indians have been rough and irresponsible; they have encouraged and directly taken part in the dismemberment of a sovereign state."[25]

The International Jurists in Geneva made similar comments on the Indian role in the Bangladesh crisis:

> In accordance with international customary law India's first duty was to maintain an attitude of neutrality and to refrain from interfering in the hostilities which had broken out in the neighbouring state. . . . The traditional rule of neutrality in respect of belligerents engaged in a civil war was applicable to India up to December 6, 1971, the date on which she recognized Bangladesh as an independent country. . . .
>
> More serious, however, from the point of view of international law is the military assistance given by India to the Bangladesh insurgents.
>
> We have already expressed the view that the principle of self-determination of peoples (under the U.N. Resolution 2625) can not be established to this situation (Bangladesh) and India's assistance to the insurgents can not, therefore, be justified under this principle.
>
> On the face of it, certain of India's actions fell within the terms of this condemnation, namely the provision of military supplies to the insurgents and granting of facilities to recruit and train guerilla forces on Indian soil. India's involvement appears to have gone further than this. *There can be no doubt that India did take military action against Pakistan before the outbreak of open war* [my italics].
>
> We find it difficult to accept that the scale of India's armed action was motivated *solely* [my italics] by military considerations based on the need to protect her national frontiers and territories. . . . This is a dangerous doctrine and would set at naught all the principles of international law enjoining neutrality on third parties in a civil war situation.[26]

REFERENCES

1. See the text of Yahya's broadcast on March 26 in *Dawn*, Karachi, March 27, 1971.
2. See press statement of Tajuddin Ahmad on April 12, 1971, published by the Bangladesh Students' Action Committee, London, 1971.
3. Z. A. Bhutto, *The Great Tragedy*, op. cit., p. 72.
4. W. H. Morris-Jones, "Pakistan Post-Mortem and the Roots of Bangladesh", *Political Quarterly*, April–June 1972.
5. See the statement by Mujib on January 8, 1972, in London, after his release from the West Pakistani prison.

6. Muhammad Hasanain Haykal, "The General who was defeated", in his weekly *Frankly Speaking* articles in Arabic, MENA, Cairo, April 19, 1973.
7. Ibid.
8. Fazal Muqueem Khan, *Pakistan's Crisis in Leadership*, op. cit., p. 73.
9. Kalim Siddiqui, *Conflict, Crisis and War in Pakistan*, Praeger, New York, 1972.
10. See *Daily Telegraph*, London, and *Washington Post*, March 30, 1971.
11. *Bangabandhu Speaks: a Collection of Speeches and Statements made by Sheikh Mujibur Rahman*, Ministry of Foreign Affairs, Government of Bangladesh, Dacca, n.d., p. 1.
12. Tajuddin Ahmad's statement on the proclamation of the "Sovereign Democratic Republic of Bangladesh", issued by Bangladesh Students' Action Committee, London, 1971.
13. *Pakistan's Crisis in Leadership*, op. cit., p. 80.
14. *Pakistan's Crisis in Leadership*, op. cit., p. 115.
15. Ibid.
16. Muhammad Hasanain Haykal, "The General who was Defeated", op. cit.
17. I was told of this by Yahya and the chief of the military intelligence in Pakistan during my second visit to Pakistan in Sept. 1971.
18. Yahya told me of Kissinger's warning to India.
19. S. Gupta, "Sino-U.S. Detente and India", *India Quarterly*, July–September 1971.
20. See *International Herald Tribune*, December 14, 1971.
21. See Oriana Fallaci's letter to the Editor, *Europa*, Milan, in February 1972.
22. See my "Emergence of Bangladesh and South Asian Triangle", *The Year Book of World Affairs*, 1973.
23. Based on personal interviews with Bengalis in London after the creation of Bangladesh.
24. I saw the contents of Yahya's peace plan to Indira Gandhi from a Pakistani official source: subsequently it was confirmed by the Bengalis who were closely associated with the exile government in Calcutta. A reference to Yahya's peace-plan (in condensed form) was made in *The New Yorker*, February 12, 1972 – see "The Birth of Bangladesh" by "Reporter at Large".
25. *Washington Post*, December 14, 1971 and see also *The Guardian* November 25–30, 1971.
26. See *The Review: The International Commission of Jurists*. "East Pakistan Staff Study" – "The Role of India", June 1972.

9

DISMEMBERMENT OF PAKISTAN, 1971: ITS INTERNATIONAL IMPLICATIONS

Changes in the boundaries of states and the emergence of new states seldom take place without outside intervention or war. A small country, confronted with an unfriendly, if not hostile, big neighbour backed by a major power, is often exposed to external threats and can hardly enjoy the "freedom from fear" which is a basic requirement for a country's stability, progress and viability. The break-up of Pakistan, the United States' "most allied ally" in the mid-1950s and subsequently China's most friendly and informal ally, in December 1971 was no doubt largely due to internal socio-economic and political developments. Yet outside influences and factors were undeniably present in the dismemberment of Pakistan. It is time that these external forces and factors connected with the civil war over Bangladesh and the third Indo-Pakistani War of 1971 were objectively assessed and their implications in the emerging balance of power in South Asia evaluated.

The tragic happenings in Pakistan which began on March 25, 1971, and ended with the triumphant entry of the Indian Army into Dacca, the capital of Bangladesh, on December 16, 1971, have aroused so much emotion, and such strong feelings of sympathy for the suffering of seventy-five million Bengalis, that there has hardly been any scope for a proper assessment of the external forces behind the tragedy. The Western press did a great service to humanity by giving wide publicity to the atrocities of the Pakistani Army in East Bengal. The result was a natural world-wide upsurge of sympathy for the cause of Bangladesh, but it also successfully camouflaged the attempt of some countries to further their narrow national interests by exploiting the tragic situation and taking advantage of the internal conflict of a smaller power.

What role did the Soviet Union play during the 1971 crisis in the subcontinent? Was it interested *only* in the "success in solving in a democratic manner the complex problems that face the country [Pakistan]?" Were the Kremlin leaders "guided by the generally recognized humanitarian principles", as claimed by President N. Podgorny in his letter to President Yahya Khan on April 2, 1971?[1] Were the Soviet roles and moves connected with the growing Sino-Soviet conflict in the area and Pakistan's refusal to be involved in it by not being associated with the Russian moves, political and economic, such as Kosygin's seemingly innocuous plan for a regional economic grouping comprising Afghanistan, India, Iran, Pakistan and the Soviet Union and Brezhnev's deliberately vague Asian Security Plan (though the Security Plan was not a vague one when presented to countries like Pakistan)? Were not the Soviet moves also linked to their close ties with India? These were formally institutionalized in the so-called Treaty of Friendship signed between Moscow and New Delhi in the midst of the civil war in Pakistan, but had been lying ready since 1969 when the Indian Foreign Minister, Dinesh Singh, went to Moscow to discuss the Soviet–Asian Security Plan and said: "India welcomes the proposal by the Soviet Union on the creation of a system of collective security in Asia. . . ."[2]

Similarly, did India have *only* a humanitarian interest in the democratic aspirations of the Bengalis? India claimed that her involvement in the Bangladesh crisis was due to the influx of "ten million" refugees. But the most pertinent issue, however, is what justification, if any, India had in extending not only moral support, which might have been understandable, but also active military support to an armed uprising in a neighbouring country. Her intervention in the Bangladesh crisis within forty-eight hours of its inception on March 25, 1971, when not a single refugee had gone to India, could hardly be described merely as furthering a desire to restore the "democratic rights" of the Bengalis. A federated unit of another country made a unilateral declaration of independence. India allowed that rebel group to form an exile government on her soil, and aided that government in its functioning by providing all facilities including a clandestine broadcasting station, and arming the forces of that government, the *Mukti-Bahini* or liberation army. How would India react if either China or Pakistan were to extend such facilities to a federating unit of the Indian union like Assam or Nagaland, if such a unit were to make a unilateral declaration of independence? Would not the Indian Government and press call it an "aggression" against the country?

During the 1971 happenings in East Bengal such issues could hardly be discussed in their true perspective because of the wide emotional feelings which had been justly aroused by the Pakistani Army's excesses while trying to suppress the secession movement, but now the true picture is emerging. The Bangladesh crisis was not merely a conflict between Pakistani nationalism and Bengali sub-nationalism. Linguistic, cultural and racial differences and tensions are not uncommon in the new Afro-Asian countries; the social order in these countries is characterized by a lack of integration due to the "ethnic, religious, racial and cultural pluralism" characteristic of these societies.[3] But if a powerful neighbour, backed by a great power, intended to take advantage of such internal tensions, the stability and territorial integrity of many Afro-Asian countries would be in danger. As an American scholar, commenting on India's role during the Bangladesh movement, recently pointed out: "In 1971 justifiable humanitarian concern became confused with analysis of a difficult political situation. Yet at no time in recent history have the internal affairs of one country been used to justify the invasion and dismemberment of another."[4]

On the Soviet role, an Indian scholar, while trying to justify it, had to admit that the Soviet "objective must have been to facilitate Indian military action in East Pakistan." One might ask why the Soviet Union was interested in such military action against Pakistan. The Indian author gives the answer: "Pakistan had become an undependable ally of any power which wants to pursue the policy of containing Chinese influence in this part of the world." Then he bluntly points out: "Kosygin supported the Bangladesh movement despite its legal and theoretical snags because he must have thought that he . . . [was] backing a winning horse."[5]

The Bangladesh crisis was interlinked with the Sino-Soviet rivalry in South and South-east Asia. It also had a bearing on the strategic and global competition in the Third World between the two super-powers in spite of recent attempts at détente in American–Soviet relations. "The operation Bangladesh was also a part of the operation for the Indian Ocean in Kosygin's global plan and he seemed to have made a clean sweep in this respect over his rivals, President Nixon and Chou En-lai, on the Bangladesh issue."[6]

Realpolitik in South Asia

Let us first look at the patterns of alignment in South Asia on the eve of the 1971 crisis. The most unfortunate aspect of international relations in South Asia had been the constant bad relations and tensions between the two regional powers in the area, India and Pakistan, which have always moved in diametrically opposite directions: if one turns to Washington, the other tries to move towards Moscow/Peking or Peking. This is the result of their corrosive quarrels and constant tensions.

The patterns of alignment in South Asia have always been greatly complicated by regional tensions in the area. On the whole, South Asia has not been what is termed a "primary tension area" involving a "big power zone";[7] but there have been a few exceptions. The first occurred during the Sino-Indian border conflict in 1962 when Nehru, confronted with a total military débacle, made an "urgent open appeal for the intervention of the United States with bomber and fighter squadrons to go into action against the Chinese" on the night of November 20, 1962.[8] There was a real risk of a general war involving the major powers, but thanks to the dramatic declaration of a unilateral cease-fire by the Chinese on November 21, a major crisis was averted. The second major risk was during the 1965 Indo-Pakistan war when China issued an ultimatum to India on September 16, 1965, threatening that unless the Indian Government dismantled within three days "all the military works for aggression" on the Chinese side of the China–Sikkim boundary or the boundary itself, it must bear full responsibility for all the grave consequences.[9] The Chinese ultimatum was interpreted as a "paper" one, but this view was false. I had the opportunity to read the Sino-Pakistani confidential messages during the war and the minutes of Ayub Khan's dialogues with Mao Tse-tung, Chou En-lai and other top Chinese leaders during Ayub's top-secret visit to China in the midst of the war, and can vouch that China meant business. It was Ayub's unwillingness or inability to carry on a prolonged war which prevented a general war in the subcontinent.[10] The latest occasion when the area seemed to be turning into a "primary tension area" was during the third Indo-Pakistani war in 1971 on Bangladesh. The U.S. Seventh Fleet, "Enterprise", was, in a rather mystifying way, moving to the Bay of Bengal while Indian troops were advancing on Dacca; and the Russians were reported to have assured the Indians of counter-measures against any move from the U.S. Fleet.

Although South Asia has on the whole, with the few exceptions noted above, remained an area without immediate crises, it has been one of active diplomatic competition between the two super-powers, and the rise of China as an emerging major power has further complicated the South Asian triangle. The region has been important politically though not militarily. But thanks to the intensified Sino-Soviet conflict, the area has also acquired military significance to Moscow and Peking. The global policies of the U.S.A., the Soviet Union and China and the regional tensions and conflicts between India and Pakistan have been interrelated. Thus within the South Asian state system, the five most populous countries in the world were, to quote Norman Palmer's words, "jockeying and jostling" with each other in a confused pattern of interrelationships.[11]

The presence of outside powers in South Asia has been a big factor in the regional conflicts between India and Pakistan. This was also the case when the Bangladesh crisis turned into another hot issue in their unending feuds. The crisis of Bangladesh no doubt resulted from Pakistan's failure to achieve national integration and find a viable political order in which the people of two geographically separated units could live together in a true federal or confederal union. But this does not mean that the external factors did not complicate the issue.

The United States, by the time Richard Nixon came to the White House in January 1969, had decided to play its role in Asia at a low profile. During his world tour in August 1969, when he visited five Asian countries including India and Pakistan, Nixon gave expression to his policy by defining the role of the United States in Asia. He explained that while the United States would, of course, honour its treaty commitments, it must avoid the kind of policy which would make Asian countries so dependent on the United States that the latter would be dragged into conflicts such as the Vietnam war. Nixon admitted that it was a difficult policy to follow, but he believed it was one which, with proper planning, could be developed. Nixon recalled some advice he had received in 1964 from the former Pakistani President, Ayub Khan, who had told him that the role of the United States in countries like Vietnam, the Philippines and Thailand – or for that matter in any other Asian country which experienced internal subversion – was to help them fight the war but not to fight the war for them. Nixon thought this a good principle.[12]

The new U.S. policy under the Nixon Doctrine was to maintain a low profile. The United States had already begun a process of disengagement from the affairs of the subcontinent since the ruinous Indo-Pakistan war of 1965; military aid to both India and Pakistan was stopped; economic aid continued but with a declining volume.

While South Asia under the new U.S. policy became a low priority area compared to South-east Asia or the Middle East, the United States did not wish to leave the initiatives in the area entirely to the Soviet Union and China. Explaining the new U.S. policy towards South Asia in 1973, James H. Noyes, Assistant Secretary of Defense for Near Eastern, African and South Asian Affairs, said: "No critical U.S. security interests are involved in South Asia. . . . Those interests the United States does have in the subcontinent are primarily political. . . . They include a basic interest in peace and stability of the region and in insuring that no outside power achieves dominance over any of the regional nations."[13]

But the Soviet Union, thanks to its growing conflict with China, seemed to have embarked on expansionist designs, seemingly in accordance with the traditional Russian interest in the subcontinent as visualized by Lord Curzon in the 1900s and as disclosed in the Soviet–Nazi documents captured by the U.S. Government after the Second World War saying: "The Soviet government shared the old czarist interests in the Persian–Indian Ocean area."[14] The Kremlin leaders throughout 1969 and 1970 were assiduously working for some economic, political and military grouping with the containment of China as its object. The main objective of new Soviet moves such as Brezhnev's Asian collective security plan seemed to be to isolate and contain China while serving its own "great-power" aspirations in the region. The Soviet–Chinese rivalry was increasingly reflected in diplomatic moves made by the U.S.S.R. in 1969 and 1970. After preaching against the military pacts for more than fifteen years, the Soviet leaders now found virtues in the concept and reverted to "Dullesism" because it suited their national interests against China.

Pakistan had special difficulties and dilemmas in responding to the new Soviet moves as she could realize that both Kosygin's plan for regional economic grouping and Brezhnev's Asian collective security plan were directed against her closest friend China which, since the U.S. embargo on military supplies to India and Pakistan, had become the principal supplier of arms to Pakistan. Pakistan and China remained opposed to a Soviet-inspired security system, and Moscow had a sizeable task in seeking to extend ties with Pakistan at China's expense.

When Pakistan finally expressed its inability to join the Russian moves against China, the brief interval of so-called "friendly relations" between Moscow and Islamabad came to an end. The soviet press and propaganda media began similar attacks to those Pakistan had experienced in the 1950s when she joined SEATO and CENTO. Between 1965 and 1970 there was some relaxation in the Soviet attacks against Pakistan. Thus Pakistan, which in the mid-1950s had been a "stooge of imperalist powers", was elevated all of a sudden to the status of "the respected southern neighbour"[15] of the Soviet Union after Ayub's first state visit in 1965, but by the beginning of 1970 the Soviet press and propaganda media reverted to their old campaign of vilification against Pakistan. The *New Times*, for instance, wrote a lengthy article on Pakistan on February

7, 1970, full of critical and hostile comment at a time when the Pakistan Government was engaged in serious political negotiations with the Bengali leader Mujibur Rahman for a political settlement between East and West Pakistan and to avoid confrontation. The *New Times* article reflected the hardening Soviet attitude towards Pakistan at this time; Pakistan's Ambassador in Moscow also began to send reports in 1970 of the Soviets' "increasing pressures" and "hardening attitude".[16] This was the Soviet attitude and policy towards Pakistan on the eve of the Bangladesh crisis and it should provide some background for understanding Soviet concern for "suffering humanity in Bangladesh". It would be naïve to think that the Kremlin leaders were moved solely by suffering humanity in Bangladesh if one recalls the Soviet atrocities in Hungary in 1956 and in Czechoslovakia in 1968, not to speak of Stalin's ruthless policy of suppression in the Central Asian republics of the Soviet Union.

Pakistan's relations with China began to grow closer after the boundary agreement between the two countries in 1963. Pakistani-Chinese friendship reached its zenith during the 1965 Indo-Pakistani war; then their relationship was affected somewhat by Ayub's acceptance of the Soviet mediatory role at the Tashkent Conference in 1966 and moving closer to Moscow in 1967 and 1968 for getting Russian arms for Pakistan. China was also in the midst of the upheaval caused by the Cultural Revolution, which had created some fears in Ayub's mind about Chinese help, though China continued to send arms supplies to Pakistan in 1967–8 notwithstanding the dislocation and disturbances it was suffering at the time. Then in 1969, when Yahya Khan began the grand assignment given him by Nixon to act as "courier" between Washington and Peking, Pakistan's relations with China again became close and intimate. Yahya's role also improved Pakistan's links with Washington, particularly as Nixon had a good appreciation of the realities and dynamics of the subcontinent in the context of the Indo-Pakistani relations. When Yahya visited Peking in November 1970, China warned him of "outside factors" working in East Pakistan for a secession movement.[17] The Pakistani intelligence services, both civil and military, also reported "outside forces" operating in East Pakistan in

1970 when Pakistan was seeking a viable political order for removing the East–West Pakistan tensions.

This was the picture of the South Asian Triangle on the eve of the crisis on Bangladesh. The Soviet Union was hostile towards Pakistan for its refusal to join in "the Soviet version of SEATO" and other anti-China moves. The Pakistan–China and Pakistan–U.S.A. relationships were cordial, and had improved in the context of Nixon's new China policy in which the Pakistani President was playing a significant role.[18] India's relationship with Moscow, which had a history of fifteen years of friendly ties behind it, was getting closer in their common objective of containment of China; India was also suspicious of Nixon's alleged "pro-Pakistan" attitude.

When the civil war over Bangladesh began on March 25, 1971, the picture as presented in the world press seemed to be that the Soviet Union and India were on the side of justice, democracy and humanitarian principles while the United States and China were supporting a military junta in Pakistan against a national liberation movement based on the democratic aspirations of the Bengalis. But the real situation was not so simple as presented in the press. The *Realpolitik* prevailing in the area had to be considered. Diplomatic considerations were given priority over any ideological factors by the great powers in the crisis on Bangladesh, as is always the case in any international crisis. The Bangladesh War in 1971 provides an example of how the major powers wage their many-faceted struggle in the Third World through proxies as well as of how the Third World might become the "tinder box" that could consume the major powers' hopes for a détente.[19] A later example was, of course, the 1973 war in the Middle East.

India and the Bangladesh Crisis

India's interest and involvement in political happenings in East Pakistan during 1969–70 were closely linked with her constantly tense and bad relations with Pakistan. As the U.N. Secretary-General U Thant pointed out in his Annual Report of 1971: "The relations between the Governments of India and Pakistan are also a major component of the problem [the Bangladesh crisis]. . . . The crisis is unfolding in the context of the longstanding and unresolved difficulties which gave rise to open warfare only six years ago [i.e. in 1965]".[20] From the very beginning of the crisis, Pakistan complained of India's involvement and calculated wish to dismember Pakistan. Her fears were confirmed by the views expressed at a symposium organized by the Indian Council of World Affairs on March 31, 1971 (i.e. within six days of the outbreak of the revolt in East Pakistan) at which some Indians agreed with the candid statement of K. Subrahmaniyam, Director of the Indian Institute of Defence Studies: "What India must realize is the fact that the break-up of Pakistan is in our interest, an opportunity the like of which will never come again."[21] It was further stated at the same symposium that the Bangladesh crisis provided India with the "opportunity of the century" to destroy her number one enemy, Pakistan.[22] Throughout 1970 All-India Radio had been broadcasting a programme every evening entitled *Apper Bangla* and *Opper Bangla* (This Side and the Other Side of Bengal), openly encouraging the secession movement in East Pakistan. All-India Radio is an official organ.

Even more significant, however, was the Indian Government's immediate reaction to the crisis. Less than forty-eight hours after the Pakistan Army action, Mrs. Gandhi said in Lok Sabha: "We are deeply conscious of the historic importance of this movement. . . . I would like to assure the honourable members who asked whether decisions would be taken *on time* [my italics], that obviously is the most important thing to do. There is no point in taking a decision when the time for it is over."[23] The "honourable members" were pressing for a decision for Indian intervention and Mrs. Gandhi's answer was self-evident. In Rayja Sabha on the same day she stated: "We are interested in the matter for many reasons. Firstly, as one member has said, Sri Mujibur Rahman has stood for the values which we ourselves cherish. . . ."[24] The head of a foreign government commented that just because the rebel leader subscribed to India's "cherished values", India must therefore "be interested" in the internal affairs of a neighbouring country. Then on March 31, 1971, the Indian Parliament passed a resolution introduced by Mrs.

Gandhi pledging full support to the rebel group: "This House expresses its profound sympathy for and solidarity with the people of East Bengal in their struggle. . . . This House records its profound conviction that the historic upsurge of the 75 million people of East Bengal will triumph. The House wishes to assure them that their struggle and sacrifices will receive the whole-hearted sympathy and support of the people of India."[25]

What justification, if any, did India have for assuring "support" to a federating unit which was rebelling against the national government in a neighbouring country? Was it not contrary to the U.N. Charter and to the 1950 and 1966 bilateral agreements between India and Pakistan, pledging not to interfere in each other's internal affairs? As pointed out earlier, the support of the Indian Government, press and public for the armed uprising in East Pakistan was given long before her economy or society was burdened with the entry of a single refugee.

India is never tired of preaching mediation, conciliation, good offices and other peaceful methods of settling disputes to other nations, particularly the Western ones. But when her own national interests are involved in any matter, whether Kashmir or Goa, or the Himalayan kingdoms of Bhutan, Sikkim and Nepal, India has consistently refused any counsel of mediation by the U.N. or by any third party. The same was true of India's record in the Bangladesh crisis. U Thant addressed letters to Mrs. Gandhi and President Yahya Khan on October 20, 1971, offering his good offices in the settlement of the crisis. The Pakistani President's reply was the immediate and unqualified acceptance of the U Thant offer: "I fully agree with your appreciation of the gravity of the situation which is worsening rapidly on the Indo-Pakistani borders. . . . It is a pity that the Indian Prime Minister has summarily rejected the proposal for withdrawal of forces of both countries from the borders. . . . I recommend that the U.N. observers on both sides should observe the withdrawal and supervise the maintenance of peace. . . . I also welcome the offer you have made for making your good offices available."[26] Whereas Yahya replied to U Thant's letter the same day, October 20, 1971, it took Mrs. Gandhi nearly a month to reply. She wrote on November 16, evading the Secretary-General's offer of good offices; on the contrary, she accused the U.N. of "the present attempt to save the military régime", and of an attempt to "side-track this main problem and convert it into an Indo-Pakistani dispute". She further told U Thant: "If you are prepared to view the problem in perspective, you will have our support in your initiatives."[27]

U Thant, in his reply of November 22, expressed surprise over Mrs. Gandhi's remarks: "I am puzzled by the reference in paragraph 5 of your Excellency's letter to 'the present attempt to save the military régime of Pakistan' and . . . to 'side-track this main problem and to convert it into an Indo-Pakistani dispute.' . . . I am also puzzled by the statement in paragraph 8 that if I am 'prepared to view the problem in perspective' I shall have the support of the Indian Government."[28]

No observer of India's record at the U.N. whenever any matter involving her interests was taken up would be "puzzled". While India made a hue and cry about her "terrible burden" as a result of the influx of millions of refugees, she repeatedly refused to allow U.N. observers to facilitate the return of refugees to their homes. India insisted that only *after* a political settlement, which must be the dismemberment of Pakistan and the creation of a new country, could the refugees return. It was an extraordinary demand.

On November 23, 1971, Yahya made an urgent appeal to the U.N. Secretary-General: "I am addressing this message to you with a deep sense of urgency in view of the grave situation which has arisen in my country as a result of unprovoked and large-scale attacks by Indian armed forces on various parts of Pakistan."[29] On November 22 Indian troops began to cross the international boundary of Pakistan in its eastern region on the pleas of "self-interest" and "self-defence" – dangerous doctrines if applied in international relations. If it is accepted, the territorial integrity of any smaller country will not be safe and it will be a negation of all the principles and premises of the U.N. Charter. It is a great pity that the same liberal point of view in Western countries which was most opposed to the U.S. involvement in the Vietnamese War did not condemn the Indian invasion of East Pakistan.

That India invaded East Pakistan is conceded even by scholars who made the most charitable interpretation of the Indian role. Thus in his assessment of the Bangladesh crisis Norman Brown candidly states: "The victory of the forces for independence was achieved through aid India rendered the East Pakistanis. This turned out to be of two kinds: one was arming of the guerrilla force known as Mukti-Bahini, 'the liberation Army'; the other was the *invasion* [my italics] of East Pakistan by the Indian army."[30]

The U.S.A., the Soviet Union, China and the Bangladesh Crisis

The Soviet hardening towards Pakistan in the preceding two years (1969–70) has already been noted, and as the Bangladesh crisis turned out to be another important issue in the Indo-Pakistan relationship, Soviet support for India on the Bangladesh crisis was almost certain.

The Soviet Union's overriding strategic interest on the subcontinent has been to maintain close relations with India with the twin objectives of protecting its southern flank and maintaining enough pressure on China. The prompt Soviet reaction to the crisis was expressed in Podgorny's letter to Yahya on April 2, 1971, within less than ten days of the outbreak of the civil war. The tone and content of the letter revealed that the Soviet posture of neutrality in Indo-Pakistani disputes, which she had adopted from April 1965 and which enabled her to play the role of peacemaker in the subcontinent at the Tashkent Conference in 1966, had been sacrificed "in the hope that in the long run it will pay political dividends". The Russians were also most conscious, above all, of the inroads made by China in Pakistan and this had a great impact on their policy alternatives in the area because of the geopolitical proximity of Pakistan to the Soviet Union.[31] Moscow seemed to have made the choice between a stable and friendly India under Mrs. Gandhi, whose electoral victory in the 1971 Indian elections was hailed in the Soviet Union, and a tottering Pakistan increasingly under the sway of Peking.

Then came the dramatic announcement of Nixon's trip to Peking and Pakistan's role in improving the Sino-American relations. The latter greatly offended the Kremlin leaders, and gave the Soviet Union opportunities to bring India closer under a "treaty of friendship" signed in August 1971. As Robert H. Donaldson commented:

> For the visit of the American President to the capital of India's "adversary number two had been faciliated through the co-operation of her enemy number one" – a fact of some concern to Mrs. Gandhi as she faced the prospect of yet another war with Pakistan. For it seemed as though the apparent convergence of interest of the two super-powers in the 1960s in supporting India as a bulwark against Chinese ambitions was being outdistanced by the events of the 1970s.
>
> The Soviets, no less concerned over the propect of Sino-American rapprochement, saw the Indian dilemma as an opportunity to gain influence in New Delhi. . . .[32]

With the signing of the "treaty of friendship", Indo-Soviet collaboration on the Bangladesh crisis became palpable. The Soviet Government began to adopt a partisan attitude in contrast to its neutrality during the 1965 Indo-Pakistan war. There were exchanges of visits between the Soviet and Indian foreign ministers; Mrs. Gandhi also went to Moscow in September 1971. The flow of Soviet arms to India increased; India was assured of Soviet help if China were to intervene in any Indo-Pakistani armed conflict. The Soviet press, in tune with official policy, joined in a chorus of condemnation of Pakistan. An article in *Izvestia* on November 15, when Indian troops had already begun to violate Pakistan's boundary in the East, put the entire blame on Pakistan. When the full-fledged Indo-Pakistan war began on December 3, the Soviet Union warned Pakistan of "grave responsibility" and said that it could not "remain indifferent to the developments in the sub-continent, as they affected her own security...."[33] Other powers were firmly told to stay out of the conflict. For China an important question was whether the Soviet Union contemplated a military intervention in Pakistan's affairs on the Czechoslavak pattern; the developments in Czechoslovakia had also been regarded by the Kremlin leaders as "affecting her security". China remarked that "the present sudden invasion of Pakistan by India with the support of the Soviet Union is precisely a repetition on the South Asian subcontinent of the

1968 Soviet invasion and occupation of Czechoslovakia."[34]

The Soviet Union, however, did not have to resort to direct military intervention. Her vetoes in the Security Council on any ceasefire till the Indian forces occupied Dacca – a ceasefire resolution was also adopted by the U.N. General Assembly by an overwhelming majority of 104 to 11 – were enough to give the Indians time to carry the Bangladesh operation though to a conclusion. The Chinese Government said: "The Soviet Government has played a shameful role in this war of aggression launched by India against Pakistan. The whole world has seen clearly that it was the backstage manager of the Indian expansionists."[35] The United States President also stated: "Soviet policy, I regret to say, seemed to show the same tendency as we witnessed before in the 1967 Middle East war and the 1970 Jordanian crisis – to allow events to boil up towards crisis in the hope of political gain."[36]

China and the Bangladesh Crisis

Just as China condemned the Soviet role in the 1971 crisis of the subcontinent, the Soviet Government and its press also made polemical attacks on China's policy and role. *Pravda* wrote on December 9 that China provoked the war between India and Pakistan "to further its chauvinist great-power line in Asia", while *Red Star* wrote on December 14 that China's foreign policy was based on ideas "dug from the garbage pit of history among obsolete geopolitical doctrines which in their days fed Nazism". Though such mutual recrimination was nothing new in Sino-Soviet relations, the debate on the Bangladesh war in the Security Council and the General Assembly carried the polemical exchanges of words into the forum of the United Nations. Other novel phenomena in the United Nations were the Sino-American identity of views and the voting on the crisis. The Bangladesh crisis provided the first example of co-operation at the U.N. between the United States and China. It was also the first demonstration of relaxed Sino-American relations.

Was the Chinese policy opposed to the legitimate hopes and aspirations of the Bengalis and did the Chinese actions and votes at the U.N. reflect her conflicts and tensions with the Soviet Union and India or any real opposition to the creation of Bangladesh? Was there any dichotomy between the Chinese ideology relating to the national liberation movement and her actual role during the Bangladesh crisis? These questions agitated the minds of many. First, as regards ideology, the Chinese views on national liberations as interpreted in the Maoist doctrine are clear.[37] According to the Chinese interpretation, the movement for Bangladesh was not truly one of "national liberation"; it had the potential of being so if the liberation war were to continue for a long time and leadership were to pass to the real representatives of the "have nots" in East Bengal. But the movement as it had started, with Indian and Soviet support under a bourgeois party, the Awami League, was not a true national liberation one. Its leader Mujib was a bourgeois leader supported by Bengali industrialists and businessmen, supplemented by the resources of their counterparts in West Bengal (India). From the standpoint of Peking it was a conflict between two bourgeois élites – one in West Pakistan and the other in East Bengal. Obviously China's preference was for the one which had supported her faithfully in the Sino-Soviet rivalry in the area.

Leaving aside ideology, it was futile for Mujib to expect any sympathy from Peking; in fact, he never cared about it. Mujib was highly critical of what he used to describe as the "provocative friendship" between Pakistan and China. His single-track devotion to New Delhi blinded him to Peking. When Chou En-lai addressed letters to Mujib and Bhutto after the 1970 elections in Pakistan urging both to make a political settlement between East and West Pakistan, Mujib received the Chinese ambassador who carried Chou's letter coolly and paid no attention to the Chinese counsel of restraint and moderation. He seemed to have decided to put all his eggs in one basket, New Delhi.

China was criticized for a lack of sympathy for the Bengali cause and for supporting a military régime. But those who knew the inside story of the political developments in Pakistan as I did can vouch that China never opposed the rights and demands of the neglected people of East Bengal. China, like any other friend of Pakistan, wished the people of both East and West Pakistan well. China was greatly dismayed by the tragic happenings in East Bengal from March 25, 1971, and behind the scenes advised the Pakistan Government to seek a political settlement of the conflict. In her various statements of *verbal* support for Pakistan, China did not approve of the policy of repression by the Pakistani Army nor did she oppose the demands for genuine regional autonomy.

China, like any other great power, could not, however, be expected to support an emerging régime in Bangladesh which was solely dependent on India and, via New Delhi, on Moscow also. One of the prime considerations behind India's quick military action in East Bengal, supported by the Soviet Union, was the possibility of transforming the movement into a real people's war. Neither the Soviet Union nor India wanted a genuine revolutionary movement in East Bengal which would have a great impact on other parts of the subcontinent.

As regards Chinese help to the Pakistan Government during the 1971 war, it was far from her pledged role in the 1965 war. China did not wish to be involved in a suicidal civil war among the peoples of the two parts of Pakistan whose friendship Peking valued. It is also unfair to say that China "provoked" the Indo-Pakistani war of 1971. Ever since the serious border clashes with the Soviet Union in 1969, China was worried about a Soviet pre-emptive strike on her frontiers where the forty-five Soviet divisions were placed. This is a constant threat to China's security. Given the present military balance of power, it was uncharitable to say that China would encourage a war in the subcontinent and thereby incur the risk of a Soviet threat, particularly after the signing of the Indo-Soviet treaty of 1971 which, notwithstanding its high-sounding nomenclature, was in reality a military pact.

How could China provoke a war in such unfavourable circumstances? China was mainly interested in checking the Soviet influence in the area, and as the Bangladesh movement was nursed by India directly and had indirect blessing from Moscow, China could hardly look upon it with favour. In fact, no great power would support a movement which had the blessing of its adversaries and which was against a friendly neighbour; it would be contrary to the general rules of international politics. China acted in the Bangladesh crisis like any other power in the same circumstances. I had read the Chinese messages to Yahya; they were all pleas for restraint and not for war. Indeed, the Chinese Foreign Minister publicly told Bhutto, when he went as Yahya's emissary to Peking to secure Chinese support in the imminent confrontation with India, that Pakistan should try to find a "rational" solution to the crisis – which by implication was a condemnation of the policy of Pakistan's military régime.

As regards the Chinese role at the U.N. when the Indo-Pakistani war broke out in December 1971, a careful analysis of the Chinese stand will prove that China's wrath was directed against the Soviet Union and India rather than against the emerging Bangladesh.

The United States and Bangladesh

The U.S. Government's policy during the Bangladesh crisis drew extremely sharp criticism from the American intellectuals and press. This was due partly to lack of understanding of the genesis of the conflict and to the dubious Indo-Soviet role in complicating the issue, so that a chain of developments would be set in motion in such a way as to further their own national interests. The prevailing mood among the so-called liberal forces in the U.S.A. depicted U.S. policy as supporting a military régime against a democratic movement: "The emotionalism which surrounded the American public understanding of it portrayed Pakistan as a complete villain and India as a knight in shining armour."[38] President Nixon became the target of public misunderstanding over his policy on the issues involved in the crisis. Nixon never condoned the Pakistan Army's action in East Bengal; indeed he put the strongest pressure on Yahya to make a political settlement of the crisis and to give up the path of repression and supression. During my two private visits to Pakistan in May and September 1971, I had lengthy conversations with Yahya, during which he showed me the contents of Nixon's letters to him, and I can say without fear of contradiction that Nixon did his best for a political solution of the crisis. Most probably the Nixon-sponsored efforts would have averted the Indo-Pakistani war on Bangladesh, which destroyed not only the economic infrastructure of Bangladesh but also its social fabric. After more than two years of independence, Bangladesh was still in a shambles.

As regards American economic aid to Pakistan in 1971, the bulk of it went to East Bengal, and without it the people there would have faced a major famine in which millions of people could have died. The U.S. economic assistance did not help the military operations by the Pakistani Army, but was utilized for humanitarian relief operations for the Bengalis, both inside East Bengal and outside, i.e. those who fled to the refugee camps in West Bengal. The U.S. Government, as disclosed by President Nixon in his Report to Congress in February 1972, stopped military supplies to Pakistan as soon as the civil war began. He told Congress: "Immediately, in early April, we ceased new commitments for economic development. This shut off $35 million worth of arms. Less than $5 million worth of spare parts, already in the pipeline under earlier licences, was shipped before the pipeline dried up completely by the beginning of November."[39]

The Indo-Pakistani war finally broke out on December 3, 1971, at a time when Nixon was "in sight of a political settlement" between Yahya Khan's régime and the Bangladesh government-in-exile in India. The U.S. efforts for a political settlement were discussed fully with Mrs. Gandhi when she visited Washington just ten days before the war began. It was reported that Nixon pleaded with her to give him a little time for a negotiated settlement and that she complied with the President's pleas. So when, less than ten days later, Mrs. Gandhi nevertheless sent her troops across the boundary into East Pakistan, the United States Government's reaction was quite naturally unfavourable to India. When the matter came up before the Security Council, the permanent U.S. representative, George Bush, said on December 5 that India was clearly "the major aggressor". The U.S. Government had proposed to both India and Pakistan that there should be a cease-fire and a mutual withdrawal of troops. The Government of Pakistan accepted the U.S. proposal without any reservation. The Government of India, however, rejected it publicly and following that rejection there was an escalation in the fighting on the subcontinent, the first incursions being made by India.[40] A White House spokesman added: "The White House believes that what has started as a tragedy in Bengal has now become an attempt to dismember a sovereign state which is a member of the United Nations."[41]

Senator Edward Kennedy, denouncing Nixon's attitude towards the war, raised the question in the Senate: "Are we so insensitive to what our country stands for that our government can actually support as well as apologize for a military régime's brutal suppression of democracy?"[42] The real position was that neither did President Nixon approve the military régime's policy of suppression nor could he approve of Mrs. Gandhi's war solution of the problem by dismembering a smaller neighbour with the military and diplomatic support of a super-power. Nixon's policy was dubbed as a "tilt" in favour of Pakistan. In reality, as Joseph S. Sisco, Assistant Secretary of State for Near Eastern and South Asian Affairs,[43] explained, it was "a tilt toward peace and to achieve and help achieve the kind of peace and stability which we think is in the interest of all countries in the area as well as the major powers who have an interest in the area".

The New Balance of Power in South Asia and its Implications

India's military success in the third Indo-Pakistani war was almost a foregone conclusion: a demoralized Pakistani Army, surrounded by the hostile local population and without any air cover, could easily be defeated. Moreover, India had the full backing of a super-power: although Pakistan had the moral and diplomatic support of Washington and Peking, she received no effective military help from them. So the Indian victory was achieved at little cost or difficulty. Though it cannot be termed a decisive military achievement for the Indian forces, it greatly boosted the Indian Army's morale after its débacles at the hands of the Chinese in 1962 and the indecisive result of the 1965 war with Pakistan.

Politically and psychologically the victory was of much greater significance: India at last was able to dismember her principal enemy and inflict a major diplomatic defeat on her number two adversary, China.

India began to claim a hegemonic role in the affairs of the subcontinent. The state of Bangladesh was treated like one of her client-states such as Bhutan, Sikkim and Nepal. Ceylon and Burma were expected to be impressed by India's new military and political stature as the dominant power in the region. Pakistan was taken for granted as a "lost rival", both in military and diplomatic competition. Indians began to talk in terms of a "confederation" or a "larger union" – a theme which the Indians can never forget after the "tragic mistake" of partition or "vivisection" of their motherland in 1947. The Indian Foreign Secretary Mr. Kaul expressed the view that "in the new era of peace, a union between India, Pakistan and Bangladesh could subsequently be extended to cover countries like Nepal which badly wanted transit facilities, as well as other countries of the region."[44] The *Hindustan Times* of New Delhi expressed the hope that the countries of South Asia could "in time assume the attributes of a confederation or commonwealth."[45]

After about two years, India's hegemony seemed to be less bright than the Indians had expected after their military victory in 1971. Pakistan has not proved to be a "lost cause", either economically or militarily. Her armed forces are reported to have made good the losses of 1971: Chinese arms including MIG 19s and tanks have continued to pour in. According to some reliable estimates, the total of Chinese military supplies to Pakistan from 1966 to the present day roughly matches what Washington had provided during the previous decade (1954–65).[46] Furthermore, the Pakistan–Iran military collaboration and the latter's huge military build-up have caused some doubts about India's absolute supremacy over Pakistan – "The Shah of Iran's interest in Pakistan deserves a careful watch."[47] The most disappointing political development for the Indian Government in the new era is the rise of anti-Indian feelings in Bangladesh.[48] India's economic situation also does not favour her role of hegemony.

The Major Powers and The New Balance in South Asia

The Soviet Union was quick to cash in on her role as the liberator of the seventy-five million people of Bangladesh, and tried to penetrate all spheres of Bangladesh life under the garb of an "economic-cultural relationship". She also provided Bangladesh with some Russian MIGs – which are, however, stationed in Calcutta, India. The Soviet contribution to the U.N. relief operations in Bangladesh in 1971–2 was only about $137 million or 10·7 per cent, compared with the U.S. contribution of about $347 million or 27·2 per cent. Yet the Russians made a lot of publicity for their "concern" for the suffering Bengalis.

The Soviet diplomatic objective in Bangladesh seems to be to include it under the umbrella of the Brezhnev Doctrine of Asian collective security. At present, Bangladesh is covered indirectly under the Russian plan through New Delhi's "Treaty of Friendship" with Bangladesh similar to the Indo-Soviet Treaty of 1971. The Russians have intensified their campaign for the Asian Security Plan through non-governmental channels. Their claim that this scheme is attracting great interest in Asia is now shored up with references to "speeches at conferences and symposia" and proposals of various parties and organizations.[49] These include the Afro-Asian Peoples' Solidarity Organization (A.A.P.S.O.) executive committee, which met in Aden in February 1973, and peace conventions in India and Nepal this year. A leading role in this campaign is being played by the World Peace Council (W.P.C.), whose "conference on Asian Security and Cooperation" in Dacca on May 23–26, 1973, was among the preliminaries to a "World Congress of Peace Forces" in Moscow in October 1973.

The unfriendly attitude of the Soviet Union towards the "new" Pakistan continues. When Bhutto visited Moscow in March 1972 he was told bluntly by his Russian hosts: "If history were to repeat itself we would again take the same position [referring to the Soviet role in the dismemberment of Pakistan] because we are convinced that it was correct."[50] This was a clear warning to Pakistan in the context of present-day turbulence in Baluchistan and the North-West Frontier Province of truncated Pakistan. The alleged Soviet role in current political unrest in the "Wild West" of Pakistan was dramatized by the seizure of Russian arms smuggled into Pakistan through the Iraqi embassy in Islamabad. Baghdad

Radio's broadcast propaganda for a "greater Baluchistan" and Kabul Radio's propaganda for Paktoonistan are some of the omens from Moscow for the further fragmentation of Pakistan. The coup in Afghanistan in 1973, which was alleged to have Soviet blessing, and the new Afghan rulers' threats to revive the old issue of Paktoonistan are regarded by Pakistan as Russian pressures to browbeat her into the Asian collective security plan. Further fragmentation of Pakistan and the creation of Soviet client-states such as Baluchistan and Paktoonistan would fulfil the old Tsarist ambition of a "warm-water" port for the Russians in the South. If this were to happen, the Russian expansionist designs in the Indian Ocean and Persian Gulf would be fulfilled and the peace and stability of the area would be threatened, for not only Pakistan but also Iran would be affected.

The United States is still committed to a low-profile policy towards South Asia. There have been suggestions that she should "no longer have any doubt about the Indian hegemony within the subcontinent and therefore about the need for what Mr. Galbraith has called a 'North American solution'" [referring to the strategic accommodation between the U.S.A., Canada and Mexico].[51] It would be a risky step in the context of Soviet expansionist designs and current Indo-Soviet collaboration. It is encouraging to note that President Nixon told Bhutto that the U.S. objectives in South Asia include the maintenance of the territorial integrity of Pakistan.

Dr. William Kintner has made a better and more realistic appraisal of the new situation in South Asia. He favoured the classic balance of power strategy and in this context he notes that "it is desirable to prevent domination of Asia by one power".[52]

China, despite having suffered a diplomatic setback in 1971, is not likely to tolerate passively a "Soviet–Indian axis". Chou En-lai predicted that the fall of Dacca to the Indian Army on December 16, 1971 "is not the end of the problems but just the start of them".[53] Chou expressed similar views to the British author, Neville Maxwell, when he said: "India would in the end taste the bitter fruit of its own making. And from then on there would be no tranquillity on the subcontinent."[54] Kintner's arguments are: "Support for China in this case [i.e. preventing Soviet expansionist designs in the area] would coincide with the classic balance of power strategy – that one supports the weaker power against the power threatening to become dominant." He then adds: "China's role as counterbalance to the U.S.S.R. has more potential than current usefulness."[55] Bhutto has warned an unnamed foreign power "to keep her hands off the warm waters of the Arabian sea on the Baluchistan Coast",[56] an obvious reference to the Soviet Union. Pakistan's viability and territorial integrity should remain, as Kintner points out, "a fundamental goal of American policy", if the developing world is an area in which the United States "intends to be a participant and not simply a bystander".[57]

REFERENCES

1. See the text of President N. Podgorny's letter to Yahya Khan in *Pravda*, April 3, 1971.
2. *Pravda*, September 21, 1969.
3. R. M. MacIver, *The Ramparts we Guard*, New York, 1950, p. 10.
4. Thomas B. Manton, "China, India and Pakistan: New Relationship," a paper submitted at the annual meeting of the Association for Asian Studies in Chicago, Illinois, March 30–31, 1971, p. 3.
5. J. A. Naik, *India, Russia, China and Bangladesh*, New Delhi, 1972, pp. 47–53.
6. Ibid.
7. Felix Gross, *World Politics and Tension Areas*, London, 1966, p. 41.
8. Neville Maxwell, *India's Chinese War*, London, 1970, p. 410.
9. See the text of the Chinese note in the *Peking Review*, September 24, 1965.
10. For a fuller account see the writer's forthcoming *The Major Powers and the Indian Subcontinent.*
11. Norman D. Palmer, *Recent Soviet and Chinese Penetration in India and Pakistan: Guidelines for Political-Military Policy*, McLean, Virginia: Research Analysis Corporation, 1970, p. 43.
12. See "The Nixon Doctrine" in *Documents on American Foreign Relations*, New York: Council on Foreign Relations, 1968.
13. See Hearing before the Subcommittee on Near East and South Asia of the Committee on Foreign Affairs, House of Representatives, March 12, 15, 20 and 27, 1973, Washington, 1973, p. 82.
14. See *Nazi–Soviet Relations, 1939–41: Documents from the Archives of the German Foreign Office* (Washington: Department of State, 1948), p. 257, cited in William J. Barnds, *India, Pakistan and the Great Powers* (New York, 1972, p. 366.

15. See *Central Asian Review*, Vol. 14, 1966.
16. Based on personal interviews and research in Islamabad during 1969–71.
17. I was a member of President Yahya Khan's entourage to Peking and this information was given to me by Yahya himself.
18. See G. W. Choudhury, "U.S. Policy towards the Subcontinent", in *Pacific Community*, October 1973.
19. See Alvin Z. Rubinstein, "Red Stars in the Third World", Soviet and Chinese Influence as a Problem in Foreign Policy Analysis", a paper submitted at the Fifth ANPACH Conference, University of Pennsylvania, October 25–26, 1973.
20. Extracts from the U.N. Secretary-General's introduction to the Annual Report on the Work of the U.N. Organization Relating to the Situation in East Bengal, September 17, 1971.
21. *Hindustan Times* (New Delhi), April 1, 1971.
22. Ibid.
23. See the text of Indira Gandhi's speech in Lok Sabha on March 27, 1971, in *Bangladesh Documents*, Vol. I, p. 669, New Delhi: Ministry of External Affairs, n.d.
24. Ibid., p. 670.
25. Ibid., p. 672.
26. Ibid., Vol. II, pp. 322–3.
27. Ibid., p. 324.
28. Ibid., p. 328.
29. Ibid., p. 329.
30. H. Norman Brown, *The United States and India, Pakistan, Bangladesh*, Cambridge, Mass., 1972, p. 218.
31. See *The Observer Foreign News Service*, London, No. 28727, April 5, 1971.
32. Robert H. Donaldson, "Soviet Political Aims in South Asia", a paper submitted to the Twenty-fifth Annual Meeting of the Association for Asian Studies, March 30–April 1, 1973, Chicago, Illinois, p. 8.
33. See *Daily Telegraph*, London, December 6, 1971.
34. See the text of the statement by the Government of China issued by its delegation at the U.N. on December 16, 1971, in the *New York Times*, December 17, 1971.
35. Ibid.
36. President Nixon's Report to the United States Congress, February 9, 1972, pp. 50–1.
37. See Peter Van Newss, *Revolution and the Chinese Foreign Policy: Peking Support for Wars of National Liberation*, London, 1971.
38. Thomas B. Manton, op. cit.
39. President Nixon's Report to the United States Congress, February 9, 1972, pp. 48–51.
40. See the statement of Mr. Charles Bray, the State Department spokesman on December 7, 1971.
41. See the USIS White House correspondent, Alexander M. Sullivan's statement on December 8, 1971.
42. *The Observer Foreign News Service*, London, No. 29487, December 8, 1971.

43. *Hearing before the Subcommittee on Near East and South Asia*, op. cit., p. 8.
44. *Far Eastern Economic Review*, February 12, 1972, p. 19.
45. Cited in ibid.
46. See Howard Wriggins, "One Year Later: India, Pakistan and Bangladesh", *World View*, May 1973.
47. See the Report of the Indian Economic and Scientific Research Foundation on National Security in the *Overseas Hindustan Times*, January 25, 1973.
48. For details of current anti-Indian feeling in Bangladesh, see *India–Bangladesh Tangle*, published by Research and Documentation Centre, P.O. 734, London, S.W.11; see also *The Statesman Weekly* Calcutta, August 25, 1973.
49. *Pravda*, April 26, 1973.
50. Ibid., March 18, 1972.
51. *Hearing Before the Subcommittee on Near East and South Asia*, op. cit., p. 125.
52. William R. Kintner, *The Impact of President Nixon's Visit to Peking on International Politics*, Philadelphia: Foreign Policy Research Institute, 1972, pp. 42–6.
53. Thomas B. Manton, op. cit.
54. N. Maxwell, "Midnight Thoughts of Premier Chou", *The Sunday Times*, London, December 5, 1971.
55. William R. Kintner, op. cit., p. 46.
56. *The Times*, London, September 10, 1973.
57. "The United States and the Changing World" by Kenneth Rush, Deputy Secretary in the *Department of State Bulletin*, April 9, 1973.

10

END OF AN ERA

Pakistan was claimed by the Indian Muslims on the principle of the right of self-determination. The state was born and baptized in blood – thousands of people were killed and millions were uprooted from their homes in 1946–7 when Pakistan finally emerged as a result of the Indian Muslims' determined struggle to achieve a state of their own where they wished to lead their lives in accordance with the broad principles of equality, social justice and fair play as taught by their religion, Islam. Pakistan was established amid great popular rejoicing and enthusiasm because for the people it was not only liberation from foreign rule; it also meant, as I wrote in one of my previous books, "freedom from the threat of majority rule in a caste-ridden social system where they would have been destined to be a permanent and stagnant religious minority".[1]

But unfortunately the people's rejoicings soon died down and their cherished homeland was plunged into political instability and confusion. Pakistan's history was one of political instability: "personal civilian dictatorship through various mutations of parliamentary government to military dictatorship, veering again towards some form of democracy. The constitutional problem has been the making of constitutions rather than their working. The political image of Pakistan has been one of controversy and instability."[2] What Dr. Spear referred to as "some form of democracy" was introduced by Ayub in his constitution of 1962, and proved a fatal blow to Pakistan's emerging nationalism. The philosophy of Ayub's constitution as he himself claimed was to "blend democracy with discipline". It implied that the people were not fit for self-rule which therefore had to be introduced by "instalments". The attitude was the same as that of a colonial power. The people of Pakistan, who had achieved their independence through a democratic process, were not willing to accept either Ayub's philosophy or the political order based on it. At first they chose to oppose the authoritarian system through the ballot box. The various opposition parties of the country were united in 1964; the East and West Pakistanis were gathered together in their opposition to an authoritarian system – thus giving a unique demonstration of the political unity of the people of East and West Pakistan. A non-Bengali presidential candidate was selected by the Combined Opposition Parties (COP) and the opposition candidate had the overwhelming support of the people of East Pakistan. If there had truly been a democratic process, Ayub would not have been elected in the 1964 election, and a non-Bengali candidate would have been elected enjoying popular mandate from both East and West Pakistan. But thanks to Ayub's political order, the unity of the people was not allowed free expression.

Following from the presidential election of 1964, Pakistan entered an era of agitational politics giving up the constitutional path; bullet was substituted for ballot. In the mean time the 1965 Indo-Pakistan war took place. As I have already pointed out this war had a most unfortunate effect on national unity in Pakistan. During the war the people of the country, both in the East and West of Pakistan, had shown a strong sense of patriotism and unity against the external aggression. But an urban élite group in East Pakistan headed by Mujib and his close party men showed utter disregard for national security and defence. When Mujib and other opposition party leaders were requested by the Pakistan Government to stand united against foreign aggression, his remarks at the Dacca Government House meeting held in the midst of the war amounted to nothing less than high treason. Similarly, some of his Awami Leaguers were secretly indulging in anti-state activity during the war.

India failed to achieve a military victory over Pakistan in the 1965 war, but saw new possibilities in East Pakistan through Mujib and his men. Less than six months after the war, Mujib produced a veiled scheme of secession under his six-point plan. The 1965 war had created for Mujib a favourable climate for such a move. Almost all the fighting in 1965 had taken place along the border between West Pakistan and India, but the East Pakistanis felt that because they had only one army division in their province, which was surrounded on three sides by India, they were at the mercy of the Indians throughout the war: "While West Pakistan was using its American tanks and American planes to fight India for the precious five million Kashmiris, 65 million Bengalis were left to fight with their bare hands if the Indians had attacked us", an East Pakistani said.[3] During the war East Pakistan was for all practical purposes isolated from the world, and the war suddenly illuminated all the disadvantages from which East Pakistan suffered because of political domination by an irresponsible ruling élite composed of West Pakistani top civil and military officers.

Mujib and his close followers began to work for secession of East Pakistan and seemed to have been assured of help and assistance from India. The internal conflict in the country was complicated and aggravated by foreign intervention. The East Pakistan crisis became "foreign-linked". The Agartala conspiracy case and Mujib's followers' direct, and his indirect involvement, as I have shown, were based on facts. It is a pity that the conspiracy case had to be withdrawn because of the internal political confusion created during the four-month-long agitation against Ayub and his political order.

The result was that Mujib, instead of being exposed, became a hero among the Bengalis. Its forced withdrawal of the case made the Pakistan Government appear to be persecuting a leader who only demanded the Bengalis' legitimate rights for regional autonomy. I have heard a tape-recorded version of Mujib's talks with his top political aides in 1970 in which he attributed to Ayub his own unique popularity among the Bengalis.

Yahya's "fantasy and blunders"[4] have been much talked about but I can vouch that under Yahya the Pakistan Government made the first and the last sincere attempt to remove the legitimate grievances of the Bengalis. I have shown that he conceded all the demands put forward by the Bengalis. If Mujib had been sincere and interested only in regional autonomy, there would have been no room for any conflict. The plan for the transfer of power as made by Yahya would have preserved the country's unity. Yahya had many limitations but he was politically honest in his dealings with Mujib; he went to the farthest extent possible to meet the demands of the Bengalis because the bulk of the Pakistan armed forces and the majority of the people did not wish to see their homeland dismembered and their cherished green and white flag pulled down in Dacca by the Indian Army. The people and the bulk of the armed forces were prepared to make real concessions to maintain the unity of the country.

The dismal failure of Yahya's plan for a genuine federal union wherein all the demands of the Bengalis were accepted was not due to the insincerity of the Pakistan Government; it was mainly due to the dubious and dishonest political roles of Mujib and Bhutto. Mujib was not sincere or straightforward in his political negotiations in 1969–70; he pledged to modify his six points and to maintain the unity of Pakistan. Yahya honestly believed in his words and allowed him a long rope to achieve his ulterior political objectives. Bhutto's unpardonable crime and cardinal mistake was to deny the Pakistan Government a chance to show its *bona fides* in its dealings with the Bengalis. His boycott of the National Assembly in March 1971 created an explosive situation and a point of no return. Yahya and his emissaries including myself, urged Bhutto to go to Dacca and to attend the national assembly. If the national assembly had met, Mujib's veiled scheme of secession could have been exposed. Yahya gave Bhutto categorical assurances that he would not allow the continuation of the assembly if Mujib tried to pass his constitutional draft, which would have amounted to splitting of the country. But Bhutto seemed too impatient to acquire power at any price, no matter whether it was in a united or a truncated Pakistan. Just as the forced withdrawal of the Agartala case in 1969 prevented Mujib from being exposed, similarly the forced adjustment of the national assembly on March 1, 1971, prevented the world from knowing the real reasons for the failure of Yahya's plan for a genuine federal union, in which the people of East and West Pakistan could live together as equal partners.

From the adjournment of the national assembly in March 1, 1971, there was a chain of tragic developments which culminated in the dismemberment of Pakistan on December 16, 1971. The Pakistan Army's atrocities have rightly been condemned so in the world's press, but a thorough analysis of the political developments of 1970–1 would reveal that responsibility for the tragic events of 1971, which meant not only the disintegration of Pakistan, the cherished homeland of the Indian Muslims, but also the destruction of the economic infrastructure and social fabric of Bangladesh, did not belong only to Pakistan or its armed forces or, least of all, to its people. It belonged to a great extent to Mujib for his dishonest game not only with the central Government but with his own people; to Bhutto's inordinate ambition to acquire power at any cost; to India's calculated plan to treat the Bangladesh crisis as an "opportunity of tthe century" to destroy Pakistan; to the Soviet wrath against Pakistan for her refusal to 'unite against Mao' in the context of the Kremlin leaders' grand designs against the People's Republic of China. Even after the outbreak of the civil war, there could have been a political settlement of the crisis under the initiatives taken in Washington with support from China and Iran, and with the approval of the Pakistan Government, but it was frustrated by Indo-Soviet collaboration to humiliate Pakistan and China, and to inflict a diplomatic setback to the United States.

The dismemberment of Pakistan and the emergence of Bangladesh have not solved the regional tensions and conflicts of the subcontinent. Jinnah's two-nation theory has not been proved incorrect because there is more anti-Hindu and anti-Indian feelings in the so-called "secular" state of Bangladesh today than there ever was in East Pakistan when it was part of the "Islamic State" of Pakistan. Peace and stability in the region have not been brought nearer by the tragic events of 1971; on the contrary, the Soviet expansionist designs have new scope in an unstable Bangladesh and an insecure "New" Pakistan. India is having the "bitter taste" (to quote Chou En-lai) of its own actions. The economic maladies of India have been aggravated by the heavy cost of the Bangladesh operation, while the Muslims of Bangladesh are again exposed to threats of domination by the *Bhadralok* (élite) from Calcutta. Mainly in the context of Sino-Soviet competition in South and

South-east Asia, interrelated regional and global conflicts in the area have become more prominent.

REFERENCES

1. See my *Pakistan's Relations with India*, London, 1968, p. 40.
2. Percival Spear, "First Steps of a Nation" in *The Times*, London, Supplement on Pakistan, August 14, 1963.
3. See *New York Times*, April 21, 1966.
4. See W. H. Morris-Jones, "Pakistan Post-mortem and the Roots of Bangladesh", *Political Quarterly*, Vol. 43, No. 2, April–June, 1972.

INDEX